Catalogue
of
Vocal Solos and Duets
Arranged in
Biblical Order

by
JAMES H. LASTER

THE SCARECROW PRESS, INC.
Metuchen, N.J., & London • 1984

Library of Congress Cataloging in Publication Data

Laster, James, 1934-
    Catalogue of vocal solos and duets arranged in
Biblical order.

    Includes index.
    1. Sacred songs--Bibliography.   2. Sacred duets--
Bibliography.   3. Church music--Bibliography.   I. Title.
ML128.S3L38   1984   016.7836'751   84-14187
ISBN 0-8108-1748-9

TABLE OF CONTENTS

PREFACE   v

OLD TESTAMENT

Genesis	1
Exodus	1
Numbers	2
Deuteronomy	2
Joshua	3
Ruth	3
I Samuel	6
II Samuel	7
I Kings	7
I Chronicles	8
II Chronicles	8
Job	8
Psalms	11
Proverbs	89
Ecclesiastes	92
Song Of Songs	94
Isaiah	98
Jeremiah	111
Lamentations	112
Ezekiel	113
Daniel	113
Hosea	113
Joel	113

Amos	114
Micah	114
Habakkuk	114
Zephaniah	114
Haggai	115
Zechariah	115
Malachi	115

THE APOCRYPHA

Wisdom Of Solomon	116
Ecclesiasticus	116

THE NEW TESTAMENT

Matthew	117
Mark	129
Luke	131
John	137
Acts	146
Romans	146
I Corinthians	148
II Corinthians	152
Galatians	153
Ephesians	154
Philippians	155
Colossians	156
I Thessalonians	157

I Timothy	157
II Timothy	157
Hebrews	158
James	159
I Peter	159
I John	160
Revelation	162
COMPOSER INDEX	167
SONG TITLE INDEX	181

ABBREVIATIONS

AMSI - Art Masters Studios, Inc.

BMI   - Broadcast Music, Inc.

GIA   - Gregorian Institute of America

ms   - manuscript

n.d. - no date

WIM   - Western International Music

iv

PREFACE

While preparing the Catalogue Of Choral Music Arranged In Biblical Order (Scarecrow Press, 1983), it became evident that a companion volume of vocal solos and duets would be a logical follow-up. A separate card file of appropriate material was begun, marking the genesis for this volume.

The format used in the earlier catalogue was continued in this volume: e.g., the texts of the solos/duets are arranged in Biblical Order, followed by the composer, title, accompaniment, language, if not in English, and publisher information.

There are two types of entries found in the Catalogue: a Main Entry and a SEE Reference. An annotated Main Entry is as follows:

> (1) Psalm 89:1-5, 15, 16   (2) (Psalm 119:52)
>   (3) PARKER, Clifton
>   (4) Blessed Is The People
>   (5) Piano/Organ   d1 - f$^{\#}$2
>   (6) Carl Fischer (1934)

(1) Biblical Reference -- Book, Chapter, Verse(s).
(2) Additional Scripture used in the solo; or the name of the author of paraphrased text, or a translator of a text will appear here.
(3) Composer's Name, including arranger and editor, if appropriate.
(4) Title.
(5) Language -- All texts are assumed to be in English unless otherwise indicated.
Accompaniment.
Range. Highest and lowest notes are given according to the system mentioned above.
(6) The name of the Publisher, the most recent date of publication, and the publisher's number appear at the end of each citation. Items where no date is given are listed as (n.d.) or left blank. Items for which there is no publisher's number are listed as (n.#.) or left blank.

An Annotated SEE Reference is as follows:
    (1) Psalm 92:4
            (2) SEE: Job 22:21
            (3) MacDERMID, James G.
            (4) Acquaint Now Thyself With Him

(1) Biblical Reference -- Book, Chapter, Verse(s).
(2) The SEE Reference which refers to the Main Scripture
     Heading where the complete citation is located.
(3) and (4) Composer and Title for the Main Heading are
     repeated in the SEE Reference.

The following chart for vocal ranges is used:

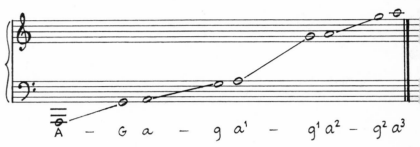

METHOD

    In order to obtain scores for this project, letters were
sent to twenty-three publishers requesting copies of vocal
solos. The author wishes to express his appreciation to the
following publishers for supplying material: Augsburg Publishing House; Boston Music Company; Carl Fischer; Concordia
Publishing House; GIA; Hope Publishing Company; Oxford University
Press; E.C. Schirmer; and Shawnee Press. Some publishers
supplied unison or two-part anthems, which would be suitable as
solos or duets. Many of these are included.

    There are several bibliographies of vocal literature
available. The following were examined for appropriate material:

    Berry, Corre, Vocal Chamber Duets: An Annotated Bibliog-
        raphy, National Association of Teachers of Singing
        (1981).

    Carman, Judith, and William Gaeddert, Rita Roesch Art Song
        In The United States (1801-1976) An Annotated
        Bibliography, National Association of Teachers of
        Singing (1976).

    Espina, Noni, Vocal Solos In Protestant Worship (2nd
        Edition), Vita d'Arte, 1866 Cedar Avenue, Bronx,
        New York, 10453 (1974).

Koopman, John, Selected Sacred Solos In Modern Idiom (2nd edition), Augsburg (1979).

Martin, Walter, Recommended Sacred Songs For the University Level Student, National Association of Teachers of Singing, (1978).

As in the Catalogue Of Choral Music, every attempt has been made to use the Biblical reference as it appears in the music as the reference for cataloging. When there were obvious errors, they were corrected. There are variations in the way publishers list scripture sources, which accounts for irregularities in listings. Many solos give as their text, 'The Psalms,' or 'from the Bible,' or 'from Scripture.' Every effort was made to locate the specific passages in these cases, but many texts are too mixed to locate. Whenever the text could be located, it is included in the Catalogue. By the same token, there are solos and duets which use Biblical texts which have been omitted because the exact Scripture reference could not be found.

In addition to publisher's contributions, and material found in Bibliographies, the author made use of the personal libraries of many voice teachers. The largest private library examined was the extensive solo collection of Mr. Louis Nicholas, of Nashville, Tennessee. Other libraries include: the Howe Library of Shenandoah College and Conservatory of Music, Winchester, Virginia; the Talbot Library of Westminster Choir College; the Sibley Library, Eastman School of Music; the Free Library of Philadelphia, Pennsylvania; and the library of the American Composer's Alliance. Appreciation is expressed to Dale Music Company, Silver Spring, Maryland; and Vester Music, Nashville, Tennessee, for allowing me to pour through their files.

The writer would like to express appreciation to Shenandoah College and Conservatory of Music for the Faculty Enrichment Grant which assisted in starting this project. Gratitude is also extended to the students who assisted in the cataloging of cards, and especially to Rebecca Whitlow, who prepared the Index of Titles. A very special word of thanks is extended to Marjorie Edmondson who typed the manuscript.

Works like this are always out of date the minute they are frozen into print. An update or revision of this Catalogue would be a logical step in keeping it current, and of greater assistance to those who will find it of use.

JHL

vii

THE OLD TESTAMENT

GENESIS

1:1
HAYDN, Joseph
In The Beginning (from The Creation)
Keyboard: LOW:a1-e2; HIGH:c1-g2
Carl Fischer (1939) also found in <u>Sacred Hour of Song</u>, Carl
Fischer.

1:26, 27 (I John 3:1, 3)
MacDERMID, James
Behold What Manner of Love
Keyboard: LOW:c1-e2; HIGH:e^{b}1 - g2
Forster (1942)

1:27 (Psalm 8:36)
HUMPHREYS, Don
Man
Keyboard: LOW:b1-d2; HIGH:d1-f2
R.D.Row (1953) in <u>Songs For Christian Science Service</u>, Book I

EXODUS

8:1
SPIRITUAL
Go Down Moses
Keyboard: LOW:d1-d2; HIGH:f$^\#$1 - F$^\#$2
Ricordi

15:00 (from)
CUMMING, Richard
The Song of Moses (#10 of We Happy Few)
Piano: BASS:G-e1
Boosey & Hawkes (1969)

15:1-2
VIADANA, Lodovico (ed. Rudolf Ewerhart)
Cantemus Domino (Drei Geistliche Konzerte)
Latin   Continuo: BASS:G - b^{b}1
Edmund Bieler Verlag (1958) #5

15:2
HANDEL, G. F.
The Lord Is My Strength
Keyboard   Duet: 2 High
John Church [Presser] (1902) found in Sacred Duets, Vol. I.

15:3 (Psalm 46:10; Psalm 74:20; Psalm 12:5; Psalm 76:6)
ANONYMOUS (ed. Marilyn Gombosi)
The Lord Is A Mighty Warrior - recitative & arioso
Keyboard: BASS: A-d1
Boosey & Hawkes (1975) a solo in Psalm of Joy, compiled by
    Johann Frederich Peter.

23:20, 22, 25 (and other)
HEAD, Michael
Behold, I Send An Angel
Organ or Piano
Boosey & Hawkes (1964)

NUMBERS

6:24
LUTKIN, Peter (arr. William Stickles)
The Lord Bless You And Keep You
Piano: c1-e2
Boston Music (1963)

6:24-26
SEE: Romans 8:38, 39
FLOYD, Carlisle
For I Am Persuaded

DEUTERONOMY

4:29 (Job 23:3)
MENDELSSOHN, Felix
If With All Your Hearts (Elijah)
Keyboard: f#1 - a3
Amsco (1940) in Everybody's Favorite Sacred Songs; also in
    The World's Best Sacred Songs; also published by G. Schirmer
    and found in 52 Sacred Songs.

4:29
RHEINTHALER, C.
The Lord Will Not Be Ever Wroth (Jephtha)
Keyboard: c1 - eb2
G. Schirmer (1929) found in Anthology of Sacred Songs - Alto.

4:29 (Job 23:3)
ROBERTS, J. E.
If With All Your Hearts
Keyboard: LOW:b1-d2; HIGH:e1-g2
Presser (1936)

6:1-5
    SEE: Matthew 6:33
    PENDLETON, Emmet
    The Kingdom of God

28:67
    SEE: Psalm 27:4
    TALMA, Louise
    Cantata: All The Days Of My Life

31:6
    BEAUMONT, V.
    Be Of Good Courage
    Keyboard: LOW:a1-d; HIGH: c1 - e^b2
    G. Schirmer

32:1-3
    MacDERMID, James G.
    My Speech Shall Distill As The Dew
    Keyboard: LOW:a1 - $f^\#2$; HIGH:c1 - $d^\#2$
    Forster (1943)

32:1-4, 9-12
    SELBY, Peter H.
    Give Ear Oh Ye Heaven
    Keyboard: b1-e2
    Willis (1973)

32:11 (Hebrews 8:10)
    MENDELSSOHN, Felix
    God Hath Led His People On
    Keyboard: c1-f2
    Coburn Press (1971) found in Lift Up Your Voice.

JOSHUA

  1:5-7
    BUTT, James
    Courage
    Organ/Piano: e1-e2
    Sphemusations (1965)

RUTH

  1:16 (and other)
    DEWEY, Richard A.
    Whither Thou Goest
    Organ: e^b1 - e^b2
    Fred Bock (1977) found in Whom God Hath Joined Together

1:16 (and other)
HALLQUIST, Gary
Song Of Ruth
Keyboard: d1-b2
Sonlife Music (1976) found in Everything For The Wedding
   Soloist

1:16
LILJESTRAND, Paul
Whither Thou Goest
Keyboard: c1-d2
Hope (1980) found in Everything For The Wedding Soloist; also
   found in Everything For The Church Soloist

1:16-17
AVERY, Lawrence
Entreat Me Not To Leave Thee
Piano/Organ: $e^b1 - e^b2$
Transcontinental (1979)

1:16, 17 (inspired by)
AVERY, Richard and Donald Marsh
I will Follow
Keyboard: c1-e2
Hope (1980) found in Everything For The Wedding Soloist

1:16-17
BLACK, Jennie Prince
The Pledge
Piano: LOW:b1-e2; HIGH:d1-g2
G. Schirmer (1943)

1:16-17
CASSLER, G. Winston
Whither Thou Goest
Organ: LOW:A1-D2; MED:c1-f2
Augsburg (1955)

1:16-17
COOK, Gerald
Ruth (to Naomi)
Piano/Organ: f1-f2
American Music Center

1:16-17
EBEN, Petr
Lied der Ruth (Song of Ruth) 1970
English/German   Organ: c1-f2
Universal (1980) 17161

1:16-17
ENGEL, James
Whither Thou Goest
Organ, Flute: e1-e2
Augsburg (1979) 11-9478 found in Three Solos For Medium Voice

1:16-17
  GIESEKE, Richard W.
  Wedding Song
  Organ: c1-f2
  Concordia (1983) 97-5786

1:16-17
  GOLDMAN, Maurice
  Song Of Ruth
  Piano: LOW:b^b1 - e^b2; HIGH:d1-g2
  Transcontinental

1:16-17
  GORE, Richard T.
  Entreat Me Not To Leave Thee
  Organ: $d^{\#}1$ - g2
  Concordia (1959) comes in high & low

1:16-17
  GOUNOD, Charles
  Entreat Me Not To Leave Thee
  Piano: LOW:c1-e2; MED:d1 - $f^{\#}2$; HIGH:e1 - $g^{\#}2$
  G. Schirmer (n.d.)

1:16-17
  GOUNOD, Charles (arr. Jack Schrader)
  Entreat Me Not To Leave Thee
  Keyboard: c1-e2
  Hope (1981) found in Everything For The Wedding Soloist

1:16, 17
  GROTON, Frederic
  Entreat Me No, Op. 10
  Keyboard: g-f2
  R. L. Huntzinger (1931) found in Choice Sacred Songs For Home
    Or Church Services

1:16-17
  HILDACH, Eugen
  Where'er Thou Goest
  Keyboard: LOW:b^b1 - e^b2; MED:c1-f2; HIGH:d1-g2
  Heinrichshofen (C.F.Peters)

1:16-17
  PEETERS, Flor
  Wedding Song
  Organ: LOW:c1-e2; MED:d1 - $f^{\#}2$; HIGH:f1-a3
  C.F.Peters (1962)

1:16-17
  PENDLETON, Emmet
  Song of Ruth, Op.12,#2 (from Light of the Lord)
  Piano: c1-f2
  Bruce Humphries (1945)

1:16-17
SAMAMA, Leo
Wither Thou Goest (Movement III - Wedding Cantata)
Organ: Tenor:g1 - e^{b}2
WIM (1974) WIM 118

1:16-17
SCHUTZ, Heinrich
A Wedding Song
Keyboard: d1-d2
G. Schirmer (1978) found in The Church Year In Song

1:16-17
SCHUTZ, Heinrich
Wedding Song
Keyboard: LOW:d1-d2; HIGH:f1-f2
Chantry (1951)

1:16-17 (taken from)
SINGER, Guy
Whither Thou Goest
Piano: b1-c2
Kavelin Music (1954)

1:16-17
WATTS, Wintter
Intreat Me Not To Leave Thee
Piano: a1 - e^{b}2
G. Schirmer (1923)

1:16-17
WEINER, Lazar
Ruth
Keyboard: e1 - b^{b}3
Transcontinental (1972)

1:16-17
WHITE, Louie
Entreat Me Not To Leave Thee
Organ: LOW:c1 - d^{b}2; HIGH:e^{b}1 - f2
Concordia (1980) found in Seven Wedding Songs

1:16-17
YOUNG, Gordon
Entreat Me Not To Leave Thee
Keyboard: f1-f2
Galaxy (1961)

I SAMUEL

2:1, 2
SCHUTZ, Heinrich
Exultavit cor meum
Latin/German Soprano with 2 Violins & Continuo: c1-f2
Barenreiter (1956) 29

II SAMUEL

1:19-27
ADLER, Samuel
Laments
Baritone & Chamber Orchestra
MS (1968) Sibley Library, Eastman

1:19-27
ROREM, Ned
Mourning Song
String Quartet: c1-g2
C.F.Peters

18:33
DIAMOND, David
David Mourns For Absalom
Piano: d1-a3
Mercury [Presser] (1947)

18:33
SCHUTZ, Heinrich
Fili mi, Absalom
Latin   Bass & 4 Trombones & Continuo: a-d1
Barenreiter (1949) 40

19:27
FROMM, Herbert
Lamentation of David (Five Songs Of Worship)
Keyboard: a1-e2
Transcontinental (1946) TV 471

23:1-5
FREUDENTHAL, Josef
The Last Words Of David
Keyboard: HIGH:g1-g2
Transcontinental (1964) TV 565

I KINGS

3:5, 7, 9, 10-13
MILLER, Merle
Solomon's Prayer
Keyboard: LOW:b1-d2; HIGH:d1-f2
R.D.Row (1954) [Free Library]

18:36-37
MENDELSSOHN, Felix
Lord God Of Abraham (Elijah)
Keyboard: $b^b - e^b1$
G. Schirmer also found in Anthology Of Sacred Songs

I CHRONICLES

29:10-11, 13-14
GREENFIELD, Alfred
Blessed Be Thou, Lord God Of Israel
Organ: $c^\#1 - f^\#2$
H.W.Gray (1932)

29:11-13
MacDERMID, James
Thine, O Lord Is The Greatness
Keyboard: LOW:d1-f2; HIGH:$f^\#1 - a3$
Forster (1944)

29:15
SEE: Psalm 27:4
TALMA, Louise
Cantata : All The Days Of My Life

II CHRONICLES

6:14, 19-21
PISK, Paul
Solomon's Prayer
Piano (Organ): $c1 - f^\#2$
American Composers Alliance

7:14
OWENS, Jimmy
If My People Will Pray
Keyboard: $c1 - g^\#2$
Lexicon (1973) found in Everything For The Church Soloist
    (Hope, 1980); also Scripture Solos For All Seasons (Lillenas,
    1980).

20:15, 17 (Isaiah 41:10, 13; II Timothy 17)
KOCH, Frederick
Be Not Afraid
Keyboard: $e^b1 - a^b3$
Boosey & Hawkes (1963)

JOB

7:6
SEE: Psalm 27:4
TALMA, Louise
Cantata: All The Days Of My Life

8:5
SEE: Job 22:21
WAY, Arthur
Acquaint Now Thyself With Him

11:13, 15, 17, 19
    SEE: Job 22:21
    WAY, Arthur
    Acquaint Now Thyself With Him

11:13-19
    PARKER, Clifton
    If Thou Prepare Thine Heart
    Keyboard: c1 - e^{b}2
    Carl Fischer (1934)

11:17
    SEE: Psalm 27:4
    TALMA, Louise
    Cantata: All The Days of My Life

14:1-2
    PINKHAM, Daniel
    Man That Is Born Of A Woman
    Guitar: g1-e2
    E.C.Schirmer (1971)

14:1, 2, 7-12
    FLOYD, Carlisle
    Man That Is Born Of A Woman
    Piano or Organ (Orchestra) a-f1
    Boosey & Hawkes (1959) from Pilgrimage

14:32-33
    CORNELIUS, Peter (ed. M.B. Stearns)
    There Is A Spirit In Man, Op.2, #3
    Keyboard: c$^{\#}$1 - f2
    Coburn Press (1971) found in Lift Up Your Voice

19:25, 26 (I Corinthians 15:20)
    HANDEL, G. F.
    I Know That My Redeemer Liveth (Messiah)
    Keyboard: e1 - g$^{\#}$2
    as a single solo, found in Everybody's Favorite Sacred Songs
        (Amsco, 1940); 52 Sacred Songs (G. Schirmer, 1939);
        Scripture Solos For All Seasons (Lillenas, 1980)

19:25-26
    PELOQUIN, C. Alexander
    I Believe
    Organ: a1-f2
    GIA (1971)

20:8a, 9
    SEE: Isaiah 2:22
    Barker, Clement W.
    Mark The Perfect Man

22:00
BUCK, Dudley
Acquaint Thyself With Him
Organ: DUET:S-T
G. Schirmer (1923)

22:00 (Psalm 99; Psalm 96; Micah 6)
HEAD, Michael
Acquaint Now Thyself With Him
Piano or Organ: LOW:b^b1 - e^b2; HIGH:d1-g2
Boosey & Hawkes (1960)

22:21 (Jeremiah 29:12, 13; Isaiah 65:19; Psalm 90:4)
MacDERMID, James
Acquaint Now Thyself With Him
Keyboard: LOW:d^b1 - e^b2; HIGH:f1-g2
Forster Music (1955)

22:21 (Job 11:13, 15, 17, 19; Job 8:5)
WAY, Arthur
Acquaint Now Thyself With Him
Organ: $c^\#1$ - $f^\#2$
Galaxy (1948)

23:3
SEE: Deuteronomy 4:29
MENDELSSOHN, Felix
If With All Your Hearts (Elijah)

23:3
SEE: Deuteronomy 4:29
ROBERTS, J. E.
If With All Your Hearts

23:3,8-9; (John 20:29)
ROWLEY, Alec
O That I Knew Where I Might Find Him
Piano/Organ: d1-g2
Boosey & Hawkes (1939)

33:15, 16
SEE: Psalm 27:1, 5, 6
BUCK, Dudley
The Lord Is My Light

36:5, 6, 7
WOOLER, Alfred
Behold, God Is Mighty
Keyboard: LOW:c1 - d^b2; HIGH: e1-a3
Arthur Schmidt (1912)

PSALMS

1:00
BONE, Gene and Howard Fenton
The First Psalm
Piano or Organ: LOW:bl-d2; HIGH: d^{b}1 - f2
Carl Fischer (1945)

1:00
BOWLING, Blanche
He Shall Be Like A Tree
Keyboard: LOW:cl - e^{b}2; HIGH:dl-f2
R.D.Row (1957)

1:00
BUTT, James
Psalm 1
Organ: f$^{\#}$1 = e2
Sphemusations (1958)

1:00
FROMM, Herbert
Psalm 1 (from Four Psalms)
Keyboard: dl-g2
Transcontinental (1971)

1:00
LUCKE, Katharine E.
Blessed Is The Man
Keyboard: cl-f2
Presser (1941)

1:00
NELHYBEL, Vaclav
Blessed Is The Man
Keyboard: cl-e2
Hope (1981)

1:00
ORE, Charles W.
Blessed Is The Man (from Lisbon Psalms)
Piano/Organ, optional descant recorder: cl-f2
Concordia (1975) Set I-piano; Set II-Organ

1:00
THIMAN, Eric
Happy Is The Man
Piano/Organ: bl-e2
Novello

1:1, 4
GREENE, Maurice (ed. Mason Martens)
Blessed Is The Man
Keyboard: DUET
Walton

2:1, 2
HANDEL, G. F.
Why Do The Nations (Messiah)
Keyboard: BASS:B-e1
Novello/G.Schirmer/Carl Fischer

2:1, 11, 13, 15, 17
MENDELSSOHN, Felix
O God Have Mercy (St. Paul)
Piano: BASS:B-d1
G. Schirmer

2:4, 9
HANDEL, G. F.
He That Dwelleth In Heaven/Thou Shalt Break Them (Messiah)
Keyboard: TENOR:e-a2
Novello/G.Schirmer/Carl Fischer

3:1-4
RAKSIM, David
Psalm on the Eve of Battle
Keyboard: LOW:a1-c2; HIGH:d1-f2
Fred Bock (1980) found in The Sanctuary Soloist

3:6-9
SCHUTZ, Henrich
Ich liege und schlafe
German   Continuo: BASS:g - e$^\flat$1
Barenreiter (1963)

3:8
GREENE, Maurice
Salvation Belongeth Unto The Lord (from Lord How Are Thy
   Increased)
Piano: f1 - e$^\flat$2
Oxford

4:00
GARLICK, Anthony
Psalm 4 (A Psalm Song Cycle)
Piano: e$^\flat$1 - f2
SeeSaw

4:00
ORE, Charles
Answer Me When I Call (Lisbon Psalms)
Piano/Organ: c1-f2
Concordia (1975) Set I-Piano; Set II-Organ

4:1 (Psalm 5:2)
SCHUTZ, Heinrich (ed. Don McAfee)
Hear Me, O Lord
English/German   Continuo: DUET
Belwin (1977) found in Eight Sacred Duets

4:2 (Psalm 5:3)
  SCHUTZ, Heinrich
  Erhore mich, wenn ich rufe
  German   Continuo: DUET
  Barenreiter (1963)

4:8
  GREENE, Maurice (ed. E. Stanley Roper)
  I Will Lay Me Down In Peace
  Keyboard: LOW:d1 - e^{b}2; HIGH:e1-f2
  Bosworth (1910) found in Seven Sacred Solos Of The Early
    English School

4:9
  SEE: Psalm 5:8
  HANDEL, G. F.
  Lead Me, Lord

5:2
  SEE: Psalm 4:1
  SCHUTZ, Heinrich
  Hear Me, O Lord

5:2
  SEE: Psalm 4:2
  SCHUTZ, Heinrich
  Erhoere mich, wenn ich rufe

5:8 (Psalm 119:3)
  HANDEL, G. F.
  Lead Me Lord
  Keyboard: e^{b}1 - e^{b}2
  R.D.Row (1959) found in Sacred Song Masterpieces

5:8 (Psalm 4:9, adapted)
  HANDEL, G. F. (arr. Fredrickson)
  Lead Me, Lord
  Keyboard: DUET
  R.D.Row (1960) found in Sacred Masterpieces

5:8 (Psalm 23:4)
  MOLIQUE, B.
  Lead Me Lord (abraham)
  Keyboard: d-e1
  G.Schirmer, found in Anthology of Sacred Song - Bass

5:8
  SEE: Psalm 103:1
  WESLEY, Samuel S.
  Praise The Lord, O My Soul

5:12
  SEE: Isaiah 1:18
  BARKER, Clement W.
  The Path Of The Just

6:00
HANSON, Howard
O Lord, Rebuke Me Not In Thine Anger
Keyboard: al-f2
Carl Fischer (1972) from Four Psalms

6:00
RUBBRA, Edmund
Psalm VI (O Lord Rebuke Me Not) Op.61
Piano/Organ: $f^{\#}1 - e2$
Lengnick from Three Psalms For Low Voice

6:00 (taken from)
SCHALIT, H.
O Lord, Return
Organ (or Harp): el-f2
H. Schalit (1952)

6:1-4
PURCELL, Henry
O Lord, Rebuke Me Not
Piano (Organ): LOW:al-e2; HIGH:cl-g2
R.D.Row found in Purcell Songs, ed. John Edmunds

6:33-37
WOOLER, Alfred
O Lord, Rebuke Me Not
Keyboard: LOW:bl-d2; MED: $c^{\#}1 - e2$; HIGH:el-g2
Arthur Schmidt (1911)

7:14-15
LADERMAN, Ezra
Behold The Wicked Man
Piano: fl-g2
Oxford (1970) from From The Psalms

8:00 (adapted)
CESTI, Marc Antonio
The Wonders Of The Universe
Keyboard: el - $g^{b}2$
G.Schirmer (1965) found in The Sunday Solo, ed. Gertrude
    Tingley

8:00
CORTESE, Luigi
Salmo VIII, Op.21
Latin   Piano, Flute, Cello: cl-a3
Edizioni Suvini Zerboni (1949)

8:00
FREED, Isadore
Psalm 8 (O Lord, How Excellent Is Thy Name)
Piano: cl-f2
Southern (1954)

8:00
HANSON, Howard
O Lord, Our Lord, How Excellent Is Thy Name
Keyboard: al - c$^{\#}$2
Carl Fischer (1972) from Four Psalms

8:00
LYON, James (ed. Gordon Myers)
Oh, Lord, Our Heavenly King
Piano or Organ: cl - e^{b}2
Eastlane Music from Six Songs of Early America

8:00
SCOTT, John Prindle
When I Consider The Heavens
Piano: LOW:dl-g2; HIGH:fl-b3
Huntzinger (1921)

8:00
WRIGHT, Norman S.
The Eighth Psalm
Piano: cl-g2
Huntzinger (1945)

8:1, 3-8
McAFEE, Don
How Excellent Is Thy Name
Keyboard: cl - e^{b}2
Sacred Music Press (1969) found in The Solo Psalmist

8:3-6
SEE: Genesis 1:27
HUMPHREYS, Don
Man

8:4
SEE: Psalm 45:1, 2
DENCKE, Jeremiah
I Speak Of The Things

8:4 (and other)
PURCELL, Henry
Lord, What Is Man (from Harmonia Sacre)
Piano: dl-a3
International Music (1958) #1699

9:00
HOFFMEISTER, Len Abbott
Arise, O Lord
Piano: LOW:al-d2; HIGH:cl-f2
G.Schirmer (1931) found in high key in 52 Sacred Songs

9:1, 2, 10
CAMPBELL-TIPTON, Louis
I Will Give Thanks Unto The Lord, Op. 25, #2
Piano: LOW:a^b1 - e^b2; MED:b^b1 - f2; HIGH:d^b1 - a^b3
G.Schirmer (1936)

9:2-3
KINGSLEY, Gershorn
I Will Give Thanks Unto The Lord (Three Sacred Songs)
Cello, Keyboard: c1-f2
Transcontinental (1969)

9:9-10 (paraphrase)
HANDEL, G.F.
God Is A Constant Sure Defense (Second Chandos Anthem)
Keyboard: d1-a3
Boosey & Hawkes (found in A Collection of Songs)

9:12, 13
SCHUTZ, Heinrich (ed. Don McAfee)
Praise To The Lord (Laudet den Herren, der du Zion wohnet)
English/German   Continuo: DUET
Belwin (1977) found in Eight Sacred Duets. Also published by
    Barenreiter in German only.

9:15
SEE: Psalm 104:5
LADERMAN, Ezra
Thou Didst Set The Earth

10:00 (Psalm 12: Psalm 16)
PERGOLESI, Giovanni B.
O Lord, Have Mercy Upon Me
Keyboard: d1-a3
Abingdon (1964) found in Select Vocal Solos For The Church
    Musician

12:00
SEE: Psalm 10
PERGOLESI, Giovanni B.
O Lord Have Mercy Upon Me

12:00
COUPERIN, Francois
Usquequo Domine
Latin   Dontinuo: TENOR:c-b2
Hugel (1972) H.32.219 (found in Neuf Motets)

12:00
WOOLER, Alfred
Consider And Hear Me
Piano: LOW:b1 - e^b2; MED:c1-f2; HIGH:e1 - a^b3
Oliver Ditson (1935)

12:1-4, 9
    HARTLEY, Walter S.
    Allegro (A Psalm Cycle)
    Piano and Flute: c1-a3
    Tenuto (Presser)

12:5
    SEE: Exodus 15:3
    ANONYMOUS
    The Lord Is A Mighty Warrior

13:00
    BEECH, Robert L.
    How Long Will Thou Forget Me, O Lord, Op. 16, #1
    Piano or Organ: d1-f2
    E.Schuberth (1940)

13:00
    HARKER, F. Flaxington
    Consider, And Hear Me, Op.49,#1
    Piano: LOW:b^{b}1 - e2; HIGH:d1-g2
    G.Schirmer (1910)

13:00 (text from)
    HOFFMEISTER, Leon Abbott
    How Long Wilt Thou Forget Me, O Lord?
    Piano: LOW:c1 - e^{b}2; HIGH:d1-g2
    Huntzinger (1928) found in Choice Sacred Songs For Home Or
        Church Service

13:00
    KAHN, Erich I.
    Psalm 13
    Piano/Organ: b^{b}1 - b3
    Composers Facsimile Edition (American Composers Alliance)

13:00 (St. Dunstan Psalter)
    LEKBERG, Sven
    How Long Wilt Thou Forget Me, O Lord
    Piano/Organ: b1-g2
    Witmark (1947)

13:00 (adapted)
    RANZZINI
    Lord, How Long Wilt Thou Forget Me?
    Keyboard: e^{b}1 - a^{b}3
    G.Schirmer (1965) found in The Sunday Solo, ed. Gertrude
        Tingley

13:00
    SACCO, Peter
    O Lord, How Long Wilt Thou Forget Me
    Piano/Organ: c1 - g$^{\#}$2
    Ostara Press (found in Three Psalms)

13:00 (taken from)
    WOOLER, Alfred
    Consider And Hear Me
    Piano: bl - e^{b}2
    Oliver Ditson (197) from Sacred Songs; also found in Choice
        Sacred Songs (ed. Wilman Wilmans)

13:1 (Psalm 102:7, 9, 12, 13)
    ROGERS, James
    How Long, O Lord Wilt Thou Forget Me?
    Piano/Organ: dl - e^{b}2
    G.Schirmer (1908)

13:1-3 (Psalm 30:1-3, 11-12)
    ARCHER, Violet
    Miserere et Jubilate
    Piano: dl - g$^\#$2
    Canadian Music Center (1954) found in Three Biblical Songs

13:1, 3, 5
    SPEAKS, Oley
    How Long Wilt Thou Forget Me?
    Piano: e^{b}1 - a^{b}3
    G.Schirmer (1911)

13:1-6
    POWELL, Robert J.
    How Long Wilt Thou Forget Me
    Keyboard: cl-f2
    Sacred Music Press (1969) found in The Solo Psalmist

13:1-6
    SOWERBY, Leo
    How Long Wilt Thou Forget Me
    Organ: a^b - e^{b}1
    H.W.Gray (1929)

13:5-6
    SCHUTZ, Heinrich (ed. Don McAfee)
    Lord, My Hope Is In Thee (Herr, ich hoffe darauf)
    English/German Continuo: DUET
    Belwin (1977) found in Eight Sacred Duets; also published by
        Barenreiter in German only.

16:00
    SEE: Psalm 10
    PERGOLESI, Giovanni B.
    O Lord Have Mercy Upon Me

16:10
    SEE: Psalm 69:20
    HANDEL, G. F.
    Thy Rebuke Hath

17:00
    GARLICK, Anthony
    Psalm 17 (A Psalm Song Cycle)
    Piano: f1-g2
    SeeSaw

18:00
    CORNELIUS, Peter (ed. M.B.Stearns)
    I Love Thee, Lord, My Strength, Op.2, #2
    Keyboard: e1-f2
    Coburn Press (1971) found in Lift Up Your Voice

18:00
    SACCO, Peter
    The Sorrows Of Death Compassed Me
    Piano/Organ: D1-C3
    Ostara Press

18:2
    NELHYBEL, Vaclav
    The Lord Is My Rock
    Organ: d1-e2
    Agape (1981) found in Psalm Settings

18:2-3, 6
    BIRCH, Robert Fairfax
    I Will Worship The Lord, Op.35, #1
    Keyboard: c1 - a^{b}3
    Joseph Patelson (1965)

18:2-7
    SCHUTZ, Heinrich
    Daily Will I Love Thee (Herzlich Lieb hab 'ich dich)
    Continuo, 2 violins: g$^\sharp$ - b^{b}2
    Bomart (Associated)

18:28
    SEE: Psalm 27:4
    TALMA, Louise
    Cantata: All The Days of My Life

18:32, 37 (Psalm 144:1-2; Psalm 91:5; Ephesians 6:11; Revelation
      21:7
    VAUGHAN-WILLIAMS, Ralph
    The Pilgrim's Psalm
    Keyboard: d1-f2
    Oxford (1952) from The Pilgrim's Progress

19:00 (based on)
    HANKS, Billie Jr.
    The Heavens Declare His Glory
    Keyboard: d1-e2
    Hope (1971) found in Everything For The Church Soloist (Hope,
      1980)

19:1-6 (Addison)
ADDISON, Joseph
The Spacious Firmament
Piano: f-e2
Oliver Ditson (1906)

19:10
COUPERIN, Francois
Domines Salvum fac regem
Latin   Continuo: Duet
Heugel (found in Neuf Motets)

19:14
SEE: Psalm 46:10a
BITGOOD, Roberta
Be Still, and Know That I Am God

19:14
HUMPHREYS, Don
My Prayer
Piano: c1 - e^{b}2
Willis (1969) found in Sing To The Lord

22:00
BLOCH, Ernest
Psalm 22 (Elohim! Why Hast Thou Forsaken Me?)
Piano: b-f1
G. Schirmer

22:2 (Matthew 27:46; and other)
SHALITT (adapted Kurt Schindler)
Eili, Eili! Invocation
English/German   Piano: MED:g$^\sharp$ - e2; HIGH:c1-f2
G.Schirmer (1917) (Free Library)

22:7
HANDEL, G.F.
All They That See Him, Laugh Him To Scorn (Messiah)
Keyboard: Tenor:f-f1
Carl Fischer; G.Schirmer; Novello

22:11
NELHYBEL, Vaclav
Be Not Far From Me
Organ: d1-f2
Agape (1981) found in Psalm Settings

22:14
SEE: Psalm 61:1
LADERMAN, Ezra
From The End Of The Earth

22:27
SEE: Psalm 57:10
HANDEL, G.F.
God's Tender Mercy Knows No Bounds

23:00
ADAMS, Joseph H.
The Lord Is My Shepherd
Keyboard: c1-f2
Paxton (1900)

23:00
ANDREWS, Mark
The Twenty-Third Psalm
Piano/Organ: $b^b1 - e^b2$
G.Schirmer (1930)

23:00 (adapted)
ARCADELT, Jacob (arr. Carl Fredrickson)
The Lord Is My Shepherd
Keyboard: d1-d2
R.D.Row (1959) found in Sacred Song Masterpieces

23:00
ARCHER, Violet
The Twenty-Third Psalm
Piano/Organ: b1-f2
B.M.I.

23:00
BAIN, James (arr. Phyllis Tate)
Brother James's Air
Piano: e1-f2
Oxford (1951)

23:00
BAIN, James (arr. Arthur Trew)
Brother James's Air
Piano: c1-d2
Oxford (1938)

23:00
BEDELL, Robert L.
The Twenty-Third Psalm
Keyboard: c1-e2
Edition Le Grand Orgue (1955)

23:00
BEN-HAIM, Paul
Psalm 23
Hebrew   Piano/Organ: g-g2
Israeli Music Pub. (1962)

23:00
 BERLINSKI, Hermann
 Psalm XXIII
 Flute: $c^{\sharp}1$ - a3
 Berlin [Merrymount] (1962)

23:00
 BETTS, Lorne
 Psalm 23
 Organ: $a^{b}1$ - f2
 Canadian Music Centre (found in Six Sacred Songs)

23:00
 BINDER, Abraham Wolf
 The Lord Is My Shepherd
 Organ: LOW:$c^{\sharp}1$ - e2; HIGH:d1-f2
 Transcontinental

23:00
 BLAIR, Kathleen
 He Restoreth My Soul
 Piano/Organ: LOW:b1-d2; HIGH:d1-g2
 G.Schirmer (1932)

23:00
 BOHN, Carl
 The Lord Is My Shepherd
 Piano: $a^{b}2$ - $e^{b}2$
 Ditson (1889) found in Choice Sacred Solos

23:00
 BROWN, Russell J.
 The Twenty-Third Psalm
 Keyboard: e1-g2
 H.W.Gray (1945)

23:00 (taken from)
 BROONES, Martin
 David's Psalm
 Keyboard: b1-d2
 Morris (1950)

23:00
 BUSS, Duane
 Psalm 23
 Piano: $d^{\sharp}1$ - g2
 American Music Center (1982)

23:00 (Baker)
 BUTT, James
 The King of Love
 Organ: e1-e2
 Sphemusations (n.d.)

23:00
CARMICHAEL, Ralph
The New 23rd Psalm
Keyboard: c1-f2
Lexicon Music (1969) found in Everything For The Church Soloist
    (Hope, 1980); also Scripture Solos For All Seasons (Lillenas, 1980).

23:00
CLARKE, Henry Leland
The Lord Is My Shepherd
Flute (or Clarinet), String Bass (or 3 Timpani): c1-a3
American Composers Alliance (1974)

23:00 (Baker)
CRAWFORD, John
The King Of Love
Piano: e1-g2
American Composers Alliance (MS)

23:00
CRESTON, Paul
Psalm XXIII
Organ/Piano: LOW:d1 - f$^\sharp$2; HIGH:f1 - a$^\flat$e
G.Schirmer (1945)

23:00
DAVYE, John J.
The Lord Is My Shepherd
Organ: e1-f2
MS (1978) from Two Psalms Of Meditation

23:00
DEACON, Mary
Beside Still Waters
Keyboard: b1-f2
H.W.Gray (1956)

23:00
DVORAK, Anton
God Is My Shepherd, Op.99, #4
Piano: LOW:b1 - c$^\sharp$2; HIGH:d1 - f$^\sharp$2
Simrock; G.Schirmer; R.D.Row; in low key in The Church Year
    In Song (G.Schirmer)

23:00
ELLIS, James G.
I Shall Not Want
Keyboard: LOW:a$^\flat$1 - d$^\flat$2; MED:b$^\flat$1 - e$^\flat$2; HIGH:d1-g2
Boston (1935)

23:00
ESPINA, Noni
Shepherd's Psalm
Piano/Organ: LOW:c1-f2; HIGH:e^{b}1 - g$^\#$2
Vita d'Arte; originally keyboard and flute

23:00
EVILLE, Vernon
I Will Dwell In The House Of The Lord
Keyboard: LOW:a1-d2; MED:b1-e2; MED-HIGH:c1-f2; HIGH:d1-g2
Boosey (1917)

23:00
FLOWERS, Geoffrey
Psalm 23
Piano/Organ: b^{b}1 - g^{b}2
Coburn Press (found in Eleven Scripture Songs)

23:00
FREUDENTHAL, Josef
The Lord Is My Shepherd
Keyboard: LOW:a1-e2; HIGH:c1-g2
Transcontinental (1959) TV 497

23:00
GARDNER, Adelaide (arr. Bob Mitchell)
The Lord Is My Shepherd
Keyboard: d1-d2
Robert Brown (1961)

23:00
GARLICK, Anthony
Psalm 23 (A Psalm Song Cycle)
Piano: e1-f2
SeeSaw

23:00
GILBERT, N.
The Lord Is My Shepherd
Keyboard: DUET
H.W.Gray

23:00
GOETZ, Marty
Psalm 23
Keyboard: b^{b}1 - d2
Alson-Flosom Music [Meadowgreen Music, Inc.] (1980) also
     found in Contemporary Christian Classics (Lorenz, 1982)

23:00
GOLDMAN, E.
Psalm 22
Piano/Organ: b1-e2
World

23:00
GOODE, Jack
Psalm 23
Piano/Organ: d1 - g#2
Abingdon (also found in Seven Sacred Solo)

23:00 (Baker)
GOUNOD, Charles
The King Of Love My Shepherd Is
Keyboard: LOW:b1-d2; MED:c1-e2; HIGH:e1-g2
Presser (n.d.) [Free Library]

23:00 (C. Becker)
HELDER, Bartholomaeus
The Lord My Shepherd Is
Organ: e1-e2
Concordia (1952) found in Wedding Blessing in either high or
low.

23:00 (Baker)
HOLLER, John
The King Of Love My Shepherd Is
Organ or Piano: c1 - f#2
H.W.Gray (1938)

23:00 (Psalm 63; paraphrase)
HUMMEL, Ferdinand
Alleluia
Piano: e^{b}1 - a^{b}3
Belwin (1969)

23:00 (Psalm 63; adapted)
HUMMEL, Ferdinand (arr. Fredrickson)
Alleluia!
Piano/Organ: DUET
R.D.Row (1960) found in Sacred Duet Masterpieces

23:00
HUMPHREYS, Don
The Lord Is My Shepherd
Piano: c1-e2
Willis (1969) found in Sing To The Lord

23:00
ISAACSON, Michael
Psalm 23
Hebrew   Piano: D1-a3
Transcontinental (1979)

23:00 (adapted)
KALMANOFF, Martin
The Lord Is My Shepherd
Piano/Organ: b^{b}1 - f2
Carl Fischer (1951)

23:00
    KINGSLEY, Gershon
    The Lord Is My Shepherd
    Organ: d1 - e^{b}2
    Transcontinental (1976) TV 576

23:00
    KOCH, John
    The Lord Is My Shepherd (Songs Of David)
    Flute & String Quartet: f1-g2
    American Music Center

23:00
    LaMONTAINE, John
    The Lord Is My Shepherd
    Organ/Piano: b^{b}1 - g^{b}2
    H.W.Gray

23:00
    LIDDLE, Samuel
    I Shall Not Want
    Piano: LOW:b1-c2; MED:c$^{\#}$1 - d2; MED-HIGH:d1 - e^{b}2; HIGH:e1-f2
    Boosey & Hawkes (1961)

23:00
    LOWE, Augustus
    Psalm 23
    Organ: e^b - f2
    Carl Fischer (1970)

23:00
    MADER, Clarence
    The Lord Is My Shepherd
    Organ: c$^{\#}$1 - f$^{\#}$2
    W.I.M. (1975) found in Three Biblical Songs, WIM-128

23:00
    MALOTTE, Albert Hay
    The Twenty-Third Psalm
    Piano: LOW:b^{b}1 - e^{b}2; MED:c1-f2; HIGH:d1-g2
    G.Schirmer (1937) also found in Everything For The Church
       Soloist (Hope, 1980) in medium key

23:00
    MARTIN, Broones
    David's Psalm
    Piano: LOW;b1-d2; HIGH:e1-g2
    Edwin H. Morris (1950)

23:00
    MATTHEWS, Thomas
    The Lord Is My Shepherd
    Organ: c1-g2
    H.T.FitzSimons (1965)

23:00
   MEEK, Kenneth
   The Lord Is My Shepherd
   Organ: c#1 - a3
   H.W.Gray

23:00 (1650 Scottish Psalter)
   MUELLER, Carl F.
   The Lord's My Shepherd (based on tune 'Crimond')
   Piano/Organ: e^{b}1 - a^{b}3
   Carl Fischer (1958)

23:00
   O'CONNOR-MORRIS, G.
   Psalm 23
   Keyboard
   Carl Fischer

23:00
   ORE, Charles W.
   The Lord Is My Shepherd (Lisbon Psalm)
   Piano/Organ: c1-f2
   Concordia (1975) Piano - Set I; Organ - Set II

23:00
   RIDDLE, Peter
   Psalm XXIII
   Piano/Organ: c1-g2
   SeeSaw

23:00
   RUBBRA, Edmund
   Psalm XXIII, Op.61
   Piano/Organ: a#1 - d2
   Lengnick (found in Three Psalms For Low Voice)

23:00
   SACCO, Peter
   The Lord Is My Shepherd
   Piano/Organ: d^{b}1 - a^{b}3
   Ostara

23:00
   SCOTT, John Prindle
   The Lord Is My Shepherd
   Piano: LOW:c1 - e^{b}2; HIGH:e1-g2
   G.Schirmer (1923)

23:00
   SHELLY, Harry Rowe
   The King Of Love My Shepherd Is
   Organ: d1-e2
   G.Schirmer (1914)

23:00 (paraphrase; W.S. Passmore)
SMART, Henry
The Lord Is My Shepherd
Piano: DUET:Sop/Alto
G.Schirmer (n.d.) [Free Library] also found in <u>Sacred Duets</u>,
   John Church [Presser] (1907); also found in <u>Choice Sacred</u>
   <u>Duets</u>, Oliver Ditson,(1936).

23:00
SOWERBY, Leo
The Lord Is My Shepherd
Piano/Organ: F - d^b1
H.W.Gray (1929)

23:00
SPENCE, William
The King Of Love My Shepherd Is
Keyboard: LOW:b^b1 - e^b2; HIGH:e^b1 - a^b3
Oliver Ditson (1906) found in low key in <u>Sacred Songs</u> [Ditson]

23:00
STEARNS, Peter Pindar (ed. M.B. Stearns)
The Lord Is My Shepherd
Organ: c1-d2
Coburn Press (1971) found in <u>Lift Up Your Voice</u>

23:00 (paraphrase)
TAYLOR, Raynor (ed. Gordon Myers)
The Lord Is My Shepherd
Piano/Organ: b1-e2
Eastlane Music (1970) found in <u>Six Songs Of Early America</u>

23:00
TCHAIKOVSKY, Peter (adapted and arranged Richard Maxwell and
   Fred Feibel)
The Lord Is My Shepherd
Keyboard: c1-d2
G.Schirmer (1939) found in <u>52 Sacred Songs</u>

23:00 (G. Herbert)
THIMAN, Eric H.
The God Of Love My Shepherd Is
Keyboard: c1-f2
Novello (1926)

23:00 (paraphrase by Watts)
THOMSON, Virgil
My Shepherd Will Supply My Need
Keyboard: d1 - $f^{\#}2$
H.W.Gray (1959)

23:00
    TRIPLETT, Robert
    The Lord Is My Shepherd
    Organ: b1-a3
    Abingdon (1968)

23:00
    VAN DE WATER, Beardsley
    The Good Shepherd
    Keyboard: LOW:a1-e2; HIGH:c1-g2
    Oliver Ditson (1935)

23:00
    VAUGHAN-WILLIAMS, Ralph
    The Bird's Song (from The Pilgrim's Progress)
    Piano: d^{b}1 - f2
    Oxford (1952)

23:00
    WIEMAR, Wolfgang
    Der Herr ist meine Hirt
    German   Organ: A - e^{b}1
    Breitkopf (1969) 6429

23:00
    WINTON, Mary
    Psalm 23
    Keyboard: d^{b}1 - f2
    E.Newgrass [Carl Fischer] (1956)

23:00
    WOLFORD, Julie Lofgren
    The Shepherd
    Keyboard: e1-f2
    Flammer (1975) found in Songs Of Praise By Contemporary
        Composers

23:00
    ZAIMONT, Judith Lang
    Psalm 23 (1979)
    Piano: Mezzo
    Allied Artists Bureau, Michael Leavitt

23:4
    KINSCELLA, Hazel Gertrude
    Yea, Though I Walk Through The Valley
    Keyboard: LOW:g - c$^{\#}$2; MED:b^{b}1 - e2; HIGH:d1 - g$^{\#}$2
    J.Fischer (1936)

23:4
    SEE: Psalm 5:8
    MOLIQUE, B.
    Lead Me Lord

23:4
SEE: Psalm 42:5
REINTHALER, C.
Why Art Thou Cast Down, O My Soul?

24:1-5
FREUDENTHAL, Josef
The Earth Is The Lord's
Keyboard: LOW:b1-e2; HIGH:d1-g2
Transcontinental (1955)

24:1-5
McAFEE, Don
The Earth Is The Lord's
Keyboard: d1-d2
Sacred Music Press (1969) found in The Solo Psalmist

24:1-7, 8-11
SEE: Psalm 130
YARDUMIAN, Richard
Symphony #2

25:00
MARZO, Eduardo
Unto Thee O Lord, Op. 146
Keyboard: LOW:c1-f2; HIGH:e1-a3
Flammer (1917)

25:00
ORE, Charles W.
Turn Thee Unto Me, (from Lisbon Psalms)
Piano/Organ: c1-f2
Concordia (1975) Set I - Piano; Set II - Organ

25:1 (Psalm 90:17; and other)
CORNELIUS, Peter
Unto Thee I Lift Up My Soul
Keyboard: $e^b1 - e^b2$
Coburn (1971) found in Lift Up Your Voice

25:4, 5
SEE: Psalm 27:4
Talma, Louise
Cantata: All The Days Of My Life

25:5
NELHYBEL, Vaclav
Hear Me When I Call
Organ: e1-f2
Agape (1981)

25:5
   PETER, Johann F.
   Lead Me In Thy Truth
   Organ (Piano) & Strings: $e^b1 - g2$
   C.F.Peters

25:16-18, 20
   DVORAK, Anton
   Turn Thee To Me And Have Mercy, Op.99
   Keyboard: LOW:$d^b1 - d^b2$; HIGH:f1-f2
   Simrock; G.Schirmer

26:8 (Psalm 27:1, 4, 5, 6b; Psalm 96:6)
   BAUMGARTNER, H. Leroy
   Lord, I Have Loved The Habitations Of Thy House, Op.48,#3
      from O Lord, My God, Thou Art Very Good
   Keyboard
   Concordia (1958)

27:00
   EDWARDS, Clara
   The Lord Is My Light
   Keyboard: LOW:$b^b1 - e^b2$; HIGH:d1-g2
   G.Schirmer (1938)

27:00
   SPEAKS, Oley
   The Lord Is My Light
   Piano: d1-g2
   G.Schirmer (1913)

27:1 (Psalm 34:22; Psalm 143:7-8; Lamentations 3:22, 37)
   VanVOLLENHOVEN, Hanna
   Hear Me Speedily, O Lord!
   Organ: LOW:c1-e2; HIGH:e1 - $g^{\#}2$
   G.Schirmer (1940)

27:1
   SEE: Psalm 130
   YARDUMIAN, Richard
   Symphony #2

27:1, 2, 3, 5
   WOLLER, Alfred
   The Lord Is My Light
   Piano: LOW:$b^b1 - d2$; MED:c1 - e^b2; MED-HIGH:$d^b1 - f2$; HIGH:
      $e^b1 - g2$
   Oliver Ditson (1917)

27:1, 3, 5
   ALLITSEN, Frances
   The Lord Is My Light
   Piano: LOW:a1 - e^b2; MED:b1-f2; MED-HIGH:c1-g2; HIGH:d1 -a^b3
   Boosey & Hawkes (1925); also G.Schirmer; also found in medium
      key in Everything For The Church Soloist (Hope, 1980)

27:1, 3, 5
    BUCK, Dudley
    The Lord Is My Light
    Keyboard: Duet
    G. Schirmer (1917)

27:1, 4, 5, 6b
    SEE: Psalm 26:8
    BAUMGARTNER, H. Leroy
    Lord, I Have Loved The Habitation Of Thy House, Op. 48, #3

27:1, 4, 6
    CHARLES, Ernest
    Psalm Of Exaltation
    Piano or Organ: e1-f2
    G.Schirmer (1951)

27:1, 4-6
    HUMPHREYS, Don
    The Lord Is My Light
    Keyboard: LOW:b^{b}1 - e^{b}2; HIGH:c1-f2
    Boston (1947)

27:1, 5, 6 (Job 33:15, 16)
    BUCK, Dudley
    The Lord Is My Light
    Organ/Piano: DUET:S-T
    G.Schirmer (1889)

27:4
    SCHUTZ, Heinrich (ed. Don McAfee)
    One Thing I Ask Of The Lord (einbitte ich vom Herren)
    English/German   Continuo: DUET
    Belwin (1977) found in Eight Sacred Songs; also German only
        by Barenreiter

27:4 (Psalm 39:5; Job 7:6; Psalm 102:11; Deuteronomy 28:67;
        Psalm 39:4; Psalm 25:4, 5; Psalm 55:17; Psalm 59:16, 17;
        Psalm 119:62; Psalm 65:8, 11; Psalm 71:15, 17; Mark 13:35;
        John 12:35; I Chronicles 29:15; John 9:4; Psalm 18:28;
        Job 11:17; Psalm 18:28; Revelation 22:5; Psalm 30:5)
    TALMA, Louise
    Cantata: All The Days of My Life (A work of seven movements)
    Piano/Celesta; Clarinet; Cello; Percussion: Tenor:c-a2
    American Music Center (n.d.)

27:7-8, 9, 11, 13-4
    BAUMGARTNER, H. Leroy
    Hear, O Lord, When I Cry With My Voice, Op. 48, #4 from O Lord
        My God, Thou Art Very Good
    Keyboard: c#1 - f2
    Concordia (1958)

27:13, 14 (Ecclesiastes 3:1-8)
SACCO, John
God's Time
Piano: d1-f2
G.Schirmer (1944)

28:00
GARLICK, Anthony
Psalm 28 (A Psalm Song Cycle)
Piano: f1 - f#2
SeeSaw

28:1
PURCELL, Henry
Unto Thee Will I Cry
English/German   Continuo, 2 Violins, Viola: Bass:d-d1
Barenreiter (1959)

29:1, 2 (Psalm 6:4)
SCHUTZ, Heinrich (ed. Richard T. Gore)
Bring To Jehovah
English/German Keyboard:e♭1 - f2
Concordia (1957) found in Five Sacred Songs

29:1, 2
SCHUTZ, Heinrich
Bringt her dem Herren
German   Continuo: c1-e2
Barenreiter (1963)

29:1-2
SCHUTZ, Heinrich (ed. Lloyd Pfautsch
Give God The Father
Piano: b1-d2
Lawson-Gould (1961) found in The Church Soloist

30:00
CORNELIUS, Peter (ed. M.B.Stearns)
Sing Unto The Lord, Op.2,#4
Keyboard: c#1 - d2
Coburn Press (1971) in Lift Up Your Voice

30:1, 2, 11
COSTA, M.
I Will Extol Thee, O Lord (Eli)
Keyboard: f1-a3
G.Schirmer, found in Anthology Of Sacred Song - Soprano

30:1-3, 11-12
SEE: Psalm 13:1-3
ARCHER, Violet
Miserere et Jubilate

30:2, 12
   SEE: Psalm 69:1
   HARRIS, Cuthbert
   Save Me, O God

30:5
   SEE: Psalm 32:11
   HUHN, Bruno
   Be Glad, O Ye Righteous

30:5
   SEE: Psalm 27:4
   TALMA, Louise
   Cantata: All The Days of My Life

30:5-6
   SCHUTZ, Heinrich (ed. Don McAfee)
   Praise Ye The Lord (Ihr Heiligen, lobsinet dem Herren)
   English/German   Continuo: DUET
   Belwin (1977) found in Eight Sacred Duets; also German only
      by Barenreiter .11

31:1, 9, 15-16
   STARER, Robert
   Have Mercy Upon Me, O Lord
   Keyboard: d1-g2
   Southern (1964) found in Two Sacred Songs

31:2, 3
   SCHUTZ, Heinrich
   In te, domine, Speravi
   Latin/German   Alto, Flute, Bassoon & Continuo: c1-d2
   Barenreiter (1965) 30

31:2, 3, 4
   BUXTEHUDE, Dietrich
   Herr, auf Dich traue ich
   German   Organ, 2 Violins: $d^{\#}1$ - a3
   Barenreiter (1949)

31:2, 3, 4
   BUXTEHUDE, Dietrich (arr. Clarence Dickinson)
   Lord, In Thee Do I Trust
   Organ, 2 Violins: $d^{\#}1$ - a3
   H.W.Gray (1950) GV 98

31:5 (Psalm 127:1; Psalm 121; Isaiah 14:7)
   VAUGHAN-WILLIAMS, Ralph
   Watchful's Song
   Keyboard: $c^{\#}1$ - e2
   Oxford (1952) from The Pilgrim's Song

31:19, 24
  BEAUMONT, Vivian
  Be Of Good Courage
  Piano: LOW:a1-d2; HIGH:c1 - e^{b}2
  G. Schirmer (1957)

32:11 (Psalm 30:5; Psalm 55:17; Psalm 145:2; I Timothy 1:17)
  HUHN, Bruno
  Be Glad, O Ye Righteous
  Keyboard: LOW:b1-d2; MED:c$^{\#}$1 - e2; HIGH:e1-g2
  Archur Schmidt (1912)

33:00
  SCHNECKER, P.A.
  Rejoice In The Lord
  Piano: DUET:A-B
  G. Schirmer (1889)

33:3
  BUXTEHUDE, Dietrich
  Sing To The Lord A New Song
  English/German   Continuo & Violin: c1-g2
  Concordia

33:3
  GORE, Richard
  O Sing Unto The Lord A New Song
  Organ: e1 - a^{b}3
  J. Fischer

33:20-22
  PELZ, Walter
  Our Soul Waits For The Lord
  Organ & Cello: e1-a3
  Augsburg (1979) 11-9477 found in Three Solos For High Voice

33:21
  POWELL, Robert
  Our Heart Shall Rejoice In The Lord
  Keyboard: d1-e2
  Concordia (1974) 97-5278 found in Three Wedding Songs

34:00
  HONEGGER, Arthur
  Benedica Dominum in Omni (Trois Psaumes)
  French   Piano: c1-c2
  Salabert (1963)

34:00
  HUMPHREYS, Don
  I Sought The Lord
  Piano: d1-f2
  Willis (1965) in Sing To The Lord

34:1-6
   DIETTERICH, Philip
   Now Will I Praise The Lord
   Keyboard: el-g2
   Abingdon (1970)

34:1-7
   SCHUTZ, Heinrich (ed. Richard T. Gore)
   Now Will I Praise The Lord
   English/German   Keyboard: cl-f2
   Concordia (1957) 98-1370 in Five Sacred Songs

34:2-7
   SCHUTZ, Heinrich
   I Will Bless The Lord At All Times (from Five Small Spiritual
      Concerts)
   Keyboard: cl-g2
   G. Schirmer (1978) found in The Church Year In Song

34:2-4
   TELEMANN, G.P. (ed. Klaus Hofmann)
   Ich will den Herren loben allezeit
   English/German   Continuo: DUET:S-A
   Hanssler 39.125

34:2-5, 7
   SCHUTZ, Heinrich
   Ich will den Herren loben allezeit
   German   Continuo: DUET
   Barenreiter (1963) 1701

34:4 (Psalm 121:8; Revelation 21:4)
   STEVENSON, Frederich
   I Sought The Lord
   Organ: LOW:bl-d2; HIGH:dl-f2
   Oliver Ditson (1916) in Choice Sacred Songs (ed. Wilmans)

34:8
   FISCHER, I.
   Taste and See that The Lord Is Good
   Piano/Organ: Dl-G2
   Composers Facsimile Edition

34:18-19, 21-22
   DEMAREST, C. Agnew
   The Lord Is Nigh Unto Them
   Organ: cl-f2
   Boston (1959)

34:22
   SEE: Psalm 27:1
   VanVOLLENHOVEN, Hanna
   Hear Me Speedily, O Lord!

36:00
HUMPHREYS, Don
How Excellent Is Thy Lovingkindness
Piano: c1 - e^{b}2
Willis (1965) found in Sing To The Lord

36:00
MacDERMID, James G.
The Shadow Of Thy Wings
Keyboard: LOW:b1 - e^{b}2; HIGH: d1 - f$^{\#}$2
Forster (1953)

36:5-7, 11
LaFORGE, Frank
Thy Mercy, O Lord, Is In The Heavens
Piano: LOW:b1-f2
Carl Fischer (1938) 1373-high:1374-low

36:9
SEE: Isaiah 1:18
BARKER, Clement W.
The Path Of The Just

37:00
HUMPHREYS, Don
Rest In The Lord
Keyboard: LOW:c$^{\#}$1 - d2; HIGH:e1-f2
R.D.Row (1960) found in Songs For Christian Science Services,
Book I

37:00
SEE: Psalm 145
FISCHER, Irwin
Delight Thyself In The Lord

37:1, 4-5, 7
MENDELSSOHN, Felix
O Rest In The Lord
Piano: b1-d2
G. Schirmer (1937) found in Anthology Of Sacred Songs; also
in 52 Sacred Songs; also Scripture Solos For All Seasons
(Lillenas, 1980)

37:1-5
SCHUTZ, Heinrich
Habe deine Lust an dem Herren
German: Continuo: DUET:S-S
Barenreiter (1963) 1138

37:9
SEE: Isaiah 1:18
BARKER, Clement W.
The Path Of The Just

37:25
    SCHUTZ, Heinrich
    Ich bin jung gewesen
    German   Continuo: 2 voices
    Barenreiter (1963) 1705

39:00
    SOWERBY, Leo
    Hear My Cry, O God
    Piano/Organ: f - e^b1
    H.W.Gray

39:4
    SEE: Psalm 27:4
    TALMA, Louise
    Cantata: All The Days of My Life

39:4-5 (Isaiah 40:6-8)
    WYNER, Yehudi
    Lord, Let Me Know My End - Memorial Music II
    3 Flutes (2 in C; 1 Alto)   al-a3
    Associated (1975) AMP 7440

39:5
    SEE: Psalm 27:4
    TALMA, Louise
    Cantata: All The Days of My Life

39:12
    SEE: Psalm 55:6
    BARNES, A.M.
    Oh That I Had Wings

39:12b
    SEE: Psalm 39:13a
    LADERMAN, Ezra
    Look Away From Me

39:13a (Psalm 39:12b; Psalm 103:13-14)
    LADERMAN, Ezra
    Look Away From Me (from From The Psalms)
    Piano: d^b1 - a3
    Oxford (1970)

40:00 (adapted)
    BECK, John Ness
    Song Of Joy
    Piano: fl-d2
    C.F.Peters (1970) 6840

40:1
    SAINT-SAENS, C.
    I Waited For The Lord
    Keyboard: cl-g2
    Abingdon (1964) APM 308 found in Select Solos For The Church
        Musician

40:1-4
    HARTLEY, Walter S.
    Andante Con Moto (from A Psalm Cycle)
    Piano & Flute: c1-a3
    Presser

40:1-4, 8, 9b, 10b, 11-12, 16
    MADER, Clarence
    I Waited Patiently For The Lord (from Three Biblical Songs)
    Organ: c1-g2
    W.I.M. (1975) WIM 128

40:14-18
    SCHUTZ, Heinrich (ed. Richard Gore)
    Haste Thee, Lord God, Haste To Save Me (Eile, mich Gott, zu
        erretten)
    English/German   Continuo: d1-g2
    Concordia (1954) 98-1370 in Five Sacred Songs; also German
        only by Barenreiter (1963) 1701

41:1-4
    HANDEL, G.F.
    Blessed Are They (Foundling Hospital Anthem)
    Keyboard: d1-g2
    Novello

42:00
    ALLITSEN, Frances
    Like As The Hart Desireth
    Keyboard: LOW:a1-c2; MED:c1-f2; HIGH:d1-g2
    Boosey (1925)

42:00
    BLAIR, Kathleen
    As The Hart Panteth
    Keyboard: f1 - g^{b}2
    H.W.Gray (1953)

42:00
    LANSING, A.W.
    As Pants The Hart
    Keyboard: DUET:A-T
    White-Smith (1912)

42:00
    LIDDLE, S.
    Like As The Hart
    Piano
    Boosey (1961) [Free Library]

42:00
    MARCELLO, Benedetto
    As Pants The Weared Hart
    Keyboard: DUET:2 high
    John Church (Presser) (1907) found in Sacred Duets, Vol. I

42:00
   SMART, Henry
   As Pants The Hart
   Piano: DUET
   Oliver Ditson (1891) found in Choice Sacred Duets

42:00
   STRICKLAND, Lily
   As Pants The Hart
   Keyboard: d1-g2
   Presser (1919)

42:00
   WEST, John A.
   Like As The Hart
   Keyboard: LOW:b^{b}1 - d2; HIGH:d1 - f$^\#$2
   Arthur P. Schmidt (1906)

42:1-2, 12
   POHLE, David (ed. Helmut Winter)
   Wie der Hirsch schreyet
   German: 2 Violins, Bassoon, Continuo: Tenor:e-g1
   Sikorski (1965) #650 Score & parts

42:1-4a
   FROMM, Herbert
   Psalm 42 (from Four Psalms)
   Keyboard: g1-g2
   Transcontinental (1971)

42:2
   STICKLES, William
   My Soul Is Athirst For God
   Piano/Organ: LOW:c1 - e^{b}2; MED:d1-f2; HIGH:f1 - a^{b}3
   Schroeder & Gunther (1923)

42:2, 3
   GAUL, A.R.
   My Soul Is Athirst For God (The Holy City)
   Keyboard: e1-a3
   G. Schirmer found in Anthology of Sacred Song - Tenor

42:5 (Psalm 23:4)
   REINTHALER, C.
   Why Art Thou Cast Down, O My Soul? (from Jephtha And His
      Daughter)
   Keyboard: d1-a3
   G. Schirmer (1901) found in Anthology of Sacred Songs - SOP

42:5
   SPICKER, Max
   Why Art Thou Cast Down, O My Soul?
   Piano: c1-f2
   G. Schirmer (1902)

42:8
  SEE: Psalm 43:3-5
  MENDELSSOHN, Felix
  Why Art Thou Cast Down, O My Soul? (in Lift Up Your Voice)

43:1-3
  HARTLEY, Walter S.
  Adagio Ma Non Troppo (from A Psalm Cycle)
  Piano & Flute: cl-a3
  Tenuto (Presser)

43:1, 2, 3, 4
  WOOLER, Alfred
  Send Out Thy Light
  Piano: bl - e^{b}2
  Ditson (1913)

43:3:5 (Psalm 42:8)
  MENDELSSOHN, Felix
  Why Art Thou Cast Down, My Soul?
  Keyboard: cl-e2
  Coburn Press (1971) found in Lift Up Your Voice

45:1-2 (Psalm 8:4)
  DENCKE, Jeremiah
  I Speak Of Things
  Organ & Strings: el-f2
  Carl Fischer found in Ten Sacred Songs

46:00
  DUNGAN, Olive
  Be Still And Know That I Am God
  Piano: cl-g2
  Presser (1955)

46:00
  HANSON, Howard
  God Is Our Refuge And Strength
  Keyboard: al-f2
  Carl Fischer (1972) from Four Psalms

46:00
  MacDERMID, James
  God Is Our Refuge
  Keyboard: d^{b}1 - e^{b}2
  Forster (1915)

46:1-6, 10
  POWERS, Margaret Westlake
  Be Still, And Know
  Piano/Organ: LOW:bl-d2; HIGH:d^{b}1 - f2
  G. Schirmer (1941)

46:8-10
STANFORD, Charles Villiers
O Come Hither
Keyboard: d^b1 - f2
Novello   from God Is Our Hope And Strength

46:9, 10
CHADWICK, George
He Maketh Wars To Cease
Keyboard: LOW:a1-d2; HIGH:c1-f2
Schmidt (1892)

46:10
SEE: Exodus 15:3
ANONYMOUS
The Lord Is A Mighty Warrior

46:10a (Psalm 145:18; Psalm 62:1; Psalm 19:14; Psalm 85:8)
BITGOOD, Roberta
Be Still, And Know That I Am God
Keyboard: LOW:b1-d2; MED:$c^{\#}1$ - e2; HIGH:e^b1 - g2
H.W.Gray (1947)

47:00
HANSON, Howard
O Clap Your Hands, All Ye People
Keyboard: e^b1 - f2
Carl Fischer (1972) from Four Psalms

47:1-2
SEE: Psalm 68:4
HORVIT, Michael
Sing To God

47:1-2, 6-7 (Psalm 48:1-2, 12-14)
HUHN, Bruno
Great Is The Lord
Piano: LOW:b^b1 - f2; HIGH:d1-a3
Boston (1923)

47:1, 5-8
McAFEE, Don
O Clap Your Hands
Keyboard: c1 - e^b2
Sacred Music Press (1969) found in The Solo Psalmist

47:1-6
SCHUTZ, Heinrich
Frohlocket
German   Continuo & 2 Violins: BASS:c-e1
Barenreiter (1936) 1088

48:1-2, 12-14
    SEE: Psalm 47:1-2, 6-7
    HUHN, Bruno
    Great Is The Lord

49:00
    ORLAND, Henry
    From Psalm 49, Op. 18, #3 (from Six Occasional Songs)
    Piano: G# - f1
    SeeSaw (197?)

49:1
    JONES, Kelsey
    Psalm Forty-Nine (1.Hear This All Ye People; 2.They That
        Trust In Their Wealth; 3.Death Shall Feed In Them; 4.And
        The Upright Shall Have Dominion)
    Piano: g-g2
    Canadian Music Center

49:16b
    SEE: Psalm 127:1
    MYERS, Gordon
    Except The Lord Build The House

50:14 (Psalm 95:1-7)
    PENDLETON, Emmet
    Sing Unto The Lord, Op.12,#4 (Light Of The Lord)
    Piano: c1 - eb2
    Bruce Humphries (1945)

51:00
    EVANS, Vincent
    Create In Me A Clean Heart
    Keyboard: e1-g2
    Abingdon (1964) APM 308 found in Select Vocal Solos For The
        Church Musician

51:00
    MENDELSSOHN, Felix
    O God Have Mercy (St. Paul)
    Keyboard: b-d1
    G. Schirmer

51:00 (metrical)
    WOOLER, Alfred
    God Be Merciful To Me
    Organ or Piano: c#1 - d2
    Oliver Ditson (1921)

51:1
    STARER, Robert
    Have Mercy Upon Me, O Lord
    Piano/Organ: d1-g2
    Southern

51:9-11
>TIMMINGS, William
>Turn Thy Face From My Sings
>Keyboard: e^{b}1 - f2
>Heidelberg Press (1921)

51:10
>SCHUTZ, Heinrich (ed. Don McAfee)
>Lord, Create In Me A Clean Heart (schaffe in mir, Gott, ein
> reines Herz) in Kleine Geistliche Konzerte
>English/German   Continuo: DUET
>Belwin (1977) found in Eight Sacred Duets; also German only
> Barenreiter (1963) 1707

51:10, 11
>BERNHARD, Christoph (ed. David Streetman)
>Create In Me A Clean Heart (Schaffe in mir, Gott, ein reines
> Herz)
>English/German   Organ, Cello, 2 Violins: b1-a3
>Concordia (1972) 97-5041

51:10-12
>BUXTEHUDE, Dietrich (ed. James Boeringer)
>Create In Me A Clean Heart
>Organ, 2 Violins, Cello: b^{b}1 - a3
>Concordia (1966) 97-9359, score & parts

51:10-12
>HANDEL, G.F.
>Make Me A Clean Heart, O God
>Keyboard: C$^{\#}$1 - f$^{\#}$2
>Coburn Press (1971) found in Lift Up Your Voice

51:10-12, 15
>POWERS, George
>Create In Me
>Organ: f1-a3
>Abingdon (1966)

51:10-13
>MUELLER, Carl F.
>Create In Me A Clean Heart
>Piano/Organ: LOW:a1-c2; HIGH:c$^{\#}$1 - e2
>G. Schirmer (1957)

51:10-15
>RIKER, Franklin
>Create In Me A Clean Heart, O Lord
>Organ: e1 - g$^{\#}$2
>Oliver Ditson (1918)

51:12, 13
BUXTEHUDE, Dietrich
Schaffe in mir, Gott, ein rein Herz
German   Continuo & 2 Violins: $b^b1 - a^b3$
Barenreiter (1968) 1753

54:00
CLERBOIS, Roger
Save Me, O Lord
Organ/Piano: LOW:c1-e2; HIGH:d1-f2
Oliver Ditson (1925)

54:00
WOLLER, Alfred
Save Me, O God
Keyboard: LOW:c1 - e^b2; HIGH:e1-g2
Arthur Schmidt (1914)

54:1
FLOYD, Carlisle
Save Me, O Lord
Piano/Organ (orchestra) $c^{\#} - f1$
Boosey & Hawkes

55:00 (adapted)
MENDELSSOHN, Felix
Hear My Prayer
Piano/Organ: LOW:$b^b1 - e^b2$; HIGH:d1-g2
G. Schirmer (1907)

55:1-8
DVORAK, Anton
Hear My Prayer, O Lord, Op. 99
Keyboard: LOW:b^b1 - e2; HIGH:e^b - a3
Simrock; G. Schirmer

55:6 (Psalm 39:12)
BARNES, A.M.
Oh, That I Had Wings
Piano: b^b1 - f2
Oliver Ditson (1903) found in Sacred Songs

55:17
SEE: Psalm 32:11
HUHN, Bruno
Be Glad, O Ye Righteous

55:17
SEE: Psalm 27:4
TALMA, Louise
Cantata: All The Days of My Life

56:13
    SEE: Isaiah 12:3, 4
    CALDER, Lee
    God Is My Salvation

57:00
    BUXTEHUDE, Dietrich
    Mein Herz ist bereit
    German   Continuo, 3 Violins, Cello: F-f1
    Barenreiter (1971)

57:00
    HEAD, Michael
    Be Merciful Unto Me (from Three Psalms)
    Organ/Piano: LOW:a1-g2; HIGH:c1 - b♭3
    Robertson (Presser)

57:1b
    SEE: Psalm 69:4b
    LADERMAN, Ezra
    What I Did Not Steal

57:7, 9
    SEE: Psalm 68:4
    HORVIT, Michael
    Sing To God

57:9-11 (adapted)
    CHAMBERS, Brent (arr. Jane Yankitis)
    Be Exalted, O God
    Keyboard or Guitar: b♭1 - e♭2
    Lillenas (1980) found in Scripture Solos For All Seasons

57:10 (Psalm 22:27)
    HANDEL, G. F.
    God's Tender Mercy Knows No Bounds (Sixth Chandos Anthem)
    Keyboard: d1 - a♭3
    Novello

59:16, 17
    SEE: Psalm 27:4
    TALMA, Louise
    Cantata: All The Days of My Life

61:00
    MULLIGAN, Harold Vincent
    Hear My Cry
    Organ: c1 - e♭2
    G. Schirmer (1943)

61:1 (Psalm 22:14; Psalm 69:3)
    LADERMAN, Ezra
    From The End Of The Earth (from From The Psalms)
    Piano: b1 - g♭2
    Oxford (1970)

61:1 (and other)
    WOOLER, Alfred
    Hear My Cry, O Lord!
    Piano: LOW:al - d^{b}2; MED:bl - e^{b}2; HIGH:dl-g2
    Oliver Ditson (1908) [Free Library]

61:1-2
    NELHYBEL, Vaclav
    Hear My Voice
    Organ: dl-e2
    Agape (1981) 536, found in Psalm Settings

61:1, 3-4 (Psalm 63:1, 4)
    DVORAK, Anton
    Hear My Prayer, O Lord, Op.99, #6
    Keyboard: LOW:bl-d2; HIGH:el-g2
    Simrock; G. Schirmer

61:1, 3, 4 (Psalm 63:1, 4)
    DVORAK, Anton (ed. M.B.Stearns)
    Hear My Prayer, Op.99, #6
    Keyboard: c$^{\#}$1 - e2
    Coburn Press (1971) found in Lift Up Your Voice

61:1-5
    SOWERBY, Leo
    Hear My Cry, O God
    Keyboard: f - e^{b}1
    Belwin (1927)

62:1
    SEE: Psalm 46:10a
    BITGOOD, Roberta
    Be Still, And Know That I Am God

62:1, 5-7 (Psalm 130:5; Isaiah 40:28-31)
    SEATON, Annette
    Thou Who Wait On The Lord
    Keyboard: bl-e2
    Lillenas (1980) found in Scripture Solos For All Seasons

63:00
    SEE: Psalm 23
    HUMMELL, Ferdinand
    Alleluia

63:1, 4
    SEE: Psalm 61:1, 3-4
    DVORAK, Anton
    Hear My Prayer, O Lord

63:1, 4
SEE: Psalm 61:1, 3-4
DVORAK, Anton (ed. M.B.Stearns)
Hear My Prayer

63:1-5
HARTLEY, Walter S.
Andante Molto (in A Psalm Cycle)
Piano & Flute: c1-a3
Tenuto (Presser)

63:6 (Matthew 5:11; I Peter 4:13, 14; and other)
ELGAR, Edward
The Sun Goeth Down (from The Kingdom)
Keyboard: e^{b}1 - b^{b}3
Novello

65:8, 11
SEE: Psalm 27:4
TALMA, Louise
Cantata: All The Days of My Life

65:9
PARKER, Harold
Thou Visitest The Earth (from the cantata, The Sower)
Keyboard: e^{b}1 - a3
Oxford

65:9, 11, 13
COWEN, F.H.
How Excellent Is Thy Loving Kindness (Ruth)
Keyboard: f1 - b^{b}3
G. Schirmer, found in Anthology of Sacred Song - Tenor

66:00
WYNER, Yehudi
Halleluya
Keyboard: a1 - f$^\#$2
Merrymount (Presser); also found in Psalm And Early Songs
(Associated, 1957)

66:1-4
WYNER, Yehudi
Psalm 66 (Psalms and Early Songs)
Keyboard: a1 - f$^\#$2
Associated (1972) AMP 7123

66:4
SEE: Psalm 29:1-2
SCHUTZ, Heinrich
Bring To Jehovah

67:00
　　BARKER, Clement
　　Bless The Lord O My Soul
　　Keyboard:　LOW:d1-d2; HIGH:f1-f2
　　R.D.Row (1948)

67:00
　　FREUDENTHAL, Josef
　　The Lord's Blessing
　　Keyboard:　LOW:b^{b}1 - e^{b}2; HIGH:d1-g2
　　Transcontinental (1952) TV 480

67:00
　　FRYXELL, Regina H.
　　Psalm 67
　　Keyboard
　　G. Schirmer

67:00
　　KOCH, John
　　God Be Merciful Unto Us (Songs Of David)
　　Flute and String Quartet:　g1-g2
　　American Music Center

67:00
　　WOLFE, Jacques
　　Psalm LXVII
　　Organ:　a1-g2
　　American Music Center

67:5-8
　　HAMMERSCHMIDT, Andreas
　　Es danken dir, Gott, die Voelker
　　German　　Organ, 2 Violins
　　Barenreiter　#459

68:00
　　ROGERS, Bernard
　　Psalm 68
　　Piano (orchestra)　a-g
　　Southern (1955)

68:1-6, 17, 18
　　COUPERIN, Francois
　　Salvum me fac Deus
　　Latin　　Continuo & 2 Violins:　b^b - e^{b}1
　　Heugel (1972) H32.219

68:4 (Psalm 57:7, 9; Psalm 47:1, 2)
　　HORVIT, Michael
　　Sing To God
　　Piano:　f1 - b^{b}3
　　Transcontinental (1977)

68:18
  HANDEL, G.F.
  Thou Art Gone Up On High (Messiah)
  Keyboard: c-e
  Carl Fischer; G. Schirmer; Novello

68:19
  GREENE, Maurice
  Praised Be The Lord
  Piano/Organ: c1-f2
  Oxford

68:19
  GREENE, Maurice (ed. E. Stanley Roper)
  Praised Be The Lord
  Keyboard: c1-f2
  Bosworth, found in Seven Sacred Songs

69:00 (adapted)
  CHARLES, Ernst
  Save Me O God
  Piano: LOW:b1 - f$^\#$2; HIGH:d1-a3
  G. Schirmer (1947)

69:1 (Psalm 30:2, 12)
  HARRIS, Cuthbert
  Save Me, O God
  Keyboard: LOW: b^{b}1 - e^{b}2; HIGH:d1-g2
  Arthur Schmidt (1925)

69:1-3, 5, 16-17, 29-30
  BUTLER, Eugene
  Save Me, O God
  Keyboard: b1-e2
  Sacred Music Press (1969) found in The Solo Psalmist

69:1-3, 14-17, 20
  FLOYD, Carlisle
  Save Me, O God, For The Waters Are Come In Unto My Soul
  Piano: G-f1
  Boosey & Hawkes (1959) from Pilgrimage

69:3
  SEE: Psalm 61:1
  LADERMAN, Ezra
  From The End Of The Earth

69:4b (Psalm 119:150; Psalm 119:148; Psalm 57:1b)
  LADERMAN, Ezra
  What I Did Not Steal (from From The Psalms)
  Piano: d1-g2
  Oxford (1970)

69:8
SEE: Psalm 104:5
LADERMAN, Ezra
Thou Didst Set The Earth

69:20 (Lamentations 1:12; Isaiah 53:8; Psalm 16:10)
HANDEL, G.F.
Thy Rebuke Hath Broken His Heart/Behold and See/He Was Cut Off/
    But Thou Didst Not Leave (Messiah)
Keyboard: $d^{\#} - g1$
Carl Fischer; G. Schirmer; Novello

70:00
SCHUTZ, Heinrich (ed. Lloyd Pfautsch)
A Psalm Of David
Piano: $a^b1 - d^b2$
Lawson-Gould (1961) found in The Church Soloist, available in
    high and low keys

70:1-5
Same As Psalm 40:14-1
SCHUTZ, Heinrich
Haste Thee, Lord God, Haste To Save Me

71:1, 9, 12, 18
SPICKER, Max
In Thee, O God, Do I Put My Trust, Op.48
Piano (or String Quartet & Organ) b1-f2
G. Schirmer (1899)

71:9, 12
SEE: Isaiah 45:1, 2, 22
VanWOERT, Rutger
Be Not Far From Me, Oh God

71:15, 17
SEE: Psalm 27:4
TALMA, Louise
Cantata: All The Days of My Life

71:16
HERBST, Johannes
I Will Go In The Strength Of The Lord
Organ: e1-g2
Boosey & Hawkes; also C.F.Peters

73:25, 26 (and other)
BUXTEHUDE, Dietrich
Herr, wenn ich nur dich habe
German   Continuo, 2 Violins, Cello: d1-g2
Barenreiter (1970)

74:20
  SEE: Exodus 15:3
  ANONYMOUS
  The Lord Is A Mighty Warrior

76:6
  SEE: Exodus 15:3
  ANONYMOUS
  The Lord Is A Mighty Warrior

78:1-3
  SCHUTZ, Heinrich
  Attendite, Popule Meus, legem Meam
  Latin   Bass & 4 Trombones & Continuo: f-c1
  Musica Rara (1962); also G. Schirmer

80:00
  PINKHAM, Daniel
  Psalm 79
  Piano/Organ: f1-g2
  Composers Facsimile Edition

81:1-4
  CHILDS, David
  Psalm 81 (from Seven Psalms for Voice & Organ)
  Organ: e1-f2
  Abingdon (1966) High:APM 390; Low:APM 385

81:9-11 (Isaiah 43:1, 25)
  STEVENSON, Frederick
  Hear, O My People
  Organ: c1 - b^{b}3
  Oliver Ditson (1921)

83:00
  SACCO, Peter
  Keep Not Thou Silence, O God
  Piano/Organ: c$^{\#}$1 - g$^{\#}$2
  Ostara Press

83:1-4, 13, 18
  CHILDS, David
  Psalm 83 (from Seven Psalms for Voice & Organ)
  Organ: c1-f2
  Abingdon (1966) Low:APM 385; High:APM390

83:1-5, 13-15, 18
  SIEGEL, Arsene
  Keep Thou Not Silence, O God
  Piano: LOW:a1-g2; HIGH:b1-a2
  Galaxy (1944)

84:00
    LIDDLE, Samuel
    How Lovely Are Thy Dwellings
    Keyboard: LOW:$bb1 - eb2$; MED:c1-f2; MED-HIGH:$db1 - gb2$;
      HIGH:$eb1 - ab3$
    Boosey & Hawkes (1936)

84:00
    GREENBAUM, Matthew
    Psalm 84
    Flute/Clarinet/Violin/Cello/Piano: c1-a3
    American Music Center

84:1
    MENDELSSOHN, Felix
    I Will Sing Of Thy Great Mercies (St. Paul)
    Keyboard: e1-f2
    Augener (Galaxy)

84:1, 2, 4
    HAYDN, Franz Josef (arr. Carl Frederickson)
    How Lovely Is Thy Dwelling Place
    Keyboard: $c1 - eb2$
    R.D.Row (1959) found in Sacred Song Masterpieces

84:1, 2, 4
    SEE: Luke:48, 49
    SCHUTZ, Heinrich (ed. Richard T. Gore)
    My Son, Wherefore Hast Thou Done This To Us?

84:1, 2, 10, 11
    deLANGE, S.
    How Beautiful Are Thy Dwellings (Moses)
    Piano: $d1 - ab3$
    G. Schirmer (1902) found in Anthology of Sacred Songs, Sop.

84:1-3
    DAVIS, Katherine K.
    How Lovely Are Thy Dwellings
    Organ/Piano
    Galaxy (1952) 1.1872.7

84:2
    SEE: Psalm 135:1-2
    HANDEL, G.F.
    Praise Him, All Ye That In His House Attend

84:3-4, 10-12
    PELZ, Walter L.
    Happy Are They Who Dwell In Your House (found in Three Solos
      For High Voice)
    Organ & Oboe: e1-e2
    Augsburg (1979) 11-9477

84:4, 5
  GREENE, Maurice (ed. E. Stanley Roper)
  Blessed Are They That Dwell In Thy House
  Keyboard: LOW:d1 - f#2; HIGH:e1 - g#2
  Bosworth (1910) found in Seven Sacred Songs Of The Early
    English School

84:10 (Psalm 103:1; and other)
  COSTA, M.
  This Night I Lift My Heart To Thee (Eli)
  Keyboard: a1 - c#2
  G. Schirmer, found in Anthology Of Sacred Song - Alto

84:12 (and other)
  HANDEL, G.F.
  Powerful Guardian
  Piano/Organ: DUET
  R.D.Row (1960) found in Sacred Duet Masterpieces

85:6-11
  ROBYN, Alfred
  Wilt Thou Not Receive Us Again
  Piano/Organ: DUET:A-T
  Oliver Ditson (1913)

85:8
  SEE: Psalm 46:10a
  BITGOOD, Roberta
  Be Still And Know That I Am God

85:8, 9
  SEE: Ezekiel 13:3
  BARKER, Clement
  Woe Unto The Foolish Prophets

86:00
  HAMBLEN, Bernard
  Hear Thou My Prayer
  Piano: LOW:a1-e2; HIGH:c1-g2
  Huntzinger (1923) also found in Selected Songs For General Use

86:4-6, 12
  VIVALDI, Antonio (ed. Lloyd Pfautsch)
  Lord To Thee Do I Lift My Soul
  Keyboard: a1-d2
  Lawson Gould (1955) found in Solos For The Church Year

89:1, 5, 8-9, 11, 14-15
  POWELL, Robert J.
  I Will Sing Of The Mercies Of The Lord
  Keyboard: c1-f2
  Sacred Music Press (1969) found in The Solo Psalmist

89:1-5, 15-18, 52
    TRIPLETT, Robert F.
    I Will Sing Of Thy Steadfast Love
    Organ: d1-a3
    Abingdon (1968) APM 603

89:1, 15, 16 (Psalm 119:105)
    PARKER, Clifton
    Blessed Is The People
    Piano/Organ: d1 - f$^{\#}$2
    Carl Fischer (1934)

89:26
    SEE: Isaiah 2:22
    BARKER, Clement W.
    Mark The Perfect Man

90:00 (Psalm 92)
    FISCHER, Irwin
    Let The Beauty Of The Lord
    Organ: e1-f2
    Coburn Press, found in Eleven Scripture Songs

90:00
    HUMPHREYS, Don
    Lord, Thou Hast Been Our Dwelling Place
    Keyboard: LOW:b1-d2; HIGH:d1-f2
    R.D.Row (1952)

90:00
    PHILLIPS, Louis Baker
    Lord, Thou Hast Been Our Dwelling Place
    Piano: b1 - g^{b}2
    Boosey (1923)

90:1, 2, 4, 16-17
    BUTT, James
    Psalm 90
    Organ: e1-e2
    Sphemusations (n.d.)

90:4
    SEE: Job 22:21
    MacDERMID, James G.
    Acquaint Now Thyself With Him

90:17
    SEE: Psalm 25:1
    CORNELIUS, Peter
    Unto Thee I Lift Up My Soul

91:00
   DAVYE, John J.
   He That Dwelleth In The Secred Place (from Two Psalms Of
      Meditation)
   Organ: f1-f2
   MS (1978)

91:00
   HUMPHREYS, Don
   He That Dwelleth In The Secret Place
   Piano/Organ: e^{b}1 - f2
   Willis (1950)

91:00 (adapted)
   MENDELSSOHN, Felix (arr. Carl Fredrickson)
   Thy Secret Place
   Keyboard: c1-c2
   R.D.Row (1959) found in Sacred Song Masterpieces

91:00
   O'CONNOR-MORRIS, G.
   Psalm 91
   Keyboard
   Carl Fischer

91:00
   SCOTT, John Prindle
   He Shall Give His Angel Charge
   Piano: LOW:d1-f2; HIGH:f1 - a^{b}3
   Huntzinger (1918)

91:00
   SOWERBY, Leo
   Whoso Dwelleth
   Organ: a - f$^\#$1
   H.W.Gray (1949)

91:1-2
   SHELLY, Harry Rowe
   He That Dwelleth In The Secret Place
   Organ: e1-g2
   G. Schirmer (1921)

91:1, 2, 4, 9, 11
   LOWE, A.F.
   Sanctuary
   Keyboard
   Carl Fischer (1951)

91:1-2, 5-6, 9-10, 14-16
   BAUMGARTNER, H. Leroy
   He That Dwelleth In The Secret Place, Op.48,#2 (from O Lord
      My God, Thou Art Very Good)
   Keyboard: e1-a3
   Concordia (1958)

91:1-4
    CHILDS, David
    Psalm 91 (from Seven Psalms for Voice & Organ)
    Organ: f1-f2
    Abingdon (1966) High:APM 390; Low:APM 385

91:1, 5, 6, 9, 10, 11, 12
    MacDERMID, James
    The Ninety-first Psalm
    Piano: LOW:b^{b}1 - e^{b}2; MED:c1-f2; HIGH:e^{b}1 - a^{b}3
    Forester (1935)

91:1, 5-7, 11-12
    ROGERS, Faith Helen
    Whoso Dwelleth In The Secret Place
    Piano/Organ: d^{b}1 - b^{b}3
    G. Schirmer (1919)

91:1, 9-10, 11, 14, 16
    NEIDLINGER, W.H.
    He That Dwelleth In The Secret Place
    Keyboard: c1-g2
    John Church (1919)

91:4, 11-12
    BUSAROW, Donald
    He Shall Give His Angels Charge Over Thee
    Organ (optional instrument in c or b^b) d1 - a^{b}3
    Concordia (1981) 97-5633, medium; 97-5634 low

91:5
    SEE: Psalm 18:32, 37
    VAUGHAN-WILLIAMS, Ralph
    The Pilgrim's Psalm

92:00
    SEE: Psalm 90
    FISCHER, Irwin
    Let The Beauty Of The Lord

90:00
    LAGOURGUE, Charles
    Psalm 92
    Keyboard
    H.C.L. Publishing Co.

90:00
    WENZEL, Eberhard
    Psalm 90
    German   Organ: all spoken
    Merseburger (1973) 895

92:00
    FROMM, Herbert (arr.)
    Praise Ye The Lord (Two Psalm Settings)
    Keyboard: f1-d2
    Hope (n.d.) SA 1400

92:1-5
    CHILDS, David
    Psalm 92 (from Seven Psalms for Voice & Organ)
    Organ: c1-g2
    Abingdon (1966) High:APM 390; Low:APM 385

92:2-3
    DISTLER, Hugo
    It Is A Precious Thing To Thank Our God, Op.17,#1
    Keyboard: b1-g2
    Concordia (1969) 97-4925, found in Three Sacred Concertos

92:12 (Psalm 128:2-4)
    FELCIANO, Richard
    Benedictio Nuptialis
    Organ/Piano: e^b1 - e^b2
    E.C.Schirmer

93:00
    PENN, Marilyn
    Psalm 93
    Piano: Bar:a - $d^\#1$
    American Music Center (1982)

95:00
    FREUDENTHAL, Joseph
    Let Us Sing Unto The Lord
    Keyboard: LOW:b1-e2; HIGH:d1-g2
    Transcontinental (1949)

95:00 (adapted)
    HANDEL, G.F. (arr. Fredrickson)
    Come, Let Us Make A Joyful Noise
    Piano/Organ: DUET
    R.D.Row (1960) found in Sacred Duet Masterpieces

95:00
    HANDEL, G.F.
    For Look As High As The Heaven (Chandos Anthem I)
    Keyboard: f1-a3
    Novello

95:1-2
    HANDEL, G.F.
    For This Our Truest Interest
    Keyboard: f1-a3
    Novello

95:1-6
    SEE: Psalm 130
    YARDUMIAN, Richard
    Symphony #2

95:1-7
    LEKBERG, Sven
    O Come, Let Us Sing Unto The Lord
    Piano/Organ: d1-g2
    Galaxy (1963)

95:1-7
    SEE: Psalm 50:14
    PENDLETON, Emmet
    Sing Unto The Lord

95:4
    MENDELSSOHN, Felix
    In His Hands Are All The Corners Of The Earth
    English/German   DUET: 2 Sopranos
    John Church [Presser] (1907) found in Sacred Duets, Vol. I:
        also in Choice Sacred Duets, Vol. II (Oliver Ditson, 1902)

95:6
    HANDEL, G.F.
    O Come Let Us Worship
    Keyboard: e1-a3
    Novello

95:6, 7, 8
    HANDEL, G.F. (ed. M.B.Stearns)
    O Come Let Us Worship
    Keyboard: D1 - f#2
    Coburn Press (1971) found in Lift Up Your Voices

96:00
    BUXTEHUDE, Dietrich (ed. N. Jenne)
    Sing To The Lord A New Song
    Keyboard & Violin: c1-g2
    Concordia (1969) 97-4897

96:00
    SEE: Job 22
    HEAD, Michael
    Acquaint Now Thyself With Him

96:00 (adapted)
    HERBERT, Muriel
    Sing Unto The Lord All The Earth
    Piano: d1-f2
    Elkan [Galaxy] (1957)

96:00 (RSV)
   WHIKEHART, Lewis
   O Sing Unto The Lord
   Organ: d1 - a^{b}3
   H.W.Gray (1959)

96:1-4
   SCHUTZ, Heinrich (ed. Fritz Ricco)
   Singet dem Herrn
   German   Continuo & 2 Violins: c1-f2
   Bornart (1949)

96:6
   SEE: Psalm 26:8
   BAUMGARTNER, H. Leroy
   Lord, I Have Loved The Habitation Of Thy House, Op. 48, #3

96:6
   SEE: Psalm 113:3
   VanDYKE, M.
   In The Beauty Of Holiness

96:7, 8
   GAUL, A.R.
   Ascribe Unto The Lord Worship and Power (The Ten Virgins)
   Keyboard: f1-a3
   G. Schirmer, found in Anthology of Sacred Song - Tenor

96:12
   SEE: Psalm 98:1, 7-8
   DVORAK, Anton
   Sing Ye A Joyful Song

97:1-2, 4-6, 8, 11
   BUTLER, Eugene
   The Lord Reigns
   Keyboard: c1 - e^{b}2
   Sacred Music Press (1969) found in The Solo Psalmist

97:2-6
   DVORAK, Anton
   Clouds and Darkness
   Keyboard: LOW:b1-d2; HIGH:d$^{\#}$1 - f$^{\#}$1
   Simrock; G. Schirmer

97:10 (Psalm 103:11)
   HANDEL, G.F.
   The Lord Preserveth The Souls/For Look as High as The Heaven
      Is (Fifth Chandos Anthem)
   Keyboard: G$^{\#}$ - d1
   Novello

98:00
GOLDMAN, Edward M.
Psalm 97 (O Sing Unto The Lord A New Song)
Piano/Organ: b1 - f$^\sharp$2
World Library (1965)

98:00 (I Corinthians 15; Revelations 1)
GORE, Richard T.
O Sing Unto The Lord A New Song
Organ: LOW:b1 - e$^\flat$2; HIGH:e1 - a$^\flat$3
J.Fischer (1948)

98:00 (Watts)
WEAVER, Powell
Joy To The World
Piano/Organ: f$^\sharp$1 - g2
Galaxy (1941)

98:1-4
BUXTEHUDE, Dietrich
Singet dem Herrn
German   Continuo & Violin: d1-g2
Barenreiter (1966)

98:1, 7-8 (Psalm 96:12)
DVORAK, Anton
Sing Ye A Joyful Song, op.99
Keyboard: LOW:c1-d2; HIGH:f1-g2
Simrock; G. Schirmer

98:4-6
BUXTEHUDE, Dietrich
Jubilate Domino
Latin   Organ Continuo
Barenreiter (1970) 6462

99:00
SEE: Job 22
HEAD, Michael
Acquaint Now Thyself With Him

99:9
HANDEL, G.F.
O Magnify The Lord (Fifth Chandos Anthem)
Keyboard: e1 - g$^\sharp$2
Novello

99:9
HANDEL, G.F.
O Magnify The Lord (Eighth Chandos Anthem)
Keyboard: e1 - g$^\sharp$2
Novello

100:00
BRITTON, D. Guyver
Know Ye That The Lord He Is God
Organ: a1 - e^{b}2
Boston (1963)

100:00
HEAD, Michael
Make A Joyful Noise (from Three Psalms)
Organ/Piano: LOW:b1-e2; HIGH:d1-g2
Roberton (Presser)

100:00
JUDASSOHN, S.
Arioso
Organ/Piano: d1-g2
G. Schirmer (1940) found in Album Of Sacred Songs

100:00
KOCH, John
Make A Joyful Noise Unto The Lord (Songs Of David)
Flute and String Quartet: e^{b}1 - a3
American Music Center

100:00
LaFORGE, Frank
Make A Joyful Noise
Piano: b1-d2
Carl Fischer (1938) V1370

100:00
MacDERMID, James
Make A Joyful Noise
Piano: LOW:b1 - e^{b}2; HIGH:e^{b}1 - g2
Forster (1946)

100:00 (adapted)
McFEETERS, Raymond
A Psalm Of Praise
Piano: d1-f2
Carl Fischer (1940)

100:00
MUELLER, Carl F.
The One Hundredth Psalm
Piano/Organ: d1-e2
Flammer (1935)

100:00
ROREM, Ned
A Psalm Of Praise
Piano: c1-g2
Associated (1946) AMP 19468-4

100:00
   SCHUTZ, Heinrich
   Jubilate deo omnis terra
   German/Latin   Continuo, 2 Flutes/Violins: $F^{\#}$ - d1
   Barenreiter (1949) #6

100:00
   SOWERBY, Leo
   O Be Joyful In The Lord (from Three Psalms)
   Organ: c1 - $e^{b}2$
   H.W.Gray (1949) GV 390

100:00 (Psalm 101; Psalm 103)
   STRANDBERG, Newton
   De David
   French   Celesta/Gong/Chimes/Bass Drum (optional chorus)
     $b^{b}1$ - f2
   American Music Center (1979)

100:00
   SUBEN, Joel
   Make A Joyful Noise
   Keyboard: $c^{\#}1$ - a3
   Belwin (1971)

100:00
   TELEMANN, G.P.
   Jauchzet dem Herrn, alle Welt
   English/German   Trumpet, Violin, Viola, Continuo: BASS
   Hanssler 39.106

100:1, 2, 4, 5
   SEE: Isaiah 63:7
   FISCHER, Irwin
   Psalm of Praise

101:00
   SEE: Psalm 100
   STRANDBERG, Newton
   De David

102:7, 9, 12, 13
   SEE: Psalm 13:1
   ROGERS, James
   How Long, O Lord, Wilt Thou Forget Me?

102:11
   SEE: Psalm 27:4
   TALMA, Louise
   Cantata: All The Days Of My Life

103:00 (adapted)
  BENATI (?)
  Bless Thou The Lord
  Keyboard: g1-g2
  G. Schirmer (1965) found in The Sunday Solo

103:00 (Lyte)
  CASSLER, C. Winston
  Praise, My Soul The King Of Heaven
  Organ: DUET
  Augsburg (1968) 11-9272 found in Sacred Duets For Equal Voices

103:00
  JORDAN, Alice
  Bless The Lord, O My Soul
  Keyboard: c1 - e^{b}2
  Abingdon (1970) APM-800

103:00
  LaFORGE, Frank
  Bless The Lord
  Keyboard: d1 - f$^{\#}$2
  Carl Fischer (1933)

103:00
  SEE: Psalm 100
  STRANDBERG, Newton
  De David

103:00
  WEIMER, Wolfgang
  Lobe den Herrn, meine Seele
  Organ & Percussion: Baritone
  Breitkopf & Hartel

103:1
  SEE: Psalm 84:10
  COSTA, M.
  This Night I Lift My Heart To Thee

103:1 (Psalm 5:8)
  WESLEY, Samuel S.
  Praise The Lord, O My Soul
  Keyboard: c1-g2
  Carl Fischer (1939) found in The Sacred Hour Of Song

103:1, 2-4
  GREENE, Maurice (ed. E. Stanley Roper)
  Praise The Lord, O My Soul
  Keyboard: LOW:d1-f2; HIGH:e1-g2
  Bosworth (1910) found in Seven Sacred Solos Of The Early English
    School

103:1-3
 McARTHUR, Edwin
 Bless The Lord, O My Soul
 Piano: c#1 - f2
 Chappell (1959)

103:1-4, 11, 13
 DAVIS, Katherine K.
 Bless The Lord, O My Soul
 Piano/Organ: c1 - eb2
 Galaxy (1952) 1.1924.7

103:1-4, 19 (adapted)
 FAURE, Gabriel
 Bless The Lord, O My Soul
 Keyboard: ab1 - f2
 Boston (1921)

103:1-5, 8, 13
 STEPHENSON, Richard T.
 Psalm 103
 Piano/Organ: c1-e2
 Carl Fischer (1949) [Free Library]

103:11
 SEE: Psalm 97:10
 HANDEL, G.F.
 The Lord Preserveth The Souls

103:11-17
 DOIG, Don
 So Great Is His Mercy
 Keyboard: d1-e2
 Hope (1980) found in Everything For The Church Soloist

103:13
 SEE: Daniel 9:9
 GAUL, A. R.
 To The Lord Our God Belong Mercies

103:13, 14
 COWEN, F. H.
 Like As A Father (from Ruth)
 Keyboard: a1-d2
 G. Schirmer (1929) found in Anthology Of Sacred Song - Alto

103:13-14
 SEE: Psalm 39:13a
 LADERMAN, Ezra
 Look Away From Me

103:13-17
SCOTT, John Prindle
Like As A Father
Piano/Organ: LOW:d1 - e♭2; HIGH: f♯1 - g2
G. Schirmer (1922)

103:20
GREENE, Maurice (ed. E. Stanley Roper)
O Praise The Lord
Keyboard: LOW:e♭1 - g♭2; HIGH:f♯1 - a3
Bosworth (1910) found in Seven Sacred Solos Of The Early English
School

103:21
HANDEL, G.F.
O Praise The Lord (Twelfth Chandos Anthem)
Keyboard: b-e1
Novello

104:00
LEDERER, Charles
Psalm 104
Keyboard
Carl Fischer

104:1, 2, 5, 24, 30
FISCHER, Irwin
O Lord, How Manifold Are Thy Works
Keyboard: e♭1 - g2
American Composers Alliance (1957)

104:1, 2, 24 (Psalm 145:9; Psalm 147:4; Romans 11:33, 36)
BAUMGARTNER, H. Leroy
O Lord, My God, Thou Art Very Great, Op.48, #1 (from O Lord,
My God, Thou Art Very Great)
Keyboard: d1-g2
Concordia (1958)

104:1, 2, 14, 33, 34
JEFFERIES, George
Praise The Lord, O My Soul
Keyboard: E-d1
Norton, found in The Solo Song

104:1, 24
STEARNS, Peter Pindar
Bless The Lord, O My Soul
Oboe, Horn, Cello: c1 - b♭3
American Composers Alliance (from Three Sacred Songs)

104:5 (Psalm 9:15; Psalm 69:8)
LADERMAN, Ezra
Thou Didst Set The Earth (from From The Psalms)
Piano: d♭1 - a♭3
Oxford (1970)

104:31-34
ARCHER, Violet
TeDeum (from Three Biblical Songs)
Piano/Organ: d1-g2
Canadian Music Centre

106:00 (Psalm 108)
BARRUS, LeMar
Praise
Keyboard: d1-e2
Flammer (1975) found in Songs Of Praise By Contemporary
Composers

106:1-4
HUMPHREYS, Don
Praise Ye The Lord
Piano: LOW:c1-f2; HIGH:e^{b}1 - a^{b}3
Willis (1953) also found in Sing To The Lord (Willis, 1960)

107:00 (from)
HUMPHREYS, Don
He Sent His Word And Healed Them
Piano: LOW:c$^{\#}$1 - d2; HIGH:e1-f2
R.D.Row (1956); also found in Songs For Christian Science
Services, Book I

107:1-2, 43
POWELL, Robert J.
O Give Thanks
Keyboard: d1-e2
Sacred Music Press (1969) found in The Solo Psalmist

107:2-4
SCHUTZ, Heinrich (ed. Stantum)
Paratum cor meum
Latin/English   Keyboard & 2 Violins: c1-e2
Hinrichsen (1952) 181

107:20
SEE: John 1:1
MacDERMID, James
He Sent His Word

108:00
SEE: Psalm 106
BARRUS, LeMar
Praise

108:00 (adapted)
FERRIS, William
My Heart Is Ready, O God
Keyboard: e^{b}1 - a^{b}3
Belwin (1974)

111:00
SCHUTZ, Heinrich
Ich danke dem Herrn von ganzem Herzen
German   Continuo: g-a2
Barenreiter

111:00
SCHUTZ, Heinrich
O God, I Will Praise Thee (in Five Sacred Songs)
English/German   Keyboard: d1-f2
Concordia (1957) 98-1370

112:00
PAER, Ferdinando (ed. Himie Voxman)
Beatus Vir
Latin   Piano & Clarinet in b♭: e♭1 - c3
Nova Music (1980) full score and orchestra parts available on
    hire from publisher

113:00
EDMUNDS, John
Praise Ye The Lord
Piano: c1-a3
Dragons Teeth Press (1975) found in Hesperides: Fifty Songs

113:3 (Psalm 96:6)
Van DYKE, M.
In The Beauty Of Holiness
Keyboard: LOW:b1-d2; HIGH:e1-g2
Boosey (1937)

113:3, 4
GREENE, Maurice (ed. E. Stanley Roper)
The Lord's Name Is Praised
Keyboard: e1-g2
Bosworth (1910) found in Seven Sacred Solos Of The Early
    School

114:00
BLOCH, Ernest
Psalm 114 (Snatched Away By Jehovah)
English/French   Piano: a2-a3
G. Schirmer (1919)

114:12-14
SEE: Acts 9:2
MENDELSSOHN, Felix
But The Lord Is Mindful Of His Own

115:3
SEE: I Corinthians 3:16-17
MENDELSSOHN, Felix
For Ye Know Not

115:13-15
  BACH, J.S.
  The Lord Bless You (Der Herr segne euch) from Cantata 196,
    Der Herr denket an un
  English/German   Organ: DUET
  Concordia (1952) 97-9240, found in Wedding Blessing

116:1-5, 7-8
  DUKE, John
  I Love The Lord
  Piano or Organ: b^{b}1 - e2
  Boosey & Hawkes (1962)

116:12-14, 17-19
  LaFORGE, Frank
  What Shall I Render Unto The Lord
  Piano/Organ: LOW:c1-d2; HIGH:f1-g2
  G. Schirmer (1942)

117:00
  SEE: Ecclesiastes 47:2
  FERRIS, William
  I Have Seen Water

118:14
  SEE: Isaiah 12:3, 4
  CALDER, Lee
  God Is My Salvation

118:14, 15 (Psalm 141:3, 4)
  SCOTT, Charles P.
  The Voice Of Joy
  Organ or Piano: LOW:d1-e2; HIGH:f1-g2
  Oliver Ditson (1935)

118:14, 24, 26, 28, 29
  HUHN, Bruno
  The Lord Is My Strength
  Piano/Organ: f1-f2
  G. Schirmer (1909) found in Seventeen Sacred Songs

118:24 (Romans 5:8; I Corinthians 10:16)
  WARREN, Clara
  Let Us Keep The Feast
  Keyboard: LOW:b^{b}1 - d2; HIGH:d1-f2
  R.D.Row (1948)

119:00 (taken from)
  HAMBLEN, Bernard
  Teach Me, O Lord
  Piano: LOW:c1-d2; HIGH:e^{b}1 - f2
  Harms (1925)

119:00 (Psalm 145)
   MacDERMID, James
   Thy Word Is A Lamp
   Keyboard: LOW:b^b1 - e^b2; HIGH:d^b1 - g^b2
   Forster (1948)

119:1-5, 8
   REGER, Max
   Wohl denen, die ohne Tadel leben
   German Organ: $e1-g2$
   Bote and Bock (1975)

119:1, 5, 18
   GREENE, Maurice (ed. E. Stanley Roper)
   Thou Hast Charged/O That My Ways
   Keyboard: LOW:e^b1 - e^b2; HIGH:$f1$ - a^b3
   Bosworth (1910) found in Seven Sacred Solos Of The Early
     English School

119:3
   SEE: Psalm 5:8
   HANDEL, G.F.
   Lead Me Lord

119:12, 18, 28, 35, 59, 68
   FISCHER, Irwin
   Lord, Teach Me Thy Statues
   Keyboard: $d1$ - $f^\#2$
   American Composers Alliance (1957)

119:25-32
   WYNER, Yehudi
   Psalm 119
   Keyboard: b^b1 - $f2$
   Associated (1973) found in Psalms And Early Songs

119:33
   LaFORGE, Frank
   Teach Me, O Lord
   Piano: LOW:$c1-d2$; HIGH:$e1-g2$
   Carl Fischer (1938)

119:33, 34, 37
   MANNEY, Charles F.
   Teach Me, O Lord
   Keyboard: LOW:$c1$ - e^b2; MED:$d1-f2$; HIGH:$e1-g2$
   Arthur Schmidt (1908)

119:50
   FREUDENTHAL, Josef
   A Lamp Unto My Feet
   Keyboard: e^b1 - $g2$
   Transcontinental (1957) TV 499

119:62
    SEE: Psalm 27:4
    TALMA, Louise
    Cantata: All The Days Of My Life

119:74, 165, 174, 176
    ROGERS, James
    Great Peace Have They Which Love Thy Law
    Organ: LOW:b1-c2; MED:d1 - e^b2; HIGH:f1 - g^b2
    G. Schirmer (1936)

119:105
    SEE: Psalm 89:1, 15, 16
    PARKER, Clifton
    Blessed Is The People

119:105
    BONE, Jean and Howard Fenton
    Thy Word Is A Lamp
    Keyboard: LOW:b^b1 - e^b2; HIGH:c1-f2
    R.D.Row (1948) R-750B

119:105
    ENGLERT, Andrew Lloyd
    Thy Word Is A Lamp
    Piano: LOW:c1-d2; HIGH:d1-e2
    R.D.Row (1962)

119:114-115, 117, 120
    DVORAK, Anton
    Lord Thou Art My Refuge, Op. 99
    Keyboard: LOW:b1-c2; HIGH:e1-f2
    Simrock; G. Schirmer

119:135, 165 (and other)
    LULLY, Jean Baptiste
    Great Peace Have They
    Keyboard: c1 - e^b2
    R.D.Row (1959) found in Sacred Song Masterpieces

119:148
    SEE: Psalm 69:4b
    LADERMAN, Ezra
    What I Did Not Steal

119:150
    SEE: Psalm 69:4b
    LADERMAN, Ezra
    What I Did Not Steal

119:165-166, 175-176
    BROWN, Allanson G. Y.
    Great Peave Have They
    Piano: c1 - e^b2
    Oliver Ditson (1945)

120:00
  ROREM, Ned
  A Song Of David: Psalm 120
  Piano: d1-g2
  Associated (1946) AMP 19469-3; also found in <u>American Art
    Songs</u> (Associated AMP-7742)

121:00
  BARTLETT, Floy Little
  I Will Lift Up My Eyes
  Keyboard: LOW:b1-c2; MED:c$^{\#}$1 - f$^{\#}$2; HIGH:d1-g2
  Arthur Schmidt (1947) [Free Library]

121:00 (and other, plus poem)
  BURNAM, Edna Mae
  I Will Lift Up Mine Eyes Unto The Hills
  Keyboard: c1-f2
  Willis (1977)

121:00
  BURNS, William K.
  Psalm 121 (from <u>Four Meditative Songs</u>)
  Keyboard: f1-g2
  Abingdon (1972) APM-515

121:00
  CHILDS, David
  Psalm 121 (from <u>Seven Psalms</u> for Voice & Organ)
  Organ: d1-g2
  Abingdon (1966) High APM-390; Low APM-385

121:00
  CROWE, B.
  One Hundred Twenty-First Psalm
  Keyboard: LOW:b^{b}1 - e^{b}2; HIGH:d1-g2
  Pro Art [Royal Palm Music] (1937)

121:00
  EVILLE, Vernon
  I Will Lift Up Mine Eyes
  Piano: LOW:c1-d2; MED:e^{b}1 - f2; HIGH:f1-g2
  Boosey & Hawkes (1943)

121:00
  FROMM, Herbert
  Psalm 121 (from <u>Four Psalms</u>)
  Keyboard: d1 - $^{\#}$2
  Transcontinental (1971)

121:00
  FROMM, Herbert
  Unto The Hills (Two Psalm Settings)
  Keyboard: d1-e2
  Hope (n.d.) SA 1400

121:00
    SEE: Ephesians 4:4
    HARKER, F. Flaxington
    I Will Lift Up Mine Eyes To The Hills, Op.34,#2

121:00
    HEAD, Michael
    I Will Lift Up Mine Eyes (from Three Psalms)
    Organ/Piano: LOW:b1-e2; HIGH:e1-a3
    Robertson [Boosey & Hawkes] (1976) 1013

121:00
    HOPSON, Hal H.
    I Lift Up My Eyes To The Hills
    Piano/Organ (optional solo instrument in C):   c1-d2
    GIA (1980) G-2239

121:00
    HUMPHREYS, Don
    I Will Lift Up Mine Eyes Unto The Hills
    Keyboard: LOW:b1-d2; HIGH:d1-f2
    Boston (1947)

121:00
    JACKSON, Stanley
    I Will Lift Up Mine Eyes
    Keyboard
    Carl Fischer

121:00 (RSV)
    JENNINGS, Kenneth
    I Lift Up My Eyes To The Hills
    Keyboard: LOW:d1-f2; HIGH:d1-g2
    Augsburg (1967)

121:00 (taken from)
    JENSEN, Adolf (arr. Carl Fredrickson)
    Lift Up Thine Eyes
    Keyboard: db1 - db2
    R.D.Row (1959) found in Sacred Song Masterpieces

121:00
    KAYDEN, Mildred
    Psalm 121
    Piano: d1 - bb3
    Mercury (1956)

121:00
    KENDRICK, Virginia
    I Will Lift Up Mine Eyes
    Keyboard: e1-f2
    Schmitt (1975)

121:00
   KOCH, John
   I Will Lift Up Mine Eyes (Songs Of David)
   Flute and String Quartet: el-f2
   American Music Center

121:00 (St. Dunstan Psalter)
   LEKBERG, Sven
   I Will Lift Up Mine Eyes
   Piano/Organ: d1-e2
   Witmark (1947)

121:00
   MENDELSSOHN, Felix (arr. Fredrickson)
   Lift Thine Eyes
   Keyboard: DUET
   R.D.Row (1960) found in Sacred Duet Masterpieces

121:00
   PARKER, Clifton
   I Will Lift Up Mine Eyes Unto The Hills
   Piano/Organ: c1-e2
   Carl Fischer (1934)

121:00
   RAIGORODSKY, Natalie
   I Will Lift Up Mine Eyes
   Piano (Organ): c1 - f#2
   Coburn Press

121:00
   REPP, Ray
   I Lift Up My Eyes
   Keyboard/Guitar: c1-d2
   FEL Publications (1970) FEL 70-500

121:00
   RUTENBER, C.B.
   I Will Lift Up Mine Eyes
   Organ: c1 - a^{b}3
   G. Schirmer (1921)

121:00
   SOWERBY, Leo
   I Will Lift Up Mine Eyes
   Organ: b1-e2
   H.W.Gray (1949)

121:00
   STANFORD, C. V.
   A Song Of Trust (Bible Songs)
   Organ: a^{b}1 - g2
   Stainer & Bell

121:00
  STEARNS, Peter Pindar
  I Will Lift Up Mine Eyes
  Organ: d#1 - d2
  Coburn Press (1971) found in <u>Lift Up Your Voice</u>

121:00
  TELEMANN, G.P.
  Ich habe meine Augen auf zu den Bergen
  English/German   Tenor or Soprano
  Hanssler 39.111

121:00
  TWINN, Sydney
  I Will Lift Up Mine Eyes
  Piano/Organ: d1-a3
  Carl Fischer (1948)

121:00
  SEE: Psalm 31:5
  VAUGHAN-WILLIAMS, Ralph
  Watchful's Song

121:00
  WATKINS, Margery
  I Will Lift Up Mine Eyes
  Piano: b♭1 - e♭2
  Oliver Ditson (1927) found in <u>Choice Sacred Songs</u>

121:00
  SEE: Psalm 130
  YARDUMIAN, Richard
  Symphony #2

121:1-4
  DVORAK, Anton
  I Will Lift Up Mine Eyes, Op.99, #9
  Keyboard: LOW:d1 - e♭2; HIGH:f#1 - g2
  Simrock; G. Schirmer; also R.D.Row (1955) RB-31

121:6 (and other)
  GREENE, Maurice
  The Sun Shall Be No More Light
  Keyboard: e1-g2
  Bosworth (1910) found in <u>Seven Sacred Solos Of The Early English</u>
    <u>School</u>

121:8
  SEE: Psalm 34:4
  STEVENSON, Frederick
  I Sought The Lord

122:00
    COUPERIN, Francois
    Ad te Levavi occulos meus
    Latin   Continuo & 2 Violins: F-d1
    Heugel (1972) H32.219 (found in Neuf Motets)

122:2, 3, 6-8
    WERNICK, Richard F.
    A Prayer For Jerusalem
    Hebrew   Percussion (Vibes, Glockenspiel, Crotales, Finger
        Cymbals): g-a3
    Presser (1975) 110-40083

122:7
    SEE: Psalm 127:1
    MYERS, Gordon
    Except The Lord Build The House

123:1-5
    CHILDS, David
    Psalm 123 (from Seven Psalms for voice and organ)
    Organ: c1-a3
    Abingdon (1966) High APM 390; Low APM 385

124:00
    STANFORD, C.V.
    A Song of Battle (Bible Songs)
    Organ: e^b1 - g2
    Stainer & Bell

126:00
    KAHN, E.I.
    Psalm 126
    Piano/Organ: a1-b3
    Composers Facsimile Edition

126:00
    BROD, Max
    Psalm CXXVI
    English/Hebrew   Piano: d1-g2
    Israeli Music Pub (1953)

126:1-2, 5-6
    HANDY, William Christopher
    They That Sow In Tears
    Piano: e^b1 - a^b3
    Handy Bros. (1950)

126:5, 6
    ROGERS, James H.
    They That Sow In Tears
    Piano: d1-f2
    G. Schirmer (1908)

127:00
    BIBER, Heinrich Ignaz Franz (ed. Wolfram Stude)
    Nisi Dominus aedificaverit domum
    Latin   Violin, Cello: BASS
    Alexander Broude (1972) 9516

127:00
    DINN, Freda
    Psalm 127
    Keyboard: c1-f2
    Schott

127:00
    GIDEON, Miriam
    The Labor Of Thy Hands (#1 in A Woman of Valor)
    English/Hebrew   Piano: f#1 - g2
    American Composers Alliance

127:1 (Isaiah 2:2; Malachi 3:10)
    MacDERMID, James
    Bring Ye All The Tithes Into The Storehouse
    Keyboard: LOW:bb1 - f2; HIGH:d1 - ab3
    Forster (1960)

127:1 (Psalm 49:16b; Psalm 122:7)
    MYERS, Gordon
    Except The Lord Build The House
    Keyboard: d1 - eb2
    Eastlane

127:1
    SEE: Psalm 31:5
    VAUGHAN-WILLIAMS, Ralph
    Watchful's Song

127:4-6
    FERRIS, William
    Behold, Thus Is The Man Blessed
    Organ: e1-f2
    GIA (1968) G-14750

128:00
    GIDEON, Miriam
    The Labor Of Thy Hands (#3 in A Woman of Valor)
    English/Hebrew   Piano: e1-a3
    American Composers Alliance

128:00
    SEE: Psalm 129
    MILHAUD, Darius
    Cantate de Psaums

128:00
SCHIAVONE, John
Happy Are You Who Fear The Lord
Keyboard: LOW:e1-d2; HIGH:g1-f2
Concordia (1980) found in Seven Wedding Songs

128:00
SINZHEIMER, Max
Blessed Are Those Who Fear The Lord
Organ: d1-f2
Concordia (1974) 97:4893

128:00
WETZLER, Robert
Psalm 128 - A Wedding S ong
Organ: c1-e2
Augsburg (1964) 11-0714

128:1
POWELL, Robert
Blessed Are Those Who Fear The Lord (found in Three Wedding
    Songs)
Keyboard: d1-e2
Concordia (1974) 97-5278

128:1-4
BENDER, Jan
Wedding Song
Organ: c1-d2
Concordia (1968) 97-4887

128:2-4
SEE: Psalm 92:12
FELCIANO, Richard
Benedictio Nuptialis

128:4-6
FERRIS, William
Behold, Thus Is The Man Blessed
Organ: c1-f2
GIA (1968) G-1475

129:00 (Psalm 128; Psalm 136; Psalm 145; Psalm 147)
MILHAUD, Darius
Cantate de Psaumes
French/German   Baritone & Orchestra
Universal (1970)

130:00
BEDELL, Robert L.
Out Of The Deep Have I Called Unto Thee
Piano/Organ: LOW:c1-d2; HIGH:e^{b}1 - f2
G. Schirmer (1938); also found in 52 Sacred Songs

130:00
  BERNHARD, Christopher
  Aus der Tiefen
  German   2 Violins, Cello: al-a3
  Barenreiter #3425

130:00
  BURNS, William K.
  Out Of The Depths (in <u>Four Meditative Songs</u>)
  Keyboard: al - e^b
  Abingdon (1972) APM-515

130:00 (based on; metrical text)
  CAMPION, Thomas
  Out Of My Soul's Depth
  Lute: f$^{\#}$1 - f2
  Roger Dean (1974) CMC 103

130:00
  HOVHANESS, Alan
  Out Of The Depths, Op.142, #3
  Keyboard: el - f$^{\#}$2
  C.F.Peters (1958)

130:00
  MARKS, J. Christopher
  Out Of The Deep
  Keyboard: LOW:a^{b}1 - d^{b}2; HIGH:d1-g2
  Novello (1905)

130:00
  ROGERS, James H.
  Out Of The Depths
  Keyboard: LOW:g-c2; HIGH:c1-f2
  Arthur P. Schmidt (1905)

130:00
  SCOTT, John Prindle
  Out Of The Depths
  Piano: LOW:c1 - e^{b}2; HIGH:e1-g2
  Huntzinger (1918) also found in <u>Choice Sacred Songs For Home
    Or Church Service</u>

130:00
  SIFLER, Paul
  De Profundis
  Organ: b^{b}1 - f2
  H.W.Gray (1953)

130:00
  STANFORD, C.V.
  A Song Of Hope (<u>Bible Songs</u>)
  Organ: e^{b}1 - g2
  Stainer & Bell

130:00
    WEINER, Lazar
    Mimaamakim (Out Of The Depths)
    Piano: c1-f2
    Transcontinental (1973)

130:00
    WOOLER, Alfred
    Out Of The Depths
    Keyboard: d1-d2
    Summy (1913)

130:00 (Psalm 24:1-7, 8-11; Psalm 27:1; Psalm 95:1, 6; Psalm 121)
    YARDUMIAN, Richard
    Symphony #2
    Medium Voice & Orchestra
    Elkan Vogel (1965)

130:1-3, 5-6
    BUTLER, Eugene
    Out Of The Depths
    Keyboard: c#1 - e2
    Sacred Music Press (1969) found in The Solo Psalmist

130:5
    SEE: Psalm 62:1, 5-7
    SEATON, Annette
    Those Who Wait On The Lord

133:00
    MATESKY, Thelma
    Behold, How Good And How Pleasant
    Keyboard: d1-g2
    Mercury [Presser] (1964)

134:00
    CHAJES, Julius
    Old Jerusalem (Psalm 134)
    Piano: e1-g2
    Transcontinental (1975)

134:00
    ROREM, Ned
    Psalm 134 (Behold, Bless Ye The Lord)
    Piano: d1-d#2
    Southern (1955) from A Cycle Of Holy Songs

134: (Milton)
    THIMAN, Eric
    How Lovely Are Thy Dwellings Fair
    Organ: DUET:S.S.
    Novello (1939) 78

134:1-4
ROSENMUELLER, Johann
Der 134 Psalm
Latin/German   Continuo, 2 Violins: a1-c2
Adolph Nagel [Schott] 81

135:00
CASSLER, G. Winston
Laudate Nomen (Oh Praise The Lord)
Organ: b1-e2
Augsburg (1965)

135 (metrical)
HANDEL, G.F.
Thy Mercy, Lord (from Sixth Chandos Anthem)
Keyboard: d1 - a^{b}3
Paterson (Carl Fischer)

135:1-2 (Psalm 84:2)
HANDEL, G.F.
Praise Him, All That In His House Attend (Sixth Chandos Anthem)
Keyboard: f1 - a^{b}3
Novello

136:00
SEE: Psalm 129
MILHAUD, Darius
Cantate de Psaume

136:1-9
STARER, Robert
Give Thanks Unto The Lord (from Two Sacred Songs)
Keyboard: d^{b}1 - a3
Southern (1964)

137:00 (paraphrase)
BACH, J.S. (arr. Austin Lovelace)
By Waters Of Babylon
Organ, Violin (Flute or Oboe): d1-e2
H.W.Gray (1967)

137:00
BLOCH, Ernst
Psalm 137 (By The Waters Of Babylon)
English/French   Piano: g^{b}1 - a3
G. Schirmer (1919)

137:00
CHAJES, Julius
By The Rivers Of Babylon
Organ (or Piano & Cello): g1-a3
Transcontinental

137:00
  EVILLE, Vernon
  By The Waters Of Babylon
  Keyboard: LOW:c1-e2; MED:d1-f2; HIGH:e1-g2
  Boosey (1928)

137:00
  RICHARDS, Stephen
  Psalm 137 - By The Waters Of Babylon
  Organ: d1-g2
  Transcontinental (1971) TV 578

137:00
  SEEGER, Charles
  Psalm 137
  Unaccompanied: b1-a3
  American Music Center

137:00
  WILDER, Alec
  By The Rivers Of Babylon
  Keyboard: b1-g2
  Edwin H. Morris (1944)

137:1-5
  DVORAK, Anton
  By The Waters Of Babylon, Op.99, #7
  Keyboard: LOW:b^{b}1 - e^{b}2; HIGH:d1-g2
  Simrock; G. Schirmer; also R.D.Row (1955) RB 31

137:1-5
  HOWELL, Charles T.
  By The Waters Of Babylon
  Piano: LOW:g - e^{b}2; MED:a1-f2; HIGH:b1-g2
  Oliver Ditson (1890)

137:1-5
  SPEAKS, Oley
  By The Waters Of Babylon
  Piano/Organ: MED:d1-d2; HIGH:g1-g2
  John Church [G. Schirmer] (1935) [Free Library]

138:00
  HONEGGER, Arthur
  Confitebor tibi, Domine (Trois Psaumes)
  French   Piano: d1-f2
  Salabert (1963)

138:00
  MAROT, Clement
  Il faut que de tour mes espirits (Trois Psaumes)
  French   Piano: f1-g2
  Salabert (1963)

138:00
MATESKY, Thelma
I Will Praise Thee With My Whole Heart
Piano: d1-a3
Mercury (1964)

138:00 (Psalm 139)
ROW, Richard D.
Thy Right Hand Shall Hold Me
Keyboard: LOW:b^{b}1 - f2;   HIGH:c1-g2
R.D.Row (1945)

139:00 (adapted)
DEMAREST, Alison
Whither Shall I Go From Thy Spirit
Piano: c1-e2
Canyon (1950)

139:00 (paraphrase)
McAFEE, Don
Psalm 139
Keyboard & Treble Obligato Instrument: LOW:c1-e2;   HIGH:c1-g2
Abingdon (1973)

139:00
MUELLER, Carl F.
Whither Shall I Go From Thy Spirit
Piano/Organ: LOW:d$^\#$1 - e2;   HIGH:f1 - f$^\#$2
Carl Fischer (1951)

139:00
SEE: Psalm 138
ROW, Richard D.
Thy Right Hand Shall Hold Me

139:00
SCHINHAN, Jan Philip
Whither Shall I Go From Thy Spirit
Piano: c$^\#$1 - g2
Brodt (1956)

139:00
WARD-STEPHEN
Search Me, O God, And Know My Heart
Piano: e^{b}1 - a^{b}3
Chappell (1917)

139:1-4
BENNETT, S.
O Lord, Thou Hast Searched Me Out (The Woman Of Samaria)
Keyboard: c1-d2
G. Schirmer, in Anthology Of Sacred Song - Alto

139:1-4, 6-10, 23-24
  FLOYD, Carlisle
  O Lord, Thou Hast Searched Me And Known Me
  Piano: b - g^{b}1
  Boosey & Hawkes (1959) from Pilgrimage

139:1, 4, 8
  LEKBERG, Sven
  O Lord, Thou Hast Searched Me
  Organ: e^{b}1 - g2
  G. Schirmer (1972)

139:4, 23-24
  DVORAK, Anton (ed. M.B.Stearns)
  Search Me O God, Op. 99, #8
  Keyboard: d1-d2
  Coburn Press (1971) in Lift Up Your Voice

139:7-10, 12, 14, 23-24
  VanNUYS, Rena
  Whither Shall I Go
  Piano/Organ: d^{b}1 - g^{b}2
  G. Schirmer (1950)

139:7-12
  MacDERMID, James G.
  Whither Shall I Go From Thy Spirit
  Keyboard: LOW:b^{b}1 - e^{b}2; HIGH:d1-g2
  Forster (1937)

139:9-11, 14, 17
  FISCHER, Irwin
  If I Take The Wings Of The Morning
  Keyboard: d1 - g$^\#$2
  American Composers Alliance (1964)

139:11
  SEE: Isaiah 26:3
  SPEAKS, Oley
  Thou Wilt Keep Him In Perfect Peace

140:00
  DeBESE, Theodore
  O Dieu donne moi deliverance (trois psaumes)
  French   Piano: c1 - a^{b}3
  Salabert (1963)

140:00
  HONEGGER, Arthur
  Eripe me Domine, ab homine malo (Trois Psaumes)
  French   Piano: c1 - a^{b}3
  Salabert (1963)

140:00
   SESSIONS, Roger
   Psalm 140
   Organ: d^{b}1 - b^{b}3
   Belwin/Mills

141:3, 4
   SEE: Psalm 118:14, 15
   SCOTT, Charles P.
   The Voice Of Joy

142:00
   ROREM, Ned
   Psalm 142 (I Cried To The Lord)
   Keyboard: b1-g2
   Southern (1955) from Cycle Of Holy Songs

142:00
   SOWERBY, Leo
   Psalm 142
   Organ: e1-a3
   H.W.Gray (1966)

143:7-8
   SEE: Psalm 27:1
   VanVOLLENHOVEN, Hanna
   Hear Me Speedily, O Lord!

144:1-2
   SEE: Psalm 18:32, 37
   VAUGHAN-WILLIAMS, Ralph
   The Pilgrim's Psalm

144:9 (Psalm 145:1-6)
   DVORAK, Anton
   I Will Sing New Songs Of Gladness, Op. 99
   Keyboard: LOW:e^{b}1 - e^{b}2; HIGH:g1-g2
   Simrock; G. Schirmer; also R.D.Row (1955) RB 31

144:9 (Psalm 145:1-6)
   DVORAK, Anton (arr. Fredrickson)
   I Will Sing New Songs Of Gladness
   Keyboard: DUET
   R.D.Row (1960) found in Sacred Duet Masterpieces

145:00
   FISCHER, Irwin
   Delight Thyself In The Lord
   Keyboard: e1-f2
   American Composers Alliance (1959)

145:00
   SEE: Psalm 119
   MacDERMID, James
   Thy Word Is A Lamp

145:00
 SEE: Psalm 129
 MILHAUD, Darius
 Cantate de Psaume

145:00
 SCHMUTZ, Albert D.
 I Will Extol Thee
 Keyboard: d1-e2
 Abingdon (1976) APM 633, found in Sacred Songs

145:1-3, 8, 9, 13b, 14, 17, 18, 21
 FOLKEMER, Stephen P.
 Psalm 145
 Organ, Trumpet: DUET
 GIA (1980) G-2337

145:1-3, 8-10, 21
 HARTLEY, Walter S.
 Allegro Con Brio
 Piano & Flute: c1-a3
 Tenuto (Presser)

145:1, 3, 16, 18-20
 MOLIQUE, B.
 I Will Extol Thee My God (Abraham)
 Keyboard: f1 - b^{b}3
 G. Schirmer (1901) found in Anthology Of Sacred Song - Sop.

145:1-6
 SEE: Psalm 144:9
 DVORAK, Anton
 I Will Sing New Songs Of Gladness

145:1, 15-18
 KAUFMANN, Julius (arr. Fredrickson)
 I Will Magnify Thee
 Piano: LOW:c1-e2; HIGH:e^{b}1 - g2
 G. Schirmer (1957) adapted from the first prelude of J.S.Bach

145:2
 SEE: Psalm 32:11
 HUHN, Bruno
 Be Glad, O Ye Righteous

145:2, 9
 HANDEL, G.F.
 Every Day Will I Give Thanks
 Organ: d1 - f$^{\#}$2
 Coburn Press (1971) found in Lift Up Your Voice

145:3-4
SCHUTZ, Heinrich (ed. & arr. Don McAfee)
Great Is The Lord (Der Herr ist gross)
English/German   Continuo: DUET
Belwin (1977) found in Eight Sacred Duets; also in German only
    Barenreiter (1963) 1138

145:9
SEE: Psalm 104:1, 2, 24
BAUMGARTNER, H. Leroy
O Lord, My God, Thou Art Very Great

145:18
SEE: Psalm 46:10a
BITGOOD, Roberta
Be Still, And Know That I Am God

146:1-2 (Psalm 148:1-3)
FLOYD, Carlisle
Praise The Lord, O My Soul
Keyboard: d - f#1
Boosey & Hawkes (1959) from Pilgrimage

147:00
CARTWRIGHT, Marion L.
Great Is Our Lord
Piano: eb1 - g2
Huntzinger (1948) found in Choice Sacred Songs For Home Or
    Church Services

147:00
GOODE, Jack
Psalm 147
Piano/Organ: c#1 - f2
Abingdon, from Seven Sacred Solos

147:00
SEE: Psalm 129
MILHAUD, Darius
Cantate de Psaume

147:4
SEE: Psalm 104:1, 2, 24
BAUMGARTNER, H. Leroy
O Lord, My God, Thou Art Very Good

148:00
ROREM, Ned
Psalm 148 (Praise Ye The Lord)
Keyboard: d1-g2
Southern (1955) from Cycle Of Holy Songs

148:1-3
    SEE: Psalm 146:1-2
    FLOYD, Carlisle
    Praise The Lord, O My Soul

148:1, 3, 7, 9, 11-13 (Psalm 150:1, 3, 4-6)
    FISCHER, Irwin
    Praise Ye The Lord
    Keyboard: c1-g2
    American Composers Alliance (1966)

148:1-6
    CHILDS, David
    Psalm 148 (from <u>Seven Psalms</u> for voice and organ)
    Organ: f#1 - a3
    Abingdon (1966) High APM 390; Low APM 385

148:1-6, 9, 11, (Psalm 149:1)
    MacDERMID, James
    Sing Unto The Lord A New Song
    Keyboard: LOW:b1-f2; HIGH:d1-a3
    Forester (1939)

149:1
    SEE: Psalm 148:1-6, 9, 11, 13
    MacDERMID, James
    Sing Unto The Lord A New Song

149:1-4
    FROMM, Herbert
    Psalm 149 (from <u>Four Psalms</u>)
    Keyboard: eb1 - g2
    Transcontinental (1971)

150:00
    BANTOK, Granville
    Praise Ye The Lord
    Organ or Piano: d1-f2
    Cramer (1924)

150:00
    BUTT, James
    Psalm 150
    Organ: e1-f2
    Sphemusations (1961)

150:00
    KOCH, John
    Praise The Lord (Songs Of David)
    Flute and String Quartet: eb1 - g2
    American Music Center

150:00
   ROREM, Ned
   Psalm 150 (Praise Ye The Lord)
   Piano: d1-a3
   Southern (1955) from Cycle Of Holy Songs

150:00
   RUBBRA, Edmund
   Psalm CL (Praise Ye The Lord)
   Piano/Organ: b♭1 - f2
   Lengnick, from Three Psalms

150:00
   SCHILLING, Hans Ludwig
   Psalm 150 in the form of a Ciacona
   Keyboard: Soprano or Tenor
   Breitkopf & Hartel

150:00 (paraphrase by Lyte)
   WEAVER, Powell
   Praise The Lord His Glories Show
   Piano/Organ: e1-g2
   Galaxy (1948) 1.666.7

150:00
   WEINBERGER, J.
   Psalm 150
   Keyboard: c1 - b♭3
   H.W.Gray

150:1, 3, 4-6
   SEE: Psalm 148:1, 3, 7, 9, 11-13
   FISCHER, Irwin
   Praise Ye The Lord

PROVERBS

   1:7-9
   LEICHTLING, Alan
   The Fear Of The Lord (Two Proverbs)
   Clarinet Trio: b1-g2
   SeeSaw

   1:20-21
   SEE: Proverbs 22:17-18
   BEALE, James
   On Wisdom

   2:19-22
   LEICHTLING, Alan
   The Lord By Wisdom Founded The Earth (Two Proverbs)
   Clarinet Trio: c1-a3
   SeeSaw

3:1, 5, 6 (and other)
   HAYDN, Franz Josef (arr. Carl Fredrickson)
   Trust In The Lord
   Keyboard: c$^\#$1 - e2
   R.D.Row (1959) found in Sacred Song Masterpieces

3:5-6
   DAVIS, Katherine K.
   Trust In The Lord
   Keyboard: LOW:b1-f2; HIGH:c1-g2
   Galaxy (1946) 1.1551.7 (high); 1.552.7 (low)

3:56 (and other)
   SULLIVAN, Arthur
   Trust In The Lord (from Light Of The World)
   Keyboard: c1-d2
   Coburn Press (1971) found in Lift Up Your Voice

3:5-6, 19-20, 25-26 (Proverbs 4:18-19)
   MacDERMID, James
   Trust In The Lord With All Thine Heart
   Keyboard: LOW:c1-f2; HIGH:e^{b}1 - a^{b}3
   Forster (1940)

3:13, 15-18
   THIMAN, Eric
   Happy Is The Man
   Organ: b1-e2
   Novello (1953) in Two Biblical Songs

3:13, 16, 17, 19, 21
   FISCHER, Irwin
   The Lord By Wisdom Hath Founded The Earth
   Keyboard: e1-f2
   American Composers Alliance (1967)

3:13-23
   MADER, Clarence
   Happy Is The Man (from Three Biblical Songs)
   Organ: d1-e2
   W.I.M. (1975) WIM 128

4:18
   SEE: Isaiah 1:18
   BARKER, Clement W.
   The Path Of The Just

4:18-19
   SEE: Proverbs 3:5-6, 19-20, 25-26
   MacDERMID, James
   Trust In The Lord With All Thine Heart

8:00 (from)
   MacDERMID, James
   Doth Not Wisdom Cry?
   Keyboard: LOW:cl-f2; HIGH:e^{b}1 - a^{b}3
   Forster (1945)

8:32, 35-36
   SEE: Proverbs 22:17-18
   BEALE, James
   On Wisdom

12:19
   BEALE, James
   On Truth (Proverbs Op. 28)
   Piano/Celeste; English Horn; Vibraphone: Bass:F$^\#$ - al
   Composers Facsimilie Edition (1960)

22:17-18 (Proverbs 1:20-21; Proverbs 8:32, 35-36; Proverbs 27:7)
   BEALE, James
   On Wisdom (Proverbs, Op. 28)
   Piano/Celeste; English Horn; Vibraphone: Bass:a - c$^\#$1
   Composers Facsimilie Edition (1960)

24:19
   SEE: Isaiah 1:18
   BARKER, Clement W.
   The Path Of The Just

24:30-31, 33-34
   BEALE, James
   On Laziness (Proverbs, op. 28)
   Piano/Celeste; English Horn; Vibraphone: Bass:g$^\#$ - e^{b}1
   Composers Facsimilie Edition

26:7
   SEE: Proverbs 22:17-18
   BEALE, James
   On Wisdom

26:21-23
   BEALE, James
   On Slander (Proverbs, Op. 28)
   Piano/Celeste; English Horn; Vibraphone: Bass:c-bl
   Composers Facsimilie Edition (1960)

31:10, 11, 17, 20, 26, 28, 30
   ZAIMONT, Judith Lang
   A Woman Of Valor
   English/Hebrew String Quartet: cl - g$^\#$2
   American Composers Alliance

31:10, 25, 28, 31
  GIDEON, Miriam
  A Woman Of Valor (II of A Woman Of Valor)
  English/Hebrew   f1 - g#2
  American Composers Alliance

31:20, 28-30
  ADLER, Samuel
  A Woman Of Valor
  Keyboard: g1-g2
  Transcontinental (1965)

31:25-31 (based on)
  WILSON, John F.
  A Worthy Woman
  Keyboard: d1-d2
  Hope (1974) found in Everything For The Church Soloist, Hope
    (1980) 804

ECCLESIASTES

1:2 (Ecclesiastes 2:22-23; Ecclesiastes 8:15)
  PINKHAM, Daniel
  Vanity Of Vanities (from Three Songs From Ecclesiastes)
  Piano (or String Quartet): b1-a3
  E.C.Schirmer (1963) 1941

2:22-23
  SEE: Ecclesiastes 1:2
  PINKHAM, Daniel
  Vanity Of Vanities (#1 of Three Songs From Ecclesiastes)

3:1-8
  GOEMANNE, Noel
  A Time For Everything
  Organ: e1-e2
  GIA (1980) G-2380

3:1-8
  PINKHAM, Daniel
  To Everything There Is A Season (#3 of Three Songs From
    Ecclesiastes)
  Piano (or String Quartet): b1-a3
  E.C.Schirmer (1963) 1941

3:1-8
  SEE: Psalm 27:13, 14
  SACCO, John
  God's Time

3:1-8
TOCH, Ernst
There Is A Season To Everything
Flute, Violin, Clarinet & Cello
Affiliated Musicians (1953)

3:19-22
BRAHMS, Johannes
One Thing Befalleth The Beasts (from Vier Ernste Gesang,
   Op. 121)
English/German   Piano: a-f1
Weaner-Levant

4:1-3
BRAHMS, Johannes
So I REturned (from Vier Ernste Gesang, Op. 121)
German/English   Piano: g - e^{b}1
Weaner-Levant

8:15
SEE: Ecclesiastes 1:2
PINKHAM, Daniel
Vanity Of Vanities (Three Songs From Ecclesiastes)

9:7-9
PINKHAM, Daniel
Go Thy Way, Eat Thy Bread With Joy (#3 of Three Songs From
   Ecclesiastes)
Piano (or String Quartet): b1-a3
E.C.Schirmer (1963) 1941

12:1-7
SCOTT, John Prindle
Remember Now Thy Creator
Piano: LOW:d1-e2; HIGH:f1-g2
Flammer (1920)

12:1-8
EGGERT, Fred E.
Remember Now Thy Creator
Piano: LOW:b1-d2; HIGH:c$^{\#}$1 - e2
Heidelberg Press (1919)

47:2 (Psalm 117)
FERRIS, William
I Have Seen Water
Organ: d1-d2
GIA (1980) G-2352 (may be solo or unison anthem)

SONG OF SONGS

2:1-3a
LaMONTAINE, John
I Am The Rose Of Sharon And The Lily Of The Valley (from Songs
   Of The Rose Of Sharon, op. 6)
Piano (orchestra reduction): d1-a3
Broude (1962)

2:1-5
BUGATCH, Samuel
Ani Chavatselet Hasharon (I Am The Rose Of Sharon)
English/Hebrew   Piano: d1-g2
Transcontinental (1967)

2:3b-5
LaMONTAINE, John
I Sat Down Under The Shadow (from Songs Of The Rose Of Sharon,
   Op. 6)
Piano (orchestra reduction): $f^{\#}1 - g2$
Broude (1962)

2:6
LaMONTAINE, John
His Left Hand Is Under My Head, And His Right Hand Doth Embrace
   Me (from Songs Of The Rose Of Sharon, Op. 6)
Piano (orchestra reduction): $f^{\#}1 - d2$
Broude (1962)

2:8-10a
LaMONTAINE, John
The Voice Of My Beloved!   Behold, He Cometh (from Songs Of The
   Rose Of Sharon, Op. 6)
Piano (orchestra reduction): $c^{\#}1 - b^{b}3$
Broude (1962)

2:8-13
BARKAN, Emanuel
Hark, My Beloved
Piano: $e^{b}1 - b2$
Transcontinental (1966)

2:10-12
KINGSLEY, Gershon
Rise Up My Love (Three Sacred Songs)
Cello and Keyboard: $b^{b}1 - f2$
Transcontinental (1969)

2:10-13
HELFMAN, Max
The Voice Of my Beloved
Piano/Organ: $c1 - a^{b}3$
Transcontinental (1969) TV 529

2:10b-13
LaMONTAINE, John
Rise Up, My Love, My Fair One, And Come Away (from <u>Songs Of</u>
<u>The Rose Of Sharon</u>, Op. 6)
Piano (orchestra reduction): d#1 - a3
Broude (1962)

2:10, 11, 12, 13b
ROCHBERG, George
Rise Up My Love (Four Songs of Solomon)
Piano: d♭1 - a3
G. Schirmer (1949)

2:10-13
SAMAMA, Leo
My Beloved Spake (<u>Wedding Cantata</u>)
Organ: Tenor:f1-a3
WIM (1974) WIM 118

2:11-13
BILCHICK, Ruth Coleman
The Song of Songs
Keyboard
American Music Center (1972)

2:13
SEE: Hosea 2:21, 22
ADLER, Samuel
I Will Betroth Thee Unto Me

2:14
LaMONTAINE, John
O My Dove, That Art In The Clefts Of The Rock (from <u>Songs Of</u>
<u>The Rose Of Sharon</u>, Op. 6)
Piano (orchestra reduction): e#1 - g#2
Broude (1962)

2:14
THOMSON, Virgil
O My Dove (III of Five Phrases from the Song of Solomon)
Percussion: e♭1 - a3
American Music Edition (1953)

2:16-17
LaMONTAINE, John
My Beloved Is Mine And I Am His (from <u>Songs Of The Rose Of</u>
<u>Sharon</u>, Op. 6)
Piano (orchestra reduction): b1 - a♭3
Broude (1962)

3:1, 2
THOMSON, Virgil
By Night (V of Five Phrases from the Song of Solomon)
Percussion: g1-g2
American Music Edition (1953)

3:1-3
   ARCHER, Violet
   Requiem (from Three Biblical Songs)
   Piano/Organ: d1-g2
   Canadian Music Centre

3:1, 3
   FOSS, Lukas
   By Night On My Bed (from The Song Of Songs)
   Piano (orchestra): d^{b}1 - a^{b}3
   Carl Fischer (1950) 03661

3:9-11
   SAMAMA, Leo
   Thou Hast Ravished My Heart (from Wedding Cantata)
   Organ: e1-a3
   WIM

4:1
   ROCHBERG, George
   Behold! Thou Art Fair (Four Songs Of Solomon)
   Piano: f1 - b^{b}3
   Presser (1975)

4:9-11
   SAMAMA, Leo
   Wedding Cantata (Movement 2)
   Organ: Tenor:a-a2
   WIM (1974) WIM 118

4:16
   FOSS, Lukas
   Awake, O North Wind (from The Song Of Songs)
   Piano (orchestra): d1-g2
   Carl Fischer (1950) 03661

6:3
   THOMSON, Virgil
   I Am My Beloved's (IV from Five Phrases from Song of Solomon)
   Percussion: g1-a3
   American Music Edition (1953)

6:13
   THOMSON, Virgil
   Return, O Shulamite! (II from Five Phrases from Song of Solomon)
   Percussion: e1-g2
   American Music Edition (1953)

7:6
   VOGEL, Howard
   Behold, How Fair And Pleasant
   Organ: c1-f2
   Belwin (1969)

7:11
    FOSS, Lukas
    Come My Beloved (from <u>The Song Of Songs</u>)
    Piano (orchestra): d1-g2
    Carl Fischer (1950) 03661

7:11
    ROCHBERG, George
    Come, My Beloved (Four Songs Of Solomon)
    Piano: c#1 - a3
    Presser (1975)

7:11-13
    OVERBY, Rolf Peter
    Come, My Beloved
    Keyboard: c1-g2
    Augsburg (1961)

8:6
    CLOKEY, Joseph
    Set Me As A Seal (from <u>A Wedding Suite</u>)
    Organ: $e^b1 - e^b2$
    J. Fischer (1951) 8607

8:6
    FOSS, Lukas
    Set Me As A Seal (from <u>The Song Of Songs</u>)
    Piano (orchestra): c1-g2
    Carl Fischer (1950) 03661

8:6
    PINKHAM, Daniel
    Wedding Song
    Organ: d#1 - g2
    C.F.Peters (1975) arranged by the composer, from <u>Wedding</u>
       <u>Cantata</u>

8:6
    ROCHBERG, George
    Set Me As A Seal (Four Songs Of Solomon)
    Piano: g1-a3
    Presser (1975)

8:6-7
    BERMAN, Judith M.
    Set Me As A Seal
    Piano/Organ: b1-e2
    Transcontinental (1978)

8:6-7
    BETTS, Lorne
    Set Me As A Seal
    Organ: b1-d2
    Canadian Music Center (found in <u>Six Sacred Songs</u>)

8:6-7
   HELFMAN, Max
   Set Me As A Seal Upon Thy Heart
   Piano: d1 - f$^{\#}$2
   Transcontinental (1973)

8:6-7
   REZNICK, Hyman
   A Seal Upon Thy Heart
   Piano: c1-f2
   Transcontinental (1953)

8:6-7
   ROCHBERG, George
   Set Me As A Seal
   Piano: g1-a3
   G. Schirmer (1958) found in Wedding Bouquet (ed. B. Taylor)

8:13
   THOMSON, Virgil
   Thou That Dwellest In The Garden (I in Five Phrases from Song
      of Solomon)
   Percussion: e1-a3
   American Music Edition (1953)

ISAIAH

1:2, 4, 18-19
   RIKER, Franklin
   Head, O Heavens, And Give Ear O Earth
   Piano: LOW:b^{b}1 - e^{b}2; HIGH:e^{b}1 - g^{b}2
   G. Schirmer (1922)

1:6, 10
   YOUNG, Walter E.
   The Wilderness
   Keyboard: LOW:b^{b}1 - e^{b}2; HIGH:d1-g2
   Arthur P. Schmidt (1919)

1:18 (Isaiah 44:22; Proverbs 4:18; Proverbs 24:19; Psalm 36:9;
      Psalm 5:12; Psalm 37:9)
   BARKER, Clement W.
   The Path Of The Just
   Keyboard: LOW:b1-c2; MED:d1 - e^{b}2
   R.D.Row (1951) [Free Library]

1:18, 20, 28
   STEBBINS, G. Waring
   Come Now And Let Us Reason Together
   Organ: d1-a3
   Oliver Ditson (1923)

2:2
SEE: Psalm 127:1
MacDERMID, James
Bring Ye All The Tithes Into The Storehouse

2:4
SCOTT, John Prindle
He Maketh Wars To Cease
Organ: f#1 - g2
Flammer (1918)

2:22 (Job 20:8a, 9; Psalm 89:26)
BARKER, Clement W.
Mark The Perfect Man
Keyboard: LOW:d1 - eb2; HIGH:eb1 - f2
R.D.Row (1946)

6:3
SEE: Psalm 29:1, 2
SCHUTZ, Heinrich
Bringt her dem Herren

7:14 (Isaiah 40:9; Matthew 1:22)
HANDEL, G.F.
Behold A Virgin Shall Conceive/O Thou That Tellest (Messiah)
Keyboard: al-b2
Carl Fischer; G. Schirmer; Novello

9:1, 5, 6
KLASS, Lillian V.
The People Who Walked In Darkness
Hebrew   Piano/Organ: bl-e2
Transcontinental (1978) 991035

9:2
SEE: Isaiah 61:1, 2
MacDERMID, James G.
The Spirit Of The Lord God Is Upon Me

9:2, 6
HANDEL, G.F.
The People That Walk In Darkness (Messiah)
Keyboard: g-el
Carl Fischer; G. Schirmer; Novello

9:2, 6, 7
SEE: Philippians 4:4
DISTLER, Hugo
O Rejoice In The Lord At All Times

9:6 (Philippians 2:5-11)
PENDLETON, Emmet
Christ Is Lord, Op. 12, #3 (from Light Of The Lord)
Bruce Humphries (1945)

11:7 (based on)
KALMANOFF, Martin
The Lion And The Lamb
Piano: b1-g2
Elkan Vogel (1970)

12:00
KRAPF, Gerhard
O Lord, I Will Praise Thee
Organ/Piano: c1-f2
Concordia

12:00
SCHMUTZ, Albert D.
And In That Day Thou Shalt Say
Keyboard: d1-e2
Abingdon (1976) APM 633, found in Sacred Songs

12:3, 4 (Psalm 118:14; Psalm 56:13; and other)
CALDER, Lee
God Is My Salvation
Piano or Organ: c1-d2
Galaxy (1961)

14:7
SEE: Psalm 31:5
VAUGHAN-WILLIAMS, Ralph
Watchful's Song

15:3, 6-8
SCOTT, John Prindle
The Voice In The Wilderness
Piano: LOW:c1-f2; HIGH:$e^b1 - a^b3$
Huntzinger

25:8
SULLIVAN, A.
The Lord Is Risen (The Light Of The World)
Keyboard: b1-e2
G. Schirmer (1929) found in Anthology Of Sacred Song - alto

25:8, 9 (adapted)
LISZT, Franz (arr. Carl Fredrickson)
God Shall Wipe Away All Tears
Piano: $b^b1 - e^b2$
R.D.Row (1959) found in Sacred Song Masterpieces

26:00
SHAWN, Allen
Thou Wilt Keep Him In Perfect Peace
Piano/Organ: $b^b1 - f2$
Coburn

26:3 (Psalm 139:11)
   SPEAKS, Oley
   Thou Wilt Keep Him In Perfect Peace
   Piano: LOW:c1-d2; MED:d1-f2; HIGH:e1-g2
   G. Schirmer (1941)

26:3, 4
   THIMAN, Eric
   Thou Wilt Keep Him In Perfect Peace
   Organ: LOW:b^{b}1 - e^{b}2; HIGH:d1-g2
   H.W.Gray (1962) GV 410, high; GV411, low

26:3-4
   WIENHORST, Richard
   Thou Wilt Keep Him In Perfect Peace
   Keyboard: LOW:b1-d2; HIGH:d1-f2
   Concordia (1980) found in Seven Wedding Songs; 97-5577 low; 97-5576 high

26:3-4, 13-14
   MacDERMID, James
   Thou Wilt Keep Him In Perfect Peace
   Keyboard: LOW:a^{b}1 - e^{b}2; MED:b^{b}1 - f2; HIGH:d^{b}1 - a^{b}2
   Forster (1921)

26:3-4, 11-12
   SCOTT, John Prindle
   Trust Ye In The Lord
   Keyboard: LOW:a^{b}1 - e^{b}2; HIGH:c1-f2
   Huntzinger (1917) also in Selected Songs For General Use

33:24 (based on)
   GRAFF, Leta Bishop
   The Inhabitants Shall Not Say I Am Sick
   Keyboard: c1-c2
   Jenkins Music (1926)

34:1
   LaFORGE, Frank
   Come Near Ye Nations
   Piano/Organ: d1 - a^{b}3
   Carl Fischer (1946) V-1828

35:00
   HUMPHREYS, Don
   The Ransomed Of The Lord
   Piano: b^{b}1 - e^{b}2
   Willis (1969) found in Sing To The Lord

35:00
   MacDERMID, James
   The Ransomed Of The Lord
   Keyboard: LOW:b^{b}1 - e^{b}2; HIGH:d1-g2
   Forster (1921)

35:1-2, 6-8, 10
   THIMAN, Eric
   The Wilderness
   Keyboard: b^{b}1 - e2
   Novello

35:5, 6 (Isaiah 40:11; Matthew 11:28, 29)
   HANDEL, G.F.
   Then Shall The Eyes Of The Blind/He Shall Feed His Flock/Come
      Unto Him (Messiah)
   Keyboard: c1-f2
   Carl Fischer; G. Schirmer; Novello; also found in Everything
      For The Church Soloist (Hope, 1980); in 52 Sacred Songs
      (G. Schirmer, 1937); and in Scriptural Solos For All Seasons
      (Lillenas, 1980)

35:10
   SEE: I Corinthians 15:20, 22
   BACH, J. S.
   Now Christ Is Risen (duet)

36:3, 4
   THIMAN, Eric
   Thou Wilt Keep Him In Perfect Peace
   Organ: LOW:b^{b}1 - e^{b}2; HIGH:d1-g2
   H.W.Gray (1946)

40:1
   DVORAK, Anton
   Comford Ye, My People
   Keyboard: f1 - a^{b}3
   Abingdon (1964) APM-308, found in Select Solos For Church
      Musicians

40:1 (and other)
   PARKER, Horatio
   Glorious Jerusalem (in Lift Up Your Voice)
   Organ: c1 - g^{b}2
   Coburn Press (1971)

40:1-3
   HANDEL, G.F.
   Comfort Ye (Messiah)
   Keyboard: Tenor:E-g1
   Carl Fischer; G. Schirmer; Novello

40:1-3
   RUBENSTEIN, Anton (arr. Carl Fredrickson)
   Comfort Ye My People
   Keyboard: B^{b}1 - d2
   R.D.Row (1959) found in Sacred Song Masterpieces

40:1-3
    RUBENSTEIN, Anton (arr. Fredrickson)
    Comfort Ye My People
    Piano/Organ: DUET
    R.D.Row (1960) found in Sacred Duet Masterpieces

40:3-5 (and poem)
    HASIDIC FOLK SONG (arr. Lyndell Leatherman)
    Enter In The Wilderness
    Keyboard: d1-e2
    Lillenas (1980) found in Scriptural Solos For All Seasons

40:3-5
    THORNE, Francis
    Prepare Ye The Way Of The Lord
    Organ: d1-f2
    Joshua (G. Schirmer)

40:3, 6, 7, 8
    SCOTT, John Prindle
    The Voice In The Wilderness
    Piano: LOW:c1-f2; MED:d1-g2; HIGH:e1 - a^{b}3
    Huntzinger (1916) also found in Selected Sacred Songs For
        General Use

40:4
    HANDEL, G.F.
    Every Valley (Messiah)
    Keyboard: d1 - g$^\#$2
    Carl Fischer; G. Schirmer; Novello

40:6-8
    PIKET, Frederick
    All Flesh Is Grass (Three Biblical Songs)
    Piano/Organ: f1 - a^{b}3
    Transcontinental

40:6-8
    SEE: Psalm 39:4-5
    WYNER, Yehudi
    Lord, Let Me Know My End

40:6, 8, 28-31
    MacDERMID, James G.
    They Shall Run And Not Be Weary
    Keyboard: LOW:b1-e2; HIGH:d1-g2
    Forster (1923)

40:9
    SEE: Isaiah 7:14
    HANDEL, G.F.
    Behold A Virgin Shall Conceive/O Thou That Tellest (Messiah)

40:11
SEE: Isaiah 35:6, 7
HANDEL, G.F.
Then Shall The Eyes Of The Blind/He Shall Feed His Flock
(Messiah)

40:11
HARKER, F. Flaxington
He Shall Feed His Flock, Op. 24, #2
Piano/Organ: DUET:S-T
G. Schirmer (1944)

40:28-31 (based on)
HAMBLEN, Bernard
On Eagles Wings
Keyboard: b1-d2
Chappell (1919)

40:28-31
LaFORGE, Frank
Hast Thou Not Known
Piano: LOW:b1-d2; HIGH:d1-g2
G. Schirmer (1939)

40:28-31
SCHMUTZ, Albert
Hast Thou Not Known
Keyboard: c1-c2
Abingdon (1976) APM-633, found in Sacred Songs

40:28-31
SEE: Psalm 62:1, 5-7
SEATON, Annette
Those Who Wait On The Lord

40:28-31
SWIFT, Robert
Hast Thou Not Known
Piano/Organ: c1-f2
Coburn Press, found in Eleven Scriptural Songs

41:10
SCHUTZ, Heinrich
Feurchte dich nicht
German   Continuo: DUET:B-B
Barenreiter (1963) 1705

41:10, 13
SEE: II Chronicles 20:15, 17
KOCH, Frederick
Be Not Afraid

42:6-7 (I Corinthians 6:11)
    BROWN, Allanson G.Y.
    Behold! The Former Things Are Come To Pass
    Keyboard: LOW:c#1 - e2; HIGH:d1 - f#2
    R.D.Row (1951)

43:1, 25
    SEE: Psalm 81:9-11
    STEVENSON, Frederick
    Hear, O My People

44:22
    SEE: Isaiah 1:18
    BARKER, Clement W.
    The Path Of The Just

45:00
    KENDRICK, Virginia
    Look Unto Me, Saith Our God
    Piano: c#1 - d2
    Coburn Press (found in Eleven Scriptural Songs)

45:1, 2, 22 (Psalm 71:9, 12)
    VanWOERT, Rutger
    Be Not Far From Me, Oh God
    Piano: c1-f2
    Chappell

45:22-23, 28
    SEE: Acts 27:22, 24, 28
    MacDERMID, James
    God That Made The World

49:7, 10 (Isaiah 53:1; Isaiah 51:12-13)
    MENDELSSOHN, Felix
    Hear Ye Israel
    Keyboard: d#1 - a#3
    G. Schirmer

50:6
    SEE: Isaiah 53:3
    HANDEL, G.F.
    He Was Despised (Messiah)

51:11b
    SEE: Matthew 13:43
    MENDELSSOHN, Felix
    Then Shall The Righteous Shine (Elijah)

51:12-13
    SEE: Isaiah 49:7, 10
    MENDELSSOHN, Felix
    Hear Ye, Israel

52:00 (taken from)
    SCOTT, John Prindle
    The Messenger Of Peace
    Keyboard: $e^b1 - a^b3$
    Flammer (1920)

52:7 (and other)
    HARKER, F. Flaxington
    How Beautiful Upon The Mountains
    Piano: LOW:bl-e2; MED:dl-g2; HIGH:el-a3
    G. Schirmer (1938) also published in Duet Version

52:7 (and other)
    MENDELSSOHN, Felix (arr. Fredrickson)
    How Beautiful On The Mountains
    Keyboard: DUET
    R.D.Row (1969) found in Sacred Duet Masterpieces

52:7
    PERRY, Julian
    How Beautiful Are The Feet
    Piano: $e^b1 - f2$
    Galaxy (1954)

52:7, 9
    FISCHER, Irwin
    How Beautiful Upon The Mountains
    Keyboard: dl - $f^\#2$
    American Composers Alliance (1951)

52:9 (Matthew 12:18-21)
    ELGAR, Edward
    The Voice Of The Wilderness
    Keyboard: el-g2
    Novello, from The Apostles

53:1
    SEE: Isaiah 49:7, 10
    MENDELSSOHN, Felix
    Hear Ye Israel

53:3 (Isaiah 50:6)
    HANDEL, G.F.
    He Was Despised (Messiah)
    Keyboard: $b^b1 - c2$
    Carl Fischer; G. Schirmer; Novello; also Anthology Of Sacred
        Song (Alto)

53:5 (and other poem by Clephane)
    CAMPION, Edward
    The Ninety and Nine
    Keyboard: LOW:cl-e2; MED:el-g2; HIGH:fl-a3
    James Rogers (1917) [Free Library]

53:5
  SEE: Lamentations 1:12
  FOSTER, Myles B.
  Is It Nothing To You?

53:8
  SEE: Psalm 69:20
  HANDEL, G.F.
  Thy Rebuke Hath Broken His Heart

54:10
  SEE: Isaiah 55:6
  MacDERMID, James G.
  For The Mountain Shall Depart

54:10
  MENDELSSOHN, Felix
  For The Mountains Shall Depart (Elijah)
  Keyboard: b-e1
  G. Schirmer; H.W.Gray; Novello

54:13
  BOWLING, Blanche
  For The Mountains Shall Depart
  Keyboard: LOW:c1-e2; HIGH:e^{b}1 - g2
  R.D.Row (1958)

55:00
  SECCHI (transcribed William Reddick)
  Bow Down Your Ear
  Organ: LOW:a^{b}1 - d^{b}2; HIGH:c1-f2
  Huntzinger (1919) found in Choice Sacred Songs For Home Or
    Church Service

55:1
  SEE: John 6:51
  KIESERLING, Richard
  I Am The Bread Of Life

55:1, 3
  CHARLES, Ernest
  Incline Thine Ear
  Piano/Organ: LOW:b^{b}1 - d2; HIGH:d^{b}1 - f2
  G. Schirmer (1948)

55:1, 3
  HANDEL, G.F. (arr. Carl Fredrickson)
  Come To The Waters
  Keyboard: d1 - e^{b}2
  R.D.Row (1959) found in Sacred Song Masterpieces

55:1, 3
   HANDEL, G.F. (arr. Fredrickson)
   Come To The Waters
   Piano/Organ: DUET
   R.D.Row (1960) found in Sacred Duet Masterpieces

55:1, 3, 10-11
   MacDERMID, James
   As The Rain Cometh Down
   Piano: LOW:d^{b}1 - f2; HIGH:f1-a3
   Forster (1948)

55:1, 3, 12
   STRICKLAND, Lily
   Incline Your Ear
   Piano/Organ: LOW:d1-d2; HIGH:f1-f2
   G. Schirmer (1958)

55:3
   PETER, Johann F.
   I Will Make An Everlasting Covenant
   German/English   Piano/Organ: d1-f2
   Boosey & Hawkes, in Three Sacred Songs For Soprano

55:6
   SEE: Matthew 11:28
   LaFORGE, Frank
   Come Unto Me

55:6
   HUMPHREYS, Don
   Seek Ye The Lord While He May Be Found
   Piano: d1-g2
   Willis (1965) found in Sing To The Lord

55:6
   LYNES, Frank
   Seek Ye The Lord
   Keyboard: LOW:d^{b}1 - e^{b}2; HIGH:f1-g2
   Arthur Schmidt (1909)

55:6 (Isaiah 54:10)
   MacDERMID, James G.
   For The Mountains Shall Depart
   Keyboard: LOW:b1-d2; MED:c$^\#$1 - e2; HIGH:e1-g2
   Forster (1908)

55:6, 7
   ROBERTS, J. Varley (adapted Carl Deis)
   Seek Ye The Lord
   Organ/Piano: LOW:c1-e2; HIGH:e^{b}1 - f2
   G. Schirmer (1948)

55:6, 7 (Isaiah 58:8, 9)
    VanDYKE, May
    Seek Ye The Lord
    Piano/Organ: LOW:c1-d2; HIGH:e♭1 - f2
    Michael Keane (1937)

58:8, 9
    SEE: Isaiah 55:6, 7
    Van DYKE, May
    Seek Ye The Lord

59:19
    SEE: Revelation 3:20
    MacDERMID, James
    Arise, Shine For Thy Light Is Come

60:00
    SCOTT, John Prindle
    Arise, Shine
    Keyboard: LOW:c1-e2; HIGH:e♭1 - g2
    Huntzinger (1923)

60:1
    HUMPHREYS, Don
    Arise, Shine For Thy Light Is Come
    Piano: LOW:c1-e2; HIGH:e1-g2
    Willis (1965) W-9622, from Sing To The Lord

60:1-3, 13, 21
    HARKER, F. Flaxington
    Arise, Shine, For Thy Light Is Come, Op. 56, #6
    Keyboard: d1-a3
    Presser (1930)

60:1-3, 18-19
    SCHMUTZ, Albert
    Arise, Shine, For Thy Light Is Come
    Keyboard: b♭1 -d2
    Abingdon (1976) APM-633, found in Scripture Songs

60:1-6
    TELEMANN, G.P.
    Ihr Volkers, Hoert
    German   Flute & Continuo: d1-e2
    Barenreiter (1961) 387, a solo cantata for Epiphany

60:2, 3
    HANDEL, G.F.
    For Behold Darkness Shall Cover The Earth (Messiah)
    Keyboard: a-d1
    Carl Fischer; G. Schirmer; Novello

60:16
HERBST, Johannes (arr. Karl Kroeger)
And Thou Shalt Know It (Du solst erfahren)
English/German   Keyboard: d1-g2
Boosey & Hawkes (1978) found in Three Sacred Songs

60:19
GREENE, Maurice
The Sun Shall Be No More Thy Light
Piano: LOW:d1-f2; HIGH:e1-g2
Bosworth (1910) from Seven Sacred Solos

60:20
PETER, Johann F.
The Days Of All Thy Sorrow
German/English   Piano/Organ: d1-a3
Boosey & Hawkes, in Sacred Songs For Soprano

61:1, 2 (Isaiah 9:2; Malachi 3:2, 3)
MacDERMID, James G.
The Spirit Of The Lord God Is Upon Me
Keyboard: LOW:b1 - f$^\sharp$2; HIGH:e^{b}1 - a^{b}3
Forster (1938)

61:1-3
FREDERICKSON, Carl
Garment Of Praise
Keyboard: LOW:b^{b}1 - e^{b}2; HIGH:d1-g2
R.D.Row (1958)

61:1-3
WETZLER, Robert
Good Tidings
Organ, Oboe or Violin: b1-e2
Augsburg (1974) 11-0740

61:1-3 (Luke 4:18, 19)
WIANT, Bliss
The Great Commission
Piano: LOW:a1-e2; HIGH:c1-g2
Abingdon (1967)

61:10 (Isaiah 62:1)
CORYELL, Marian
The Robe Of Righteousness
Piano/Organ: LOW:c1-f2; HIGH:d^{b}1 - a^{b}3
Carl Fischer (1957)

62:1
SEE: Isaiah 61:10
CORYELL, Marian
The Robe of Righteousness

63:7 (James 1:17; Psalm 100:1, 2, 4, 5)
   FISCHER, Irwin
   Psalm of Praise
   Keyboard: e1-f2
   American Composers Alliance (1951)

65:17-22A, 25
   WOLPE, Stefan
   Isaiah (#5 of Six Songs From The Hebrew)
   Piano: b^b - e^{b}1
   McGinnis & Marks (1962)

65:19
   SEE: Job 22:21
   MacDERMID, James G.
   Acquaint Now Thyself With Him

JEREMIAH

1:1-5 (Jeremiah 2:8-11)
   ROSENMULLER, Johann
   Lamentationes Jeremiae Prophetae
   Latin/German   Continuo
   Nagel (1929)

1:8
   SEE: Revelation 2:10
   MENDELSSOHN, Felix
   Be Thou Faithful Unto Death

2:8-11
   SEE: Jeremiah 1:4-5
   ROSENMULLER, Johann
   Lamentatines Jeremiae Prophetae

5:15-22
   PISK, Paul
   Lamentation
   Piano/Organ: b^{b}1 - f2
   American Composers Alliance

8:22
   Spiritual (arr. Burleigh)
   Balm In Gilead
   Piano: LOW:g-d2; HIGH:b^{b}1 - f2
   Belwin (1960)

8:22
   Spiritual (arr. Hall Johnson)
   Balm In Gilead
   Keyboard: LOW:g-d2; HIGH:b^{b}1 - f2
   G. Schirmer, found in Thirty Negro Spirituals

9:23-24
SEE: Jeremiah 31:31, 33-34
MacDERMID, James G.
Let Not The Wise Man Glory In His Wisdom

23:29
MENDELSSOHN, Felix
Is Not His Word Like A Fire? (Elijah)
Keyboard: b-f1
G. Schirmer, found in Anthology Of Sacred Songs

29:12, 13
SEE: Job 22:21
MacDERMID, James G.
Acquaint Now Thyself With Him

29:13
MENDELSSOHN, Felix
Ye People Rend Your Hearts/If With All Your Hearts (Elijah)
Keyboard: f$^\#$1 - a^{b}3
G. Schirmer, found in Anthology Of Sacred Song; also found in
   Everything For The Church Soloist (Hope) 1980

31:6, 16 (and other)
BUCK, Dudley
Fear Not Ye, O Israel
Piano/Organ: LOW:d1-e2; MED:f$^\#$1 - g2; HIGH:g$^\#$1 - a3
G. Schirmer (1917) also found in Seventeen Sacred Songs

31:31, 33, 34 (Jeremiah 9:23, 24)
MacDERMID, James
Let Not The Wise Man Glory In His Wisdom
Keyboard: LOW:b1-e2; HIGH:d1-g2
Forster (1924)

LAMENTATIONS

1:12 (Isaiah 53:5; John 3:16)
FOSTER, Myles B.
Is It Nothing To You?
Keyboard: DUET
John Church [Presser] (1907) found in Sacred Duets, Vol. 2

1:12
SEE: Psalm 69:20
HANDEL, G.F.
Thy Rebuke Hath Broken His Heart

1:12, 13
DUBOIS, Theodore
O Vos Omnes (from Seven Last Words)
Latin/English   Piano: g1-g2
G. Schirmer (1926) 186

3:22, 37
SEE: Psalm 27:1
VanVOLLENHOVEN, Hanna
Hear Me Speedily, O Lord!

EZEKIEL

13:3 (Psalm 85:8, 9; and other Old Testament passages)
BARKER, Clement
Woe Unto The Foolish Prophet
Piano: LOW:g - e^{b}2; HIGH:d^{b}1 - gb2
G. Schirmer (1943)

37:00 (based on)
WOLFE, Jacques (arr.)
Bone Come A-knittin'
Piano: LOW:b^{b}1 - e^{b}2; HIGH:d1-g2
Flammer (1933)

DANIEL

3:00 (based on)
MacGIMSEY, Robert
Shadrach
Piano: LOW:c1-g2; HIGH:d1-a3
Carl Fischer (1937)

9:9 (Psalm 103:13)
GAUL, A.R.
To The Lord Our God Belong Mercies (The Holy City)
Keyboard: e1-g2
G. Schirmer, in Anthology Of Sacred Song - Tenor

HOSEA

2:21, 22 (Song Of Songs 2:13)
ADLER, Samuel
I Will Betroth Her Unto Me
Piano/Organ: d1-a3
Transcontinental (1965)

JOEL

2:12, 13, 15-17
ANDREWS, Mark
Blow Ye The Trumpet
Organ: f1-g2
G. Schirmer (1906)

2:15 (Matthew 11:29)
PURCELL, Henry
Blow Ye The Trumpet
Keyboard: al-d2
R.D.Row (1959) found in Sacred Song Masterpieces

AMOS

5:24
KINGSLEY, Gershon
Prepare To Meet Thy God (Three Sacred Songs)
Cello and Keyboard: bl-f2
Transcontinental (1969)

MICAH

6:00
SEE: Job 22
HEAD, Michael
Acquaint Now Thyself With Him

6:6-8
FREUDENTHAL, Josef
The Precepts Of Micah
Keyboard: LOW:cl - e^{b}2; HIGH:el-g2
Transcontinental (1961) TV 559

6:7-8
BANKS, Harry C.
He Hath Shewed Thee O Man
Keyboard: LOW:dl-e2; HIGH:fl - g^{b}2
Heidelberg Press (1923)

HABAKKUK

2:20
PETER, Johann F.
The Lord Is In His Holy Temple
Organ or Piano & Strings: e^{b}1 - f2
C.F.Peter (found in Ten Sacred Songs); also Boosey & Hawkes

ZEPHANIAH

3:00
MacDERMID, James
Sing, O Daughters Of Zion
Keyboard: LOW:cl-f2; HIGH:e^{b}1 - a^{b}3
Forster (1952)

HAGGAI

2:6, 7 (Malachi 3:1, 2)
HANDEL, G.F.
Thus Saith The Lord/But Who May Abide (Messiah)
Keyboard: a-d1
Carl Fischer; G. Schirmer; Novello

ZECHARIAH

9:9-10
HANDEL, G.F.
Rejoice Greatly (Messiah)
Keyboard: e1-a3
Carl Fischer; G. Schirmer; Novello; also found in Anthology
    Of Sacred Songs (Soprano)

MALACHAI

1:11
GREENE, Maurice (ed. E. Stanley Roper)
The Lord's Name Is Praised
Piano: LOW:c#1 - e2; HIGH:e1-g2
Bosworth, found in Seven Sacred Solos

3:1, 2
SEE: Haggai 2:6, 7
HANDEL, G.F.
Thus Saith The Lord (Messiah)

3:2, 3
SEE: Isaiah 61:1, 2
MacDERMID, James G.
The Spirit Of The Lord God Is Upon Us

3:10
SEE: Psalm 127:1
MacDERMID, James G.
Bring Ye All The Tithes Into The Storehouse

4:1-2
SEE: II Timothy 1:12
SCOTT, John Prindle
I Know In Whom I Have Believed

4:2 (Wesley)
BUTT, James
Christ Whose Glory
Keyboard: f1-f2
Sphemusations (n.d.)

THE APOCRYPHA

WISDOM OF SOLOMON

18:14, 15 (and poem)
STEVENSON, Frederick
Light, Op. 58
Organ: al - f$^{\#}$2
Oliver Ditson (1910)

ECCLESIASTICUS (or SIRACH)

24:3-7, 12-14
STANFORD, C.V.
A Song Of Wisdom
Organ: LOW:cl-e2; HIGH:e^{b}1 - g2
Stainer & Bell (1909)

41:1-2
BRAHMS, Johannes
O Death How Bitter (Vier Ernste Gesang)
German/English   Piano: b - f$^{\#}$1
Weaner-Levant

44:00
VAUGHAN-WILLIAMS, Ralph
Let Us Now Praise Famous Men
Organ: el - g$^{\#}$2
Curwen

THE NEW TESTAMENT

MATTHEW

1:21
    BURROUGHS, Bob
    Christmas Prophecy
    Keyboard: d1 - c#2
    Hope (1970) 501, found in New Testament Songs

1:23
    SEE: Isaiah 7:14
    HANDEL, G.F.
    Behold A Virgin Shall Conceive/O Thou That Tellest

1:23 (Luke 2:14)
    LaMONTAINE, John
    Behold, A Virgin Shall Be With Child
    Keyboard: bb1 - eb2
    H.W.Gray, found in Songs Of The Nativity

3:1, 2, 7, 8, 11, 12
    SCOTT, John Prindle
    Repent Ye
    Piano: LOW:a1-d2; MED:b1-e2; HIGH:d1-g2
    G. Schirmer (1917)

3:16 (and poem by W.A.Luce)
    BARKER, Clement W.
    Behold The Lamb Of God
    Organ: LOW:c1 - cb2; HIGH: e1-g2
    Carl Fischer (1969) V-2394, low; V-2395, high

4:4 (I John 3:1)
    FICHTHOIN, Claude
    Behold What Manner Of Love
    Organ: d1 - g#2
    Church (1942)

4:10
    BENDER, Jan
    Begone Satan
    Organ/Piano: c1-d2
    Concordia

4:23
  SEE: James 5:16
  CURRAN, Pearl G.
  Prayer

5:1, 2
  SEE: James 5:16
  CURRAN, Pearl G.
  Prayer

5:1-10
  HUMPHREYS, Don
  The Beautitudes
  Keyboard: LOW:c1-e2; HIGH:e^{b}1 - g2
  R.D.Row (1953)

5:1-10, 12
  WOOD, Don
  The Beatitudes
  Piano/Organ: LOW:c1-d2; HIGH:e^{b}1 - f2
  G. Schirmer (1959)

5:1-12
  BROWNING, Mortimer
  The Beatitudes
  Organ: LOW:c1-f2; HIGH:e1-a3
  Carl Fischer (1939)

5:1-12
  KAVANAUGH, Patrick
  The Beatitudes
  Cello: SA Duet
  American Music Center (n.d.)

5:3 (based on)
  WARD-STEPHEN
  Blessed Are The Poor In Spirit (from The Beatitudes)
  Piano: e^{b}1 - f2
  G. Schirmer (1921)

5:3-6
  MALOTTE, Albert Hay
  The Beatitudes
  Piano: LOW:c1 - e^{b}2; HIGH:e1-g2
  G. Schirmer (1938)

5:3-11 (based on by Irwin Rowan)
  WOLFE, Jacques
  The Blessed
  Piano: LOW:b1-d2; HIGH:e1 - f$^{\#}$2
  G. Schirmer (1954)

5:5 (based on)
  WARD-STEPHENS
  Blessed Are The Meek (from <u>The Beatitudes</u>)
  Piano: b1-d2
  G. Schirmer (1921)

5:6 (based on)
  WARD-STEPHENS
  Blessed Are They Which Do Hunger (from <u>The Beatitudes</u>)
  Piano: d1-a3
  G. Schirmer (1921)

5:7 (based on)
  WARD-STEPHENS
  Blessed Are The Merciful (from <u>The Beatitudes</u>)
  Piano: $b^b1 - e^b2$
  G. Schirmer (1921)

5:9 (based on)
  WARD-STEPHENS
  Blessed Are The Peacemakers (from <u>The Beatitudes</u>)
  Piano: a1-e2
  G. Schirmer (1921)

5:9-10
  SACCO, Peter
  Blessed Are The Peacemakers
  Piano/Organ: $d^b1 - a^b3$
  Ostara Press

5:10 (based on)
  WARD-STEPHENS
  Blessed Are They Which Are Persecuted (from <u>The Beatitudes</u>)
  Piano: $e^b1 - e^b2$
  G. Schirmer (1921)

5:11
  SEE: Psalm 63:6
  ELGAR, Edward
  The Sun Goeth Down

5:14-16, 43-45, 48
  LaFORGE, Frank
  Ye Are The Light Of The World
  Piano/Organ: d1-f2
  G. Schirmer (1944)

6:6-13
  SEE: James 5:16
  CURRAN, Pearl G.
  Prayer

6:9-13
ALBRECHT, M.
The Lord's Prayer
Organ/Piano: C1-E2
GIA

6:9-13
Ancient Galic Folk Hymn (arr. Richard Proulx)
The Lord's Prayer (Ar Nathir)
Organ: d1-e2
GIA (1972) G-1705

6:9-13
ANDERSON, Leroy and Alfred Heller
The Lord's Prayer
Organ: f1-g2
Mercury

6:9-13
BANTOCK, Granville
The Lord's Prayer
Keyboard: d1 - e^b2
Paxton (1943)

6:9-13
BARNES, Milton
The Lord's Prayer
Piano/Organ: $f^\#1$ - d2
Candian Music Centre

6:9-13
CADZOW, Dorothy
The Lord's Prayer
Keyboard: d1-d2
Century Music (1949)

6:9-13
CORY, George
The Lord's Prayer
Piano/Organ: e^b1 - e^b2
General Music (G. Schirmer)

6:9-13
DAME, William
Our Father
Piano/Organ: d1 - $f^\#2$
Carl Fischer (1955)

6:9-13
EARLS, Paul
The Lord's Prayer (soprano solo or children's choir)
Organ or Brass Sextet: d^b1 - e^b2
E.C.Schirmer (1970) 2162

6:9-13
FLOWERS, Geoffrey
The Lord's Prayer
Piano/Organ: f1 - e^{b}2
Coburn Press, found in Eleven Scripture Songs

6:9-13
FORSYTH, Josephine
The Lord's Prayer
Piano: a1 - e^{b}2
G. Schirmer (1929) found in 52 Sacred Songs

6:9-13
FRANCO, Johan
The Lord's Prayer
Piano/Organ: c1 - f$^\#$2
Composers Facsimile Edition

6:9-13
GASKILL, Clarence
Our Father
Keyboard: c1-d2
Bergman (1946)

6:9-13
GATES, B. Cecil
The Lord's Prayer
Piano with Violin obligato: LOW:b^{b}1 - e^{b}2; MED:c1-f2; HIGH:
    d1-g2
Choir Publishing Co. (1937)

6:9-13
HAMBLEN, Bernard
The Lord's Prayer
Organ/Piano: d^{b}1 - f2
Belwin (1946) also available in choral arrangement

6:9-13
HEAD, Michael
The Lord's Prayer
Piano/Organ: b^{b}1 - e^{b}2
Boosey & Hawkes (1956)

6:9-13
HENSCHEL, Georg
The Lord's Prayer
Keyboard: b^{b}1 - e2
Bayley & Ferguson (1919) found in The Sacred Hour Of Song

6:9-13
HEILLER, Anton
Pater Noster
Latin   Keyboard: c1 - c$^\#$2
Doblinger (1963)

6:9-13
HINES, Jerome
The Lord/s Prayer (from I Am The Way)
Piano
Carl Fischer (1965)

6:9-13
HOFFMEISTER, Leon Abbott
The Lord's Prayer
Piano: LOW:c1-d2; HIGH:e^{b}1 - f2
Huntzinger (1929) also found in Sacred Songs For General Use

6:9-13
ISENSEE, Paul R.
The Lord's Prayer
Keyboard: b1-d2
Hope (1981) 911, found in Everything For The Wedding Soloist

6:9-13 (traditional & ICET text)
JOHNSON, David N.
Lord's Prayer
Keyboard (optional bass): c1-d2
Augsburg (1974) 11-0742

6:9-13
JORGENSEN, Philip
The Lord's Prayer
Keyboard: f1-g2
Calumet (1941)

6:9-13
KREBS, Karl August
Our Father
English/German   Keyboard: d^{b}1 - g^{b}2
C.F.Peters, found in Kirchen-Arien Und Lieder

6:9-13
MacGIMSEY, Robert
Our Father
Piano: c1-f2
Carl Fischer (1950)

6:9-13
MALOTTE, Albert Hay
The Lord's Prayer
Organ: LOW:g-c1; MED-LOW:b^{b}1 - e^{b}2; MED:c1-f2; MED-HIGH:d^{b}1 -
g^{b}2; HIGH:e^{b}1 - a^{b}3
G. Schirmer (1935); also found in Everything For The Church
Soloist (Hope), 1980 in Med-Low key

6:9-13
 MAYFIELD, Larry
 O Father In Heaven
 Keyboard: cl-f2
 Lillenas (1977) 911; also found in Everything For The Wedding
   Soloist (Hope) 1981; also found in Everything For The Church
   Soloist (Hope, 1980) 804

6:9-13
 MERBECKE, John (arr. Everett Jay Hilty)
 The Lord's Prayer
 Piano or Organ: d1 - b^{b}2
 Oxford (1971) 96.20Z

6:9-13
 MYERS, Gordon
 The Lord's Prayer
 Piano/Organ: e^{b}1 - e^{b}2
 Eastland Music Co.

6:9-13
 PEETERS, Flor
 Pater Noster, Op. 102
 Latin/English   Organ: LOW:b^{b}1 - d2; MED:c1-d2; HIGH:e1-f2
 C.F.Peters (1962)

6:9-13
 PROULX, Richard (arr.)
 The Lord's Prayer
 Organ: d1-e2
 GIA (1972) G-1705

6:9-13
 ROREM, Ned
 The Lord's Prayer
 Piano/Organ: c1-g2
 Henmar [C.F.Peters] (1957) 6371

6:9-13
 SHENK, Louis
 The Lord's Prayer
 Keyboard: LOW:b1-e2; HIGH:d1-g2
 Presser (1951)

6:9:13
 SIBELIUS, Jan (arr. R.D.Row)
 The Lord's Prayer
 Keyboard
 R.D.Row (1942)

6:9-13
 WILLAN, Healey
 The Lord's Prayer
 Organ: d^{b}1 - b^{b}2
 Concordia, found in A Third Morning Star Choir Book

6:9-13
WILLIAMSON, Inez McC.
The Lord's Prayer
Keyboard: f1-a3
Fred Bock (1972) found in Whom God Hath Joined Together

6:25-33
FISHER, William Arms
Seek Ye First The Kingdom Of God, Op. 16, #2
Organ: c#1 - f#2
Oliver Ditson (1913) also found in Choice Sacred Songs

6:25, 26, 28, 29
TOPLIFF, Robert
Consider The Lilies
Piano: a1-d2
G. Schirmer (1924) found in Seventeen Sacred Songs

6:28-34
SCOTT, John Prindle
Consider The Lilies
Piano/Organ: LOW:c1-e2; HIGH:e♭1 - g2
G. Schirmer (1949)

6:30
LAFFERTY, Karen
Seek Ye First
Keyboard: d1-a2
Karen Lafferty (1972) found in Everything For The Church
    Soloist (Hope) 1980

6:31, 32b, 33
FOSTER, M.B.
Seek Ye First The Kingdom Of God (Seed Time and Harvest)
Keyboard: f1-g2
G. Schirmer, in Anthology Of Sacred Song - Tenor

6:33 (Deuteronomy 6:1-5)
PENDLETON, Emmet
The Kingdom Of God, Op. 12, #1 (from Light Of The Lord)
Piano: c1 - a#3
Bruce Humphries (1945)

9:28-30
RUTENBER, C.B.
Come Unto Me
Organ: e1-f2
G. Schirmer (1921)

9:36b, 37
BURROUGHS, Bob
The Commission
Keyboard: e♭1 -f2
Hope (1970) 501, found in New Testament Songs

10:29-31 (plus text by W.S.Passmore)
  ABT, Franz
  Not A Sparrow Falleth
  Keyboard: c1-f2
  Amsco (1940) found in Everybody's Favorite Sacred Songs

11:27-28
  SEE: Revelation 3:20
  BRYANT, Verna Mae
  Behold, I Stand At The Door

11:28
  COENEN, William
  Come Unto Me
  Piano: e^{b}1 - f2
  G. Schirmer (1940) found in Album Of Sacred Songs

11:28 (Isaiah 55:6)
  LaFORGE, Frank
  Come Unto Me
  Piano: e^{b}1 - e2
  Carl Fischer (1942)

11:28-29
  SEE: Isaiah 25:5, 6
  HANDEL, G.F.
  Then Shall The Eyes Of The Blind/He Shall Feed His Flock/Come
    Unto Him

11:28-30
  BEETHOVEN, L. (adapted Alexander Aslanoff)
  Come To Me, Op. 27, #2
  Piano: LOW:b1-e2; HIGH:d1-g2
  G. Schirmer (1933) adapted from the 'Moonlight Sonata,' first
    movement; also found in 52 Sacred Songs (G. Schirmer, 1933)
    in high key

11:28-30 (and poem)
  COENEN, William
  Come Unto Me
  Piano: e1-f2
  G. Schirmer

11:28-30
  SCARLATTI, Alessandro
  Come Unto Me
  Keyboard: e1-e2
  Carl Fischer (1939) found in The Sacred Hour Of Song

11:28-30
  SCHUTZ, Heinrich
  Venite ad me
  Latin/German   Tenor & 2 Violins & Continuo: c-g1
  Barenreiter (1949) 29

11:28-30
    WILLAN, Healey
    Come Unto Me, All Ye That Labor
    Organ: e1-e2
    Concordia, found in A Third Morning Star Choir Book

11:29
    SEE: Joel 2:15
    PURCELL, Henry
    Blow Ye The Trumpet

12:18-21
    SEE: Isaiah 52:9
    ELGAR, Edward
    The Voice Of The Watchman

13:43 (Isaiah 51:11b)
    MENDELSSOHN, Felix
    Then Shall The Righteous Shine (Elijah)
    Keyboard: $e^b1 - a^b3$
    G. Schirmer, found in Anthology Of Sacred Songs

18:1-4, 6 (Mark 10:14)
    DAY, Stanley A.
    Suffer The Little Children
    Piano: $d^b1 - f2$
    Boston (1951)

18:10
    SEE: Mark 10:13, 14
    UNDERHILL, Charles D.
    Suffer Little Children

19:1-2, 13-15
    LaFORGE, Frank
    Suffer Little Children
    Piano/Organ: LOW:c1-e2; HIGH:$e^b1 - g2$
    Carl Fischer (1950)

19:14
    FISCHER, I.
    Suffer The Children To Come Unto Me
    Piano/Organ: d1-g2
    Composers Facsimile Edition

19:14 (Mark 10:15)
    SCHULTZ, A. L.
    Suffer The Little Children
    Keyboard: $e^b1 - e^b2$
    Tullan-Meredith (1902)

21:8, 9
  LEKBERG, Sven
  And A Great Multitude
  Keyboard: c1-f2
  Witmark

21:9
  CARR, Arthur
  Hosanna To The Son Of David
  Keyboard
  G. Schirmer

21:0
  GRIMM, Heinrich
  Hosianna, dem Sohne David
  German   Continuo: Duet
  Barenreiter (1974) 6460

21:9 (text by Parks)
  ROGERS, Sharon Elery
  Song of Hosanna
  Keyboard: d1-g2
  Hope (1970) 501, found in New Testament Songs

22:37-39
  McAFEE, Don
  The Two Commandments
  Keyboard: e1-f2
  Hope (1970) 501, found in New Testament Songs

22:37-39 (I Corinthians 13:4-5, 13)
  VanDYKE, May
  Love
  Keyboard: LOW:d1 - e^{b}2; HIGH:f1-g2
  Boosey (1932)

23:37
  MENDELSSOHN, Felix (ed. Lloyd Pfautsch)
  Jerusalem
  Keyboard: d1-d2
  Lawson-Gould (1955) found in Solos For The Church Year

23:37
  MENDELSSOHN, Felix
  Jerusalem
  Keyboard: f1-f2
  G. Schirmer, found in Anthology Of Sacred Song - Sop

24:29 (paraphrase)
  SPIRITUAL
  My Lord What A Morning
  Keyboard: LOW:d1-d2; HIGH:f1-f2
  Fitzsimons

25:1-6 (Matthew 45:11; Philippians 4:7)
DENCKE, Jeremiah
Go Forth In His Name
Keyboard & Strings: f1-f2
C.F.Peters (in Ten Sacred Songs)

25:1-13
BENDER, Jan
Lord, Lord Open To Us
Piano/Organ: f1-e2
Concordia

25:34
GAUL, A.R.
Come Ye Blessed (from The Holy City)
Keyboard: d1-d2
Amsco (1940) found in Everybody's Favorite Sacred Songs

25:34-36
SCOTT, John Prindle
Come Ye Blessed
Piano: LOW:b^{b}1 - e^{b}2; MED: c1-f2; HIGH:e^{b}1 - a^{b}3
G. Schirmer (1940) also found in Seventeen Sacred Songs

25:41-45
SCOTT, John Prindle
Depart From Me
Piano: LOW:c1-e2; HIGH:e1-g2
Flammer (1919)

26:26-29
BACH, J.S.
Sacrament (from St. Matthew Passion)
Keyboard: c1-g2
Carl Fischer (1939) found in The Sacred Hour Of Song

27:28, 62-66
ROREM, Ned
Resurrection
Piano: b^{b}1 - a^{b}3
Southern Music (1956) a solo cantata

27:45-46
NYSTEDT, Knut
Tenebrae factae sunt
Latin   Organ: A-f1
Norsk Musikforlag (1978) NMO 9021

27:46 (and other)
DUBOIS, Theodore
God, My Father (from Seven Last Words)
Latin/English: d-f1
G. Schirmer (1926) 186

27:46
  SEE: Psalm 22:2
  SCHALITT
  Eili, Eili! Invocation

28:1-6
  COOMBS, C. Whitney
  As It Began To Dawn
  Piano or Organ: f#1 - f2
  G. Schirmer (1914)

28:1-6
  SPEAKS, Oley
  In The End Of The Sabbath
  Organ or Piano: LOW:a1-f2; HIGH:c1-a3
  G. Schirmer (1918)

28:1-7 (and hymn)
  HARKER, F. Flaxington
  As It Began To Dawn
  Piano: LOW:c1-d2; HIGH:e1 - f#2
  G. Schirmer (1905)

28:5-6 (and hymn)
  SCOTT, John Prindle
  Angels Roll The Rock Away
  Piano: LOW:c1-g2; HIGH:e1-a3
  Huntzinger (1918)

28:5-7 (John 20:13, 15)
  PHILLIPS, Madalyn
  He Is Risen, As He Said
  Keyboard: d1-f2
  Witmark

28:19-20
  SEE: Luke 24:36c, 49
  ELGAR, Edward
  Peace Be Unto You

45:11
  SEE: Matthew 25:1-6
  DENCKE, Jeremiah
  Go Ye Forth In His Name

MARK

5:24-29, 34
  HART, Theron Wolcott
  The Healing Of The Woman In The Throng
  Piano/Organ: eb1 - a3
  G. Schirmer

6:50
BERTRAND-BROWN
Be Not Afraid
Piano: e^{b}1 - f2
Boston (1923)

10:00
SEE: John 3:13
MOZART, W.A. (ed. M.B.Stearns)
Behold The Son Of God K.146

10:4
BENDER, Jan
Let The Children Come Unto Me (Two Solos For Baptism)
Organ/Piano: e1 - f$^\#$2
Chantry

10:4
SEE: Matthew 18:1-4, 6
DAY, Stanley A.
Suffer The Little Children

10:13, 14 (Matthew 18:10)
UNDERHILL, Charles D.
Suffer Little Children
Piano: LOW:a^{b}1 - e^{b}2; MED:b^{b}1 - f2; HIGH:c1-g2
White-Smith (1900)

10:13-16
HAUSMAN, Ruth L.
Suffer The Little Children
Piano: c1-f2
G. Schirmer (1931) found in 52 Sacred Songs

10:14
SEE: Matthew 18:1-4, 6
DAY, Stanley A.
Suffer The Little Children

10:14-15
BENDER, Jan
Whosoever Does Not Receive The Kingdom (Two Solos For Baptism)
Organ/Piano: e1 - f$^\#$2
Chantry

10:15
SEE: Matthew 19:14
SCHULTZ, A.L.
Suffer The Little Children

10:17-24
DAVIS, Katherine K.
Treasure In Heaven
Keyboard: LOW:b^{b}1 - e^{b}2; HIGH:d1-g2
R.D.Row (1951)

13:35
  SEE: Psalm 27:4
  TALMA, Louise
  Cantata: Al The Days Of My Life

14:24
  DEMAREST, Victoria
  Hymn Of The Last Supper
  Piano/Organ: b^{b}1 - e^{b}2
  Oliver Ditson (1977) found in Choice Sacred Songs

LUKE
  1:46-47
  BURKHARD, Willy
  Magnificat
  Latin   Organ: e^{b}1 - a3
  Barenreiter (1973) 6476

  1:46-47
  DENCKE, Jeremiah
  My Soul Doth Magnify The Lord
  Organ & Strings: a2-f2
  Carl Fischer; also C.F.Peters (found in Ten Sacred Songs)

  1:46-47
  GASLINI, Giorgio
  Magnificat (1963)
  Latin   Saxophone, Bass, Piano: d1 - f$^{\#}$2
  Universal (1970) 13589

  1:46-47 (based on)
  GOUNOD, Charles
  Ave Maria
  English Text is based on Magnificat
  Keyboard: LOW:a1 - f$^{\#}$2; MED:b^{b}1 - g2; MED-HIGH:c1-a3; HIGH:d1-b4
  G. Schirmer

  1:46-47
  SANDRESKY, Margaret
  My Soul Doth Magnify
  Keyboard: e1-a3
  H.W.Gray (1959)

  1:46-47
  SAVIONI, Mario
  Magnificat
  Continuo: d1-a3
  Smith College (1972) found in Thirteen Motets For Solo Voice

1:46-47
SCHUTZ, Heinrich
Meine Seele erhebt den Herren (from Symphoniae Sacrae II)
German   2 Violins & Continuo
Barenreiter #4335

1:46-47
THOMPSON, Randall
My Soul Doth Magnify The Lord (from The Nativity According
    To St. Luke)
Piano: bᵇ1 - g2
E.C.Schirmer (1962) 124

1:46-47
THORNE, Francis
Magnificat
Keyboard: a1-a3
Joshua Corporation [General Music] (1972)

1:46-49
BURNS, William K.
My Soul Doth Magnify The Lord (in Two Sacred Songs)
Organ or Piano: LOW:b1-e2; HIGH:d1-g2
Abingdon (1967)

1:46-55
DUKE, John
Magnificat
Organ: c1-f2
Boston Music Co.

1:46-55
HATCH, Verna
My Soul Doth Magnify The Lord!
Keyboard: e1-g2
Flammer (1975) found in Songs Of Praise By Contemporary
    Composers

1:46-55
HOVLAND, Egil
Magnificat
Latin: Alto Flute & Harp: g-f2
Norsk Musikforlag (1966)

2:8
BOEX, Andrew J.
And There Were Shepherds
Keyboard: E1-f2
George B. Jennings (1902)

2:8-13
HANDEL, G.F.
There Were Shepherds (recitative & arioso) (Messiah)
Keyboard: a2-a3
Carl Fischer; G. Schirmer; Novello

2:8-14
  LaFORGE, Frank
  And There Were Shepherds Abiding In The Fields
  Piano: d1-g2
  Carl Fischer (1938) V-1367

2:8-14
  SCHUTZ, Heinrich (ed. M.B.Stearns)
  Recitative And Angel's Message To The Shepherds (from Christmas
    Story
  Keyboard: c$^\#$1 - f$^\#$2
  Coburn Press (1971) found in Lift Up Your Voice

2:8-15 (metrical version by Tate)
  BELCHER, Supply (ed. Gordon Myers)
  Piano: b1-e2
  Abingdon (1964) APM-372

2:8-15
  SCOTT, John Prindle
  There Were Shepherds
  Organ: LOW:d1-f2; HIGH:f1 - a^{b}3
  Flammer (1917)

2:9
  HANDEL, G.F.
  And Lo! The Angel Of The Lord Came Upon Them (Messiah)
  Keyboard: f1-g2
  Carl Fischer; G. Schirmer; Novello

2:9-15
  ROREM, Ned
  An Angel Speaks To The Shepherd
  Piano: a1 - a^{b}3
  Southern (1956)

2:10, 11
  HANDEL, G.F.
  And The Angel Said Unto Them (Messiah)
  Keyboard: g$^\#$1 - f$^\#$2
  Carl Fischer; G. Schirmer; Novello

2:10-12
  SCHUTZ, Heinrich
  Be Not Afraid (from The Christmas Story)
  Keyboard: d1-e2
  G. Schirmer

2:10-14
  HARKER, F. Flaxington
  Glory To God In The Highest
  Piano: LOW:b^{b}1 - c2; HIGH:e^{b}1 - f2
  G. Schirmer (1910)

2:13
HANDEL, G.F.
And Suddenly There Was With The Angel (Messiah)
Keyboard: a2-a3
Carl Fischer; G. Schirmer; Novello

2:13-14 (and other)
BOEX, Andrew J.
Now Let All Christian Men Rejoice
Keyboard: d1-g2
J. Church (1896)

2:14
SEE: Matthew 1:23
LaMONTAINE, John
Behold A Virgin Shall Be With Child

2:29
THORNE, Francis
Nunc Dimittis
Organ: g1 - a^{b}3
Joshua (G. Schirmer)

2:29-30
SCHUTZ, Heinrich
Herr, nun lassert du deinen, Diener im Friede fahren (SWV 352)
German   Continuo, 2 Violins: D-d1
Barenreiter 630; also English/German edition published by
   Hanssler (1968)

2:29-32
BUXTEHUDE, Dietrich
Herr, Nun Lassert du deinen diener
German   Organ, 2 Violins: TENOR:c-g1
Barenreiter (1969)

2:29-32
BURGON, Geoffrey
Nunc Dimittis
Organ (optional Trumpet): e1-e2
J & W Chester (1979) JWC 55243

2:42 (Tate)
PURCELL, Henry
The Blessed Virgin's Expostulation (from Sacred Songs)
Piano: LOW:b^{b}1 - e^{b}2; HIGH:d^{b}1 - g^{b}2
International, found in 40 Songs (ed. Kagen)

2:48, 49 (Psalm 84:1, 2, 4)
SCHUTZ, Heinrich (ed. Richard T. Gore)
My Son, Wherefore Hast Thou Done This To Us? (Meine Seele,
   warum hast du uns das getan?)
English/German   Continuo, 2 Violins: TRIO SAB
Concordia (1962) 97-9347

4:18, 19
  SEE: Isaiah 61:1-3
  WIANT, Bliss
  The Great Commission

4:18, 21 (John 12:33, 40, 44)
  SULLIVAN, Arthur (ed. M.B.Stearns)
  The Spirit Of The Lord Is Upon Me (from Light Of The World)
  Keyboard: e1-e2
  Coburn Press (1971) found in Lift Up Your Voice

5:1-11
  KRAPF, Gerhard
  Master, We Have Toiled All Night
  Organ/Piano: b1-e2
  Concordia

5:5
  SCHUTZ, Heinrich
  Meister, wir haben die ganze Macht gearbeitet
  German   Continuo: DUET
  Barenreiter

6:36-42
  KRAPF, Gerhard
  Be Merciful, Even As Your Father Is Merciful
  Organ/Piano: e1-e2
  Concordia

7:11-17
  KRAPF, Gerhard
  Jesus Said To The Widow, "Do Not Weep"
  Organ/Piano: e^{b}1 - e2
  Corcordia

7:22
  SEE: John 14:6, 8-9
  WARREN, Clara
  Hast Thou Not Known Me?

7:36-40, 47-48
  WARREN, Raymond
  Drop, Drop Slow Tears
  Piano & Flute: b^{b}1 - f2
  Novello

9:28:29, 35 (and other)
  ELLIS, James G.
  Transfiguration
  Keyboard: d1-f2
  Boston (1939) 9190

12:24, 27, 29, 32
    BACH, J.S. (ed. M.B. Stearns)
    Fear Not, Little Flock
    Keyboard: b^b1 - e^b2
    Coburn Press (1971) found in <u>Lift Up Your Voice</u>

14:16-24
    KRAPF, Gerhard
    At The Time Of The Banquet
    Organ/Piano: d1-e2
    Concordia

15:11:25
    VanDeWATER, Beardsley
    The Penitent
    Keyboard: LOW:b1-f2; HIGH:d1-a3
    Oliver Ditson (1892) also found in <u>Choice Sacred Songs</u>

    15:17-19
    SULLIVAN, Arthur
    How Many Hired Servants (from <u>The Prodigal Son</u>)
    Piano: g1-g2
    Oliver Ditson

16:19-31
    KRAPF, Gerhard
    Father Abraham, Have Mercy On Me
    Organ/Piano: d1-e2
    Concordia

18:10-14
    VanDeWATER, Beardsley
    The Publican
    Keyboard: LOW:c1-e2; HIGH:E^b1 - g2
    Oliver Ditson (1936) also found in <u>Sacred Songs</u>

18:15, 16
    SCOTT, Charles P.
    Suffer The Little Children
    Keyboard: LOW:b^b1 - d2; HIGH:e^b1 - g2
    Lorenz (1924)

21:25, 26, 33
    BENDER, Jan
    And There Will Be Sound
    Organ (Piano): c1 - $f^\#2$
    Concordia

21:34-36
    SCHUTZ, Heinrich
    Heutet euch
    German   Continuo & 2 Violins: E-e1
    Barenreiter (1936) 1088

22:17-20
McGUIRE, Bobby
Communion Song
Keyboard: bb1 - c2
Lillenas (1980) found in Scripture Solos For All Seasons

23:28, 29a (John 16:33)
SULLIVAN A.
Daughter Of Jerusalem (The Light Of The World)
Keyboard: d - f#1
G. Schirmer, in Anthology Of Sacred Song - Bass

24:00 (Wesley)
SCOTT, John Prindle
The First Easter Morn
Organ: LOW:d1-e2; HIGH:f1-g2
G. Schirmer (1950)

24:13-31
WEINBERGER, Jaromir
The Way To Emmaus
Organ: d1-a3
Belwin (1940) a 14 minute solo cantata

24:36c, 49 (Matthew 28:19-20)
ELGAR, Edward
Peace Be Unto You (from The Apostle)
Keyboard: c-f1
Novello

JOHN

1:1 (Hebrews 11:3, Psalm 107:20; Hebrews 4:12)
MacDERMID, James
He Sent His Word
Keyboard: LOW:b1 - eb2; HIGH:e1-g2
Forster (1921)

1:5
McAFEE, Don
When All Things Began
Keyboard: d1-f2
Abingdon (1968) from Two Songs For Medium Voice

1:1-14
ROBINSON, McNeil
In The Beginning Was The Word
Piano/Organ: c1-g2
Coburn Press, found in Eleven Scriptural Songs

1:29
BIZET, Georges
Agnus Dei
Latin/English   Piano: LOW:b1-g2; MED:c1 - a^{b}3; HIGH:d1-b3
ProArt (1948)

1:29
HERBST, Johannes (arr. Karl Kroeger)
See Him, He Is The Lamb Of God (Siehe das ist Gottes Lamm)
English/German   Keyboard: d1-f2
Boosey & Hawkes (1978) found in Three Sacred Songs

3:5, 6, 7, 16 (John 14:6)
MacDERMID, James
God So Loved The World
Keyboard: LOW:b^{b}1 - e^{b}2; MED:c1-f2; HIGH:e^{b}1 - a^{b}3
Forster (1924)

3:13 (Romans 8; Mark 10)
MOZART, W.A. (ed. M.B.Stearns)
Behold The Son Of God, K.146
Keyboard: d1-e2
Coburn Press (1971) found in Lift Up Your Voice

3:14-15
BUXTEHUDE, Dietrich
Sicut Moses
Latin   Organ: d1-b3
Barenreiter

3:16
BUXTEHUDE, Dietrich
Also hat Gott die Welt geliebt
German   Continuo, 2 Violins: d1-g2
Barenreiter #288

3:16
FISCHER, I.
God So Loved The World
Keyboard: c$^\#$1 - g2
Composers Facsimile Edition

3:16
SEE: Lamentations 1:12
FOSTER, Myles B.
Is It Nothing To You?

3:16, 17
BURROUGHS, Bob
God's Love
Keyboard: d1-g2
Hope (1970) 501, found in New Testament Songs

3:16, 17
STAINER, John
God So Loved The World (from The Crucifixion)
Organ or Piano: LOW:b^{b}1 - e^{b}2; HIGH:d^{b}1 - g^{b}2
G. Schirmer (1960); also found in Songs For The Easter Season
   (Columbia Pictures)

3:16, 17
STAINER, John (arr. Fredrickson)
God So Loved The World
Piano/Organ: DUET
R.D.Row (1960) found in Sacred Duet Masterpieces

4:23, 24
HOPEKIRK, Helen
God Is A Spirit
Piano: d1 - f$^\#$2
Boston Music (1917)

4:23, 24
McARTHUR, Edwin
God Is A Spirit
Keyboard: c1-f2
R.D.Row (1956)

4:23, 24
MOURANT, Walter
The Hour Cometh
Piano: G-d1
American Composers Alliance (1970)

4:23, 24 (Revelation 20:17)
ROBERTS, J.E.
God Is A Spirit
Keyboard: LOW:c1-d2; MED:d1-e2; HIGH:f1-g2
Arthur P. Schmidt (1928)

4:23, 24
SCOTT, Charles P.
God Is A Spirit
Piano/Organ: c1 - d^{b}2
Oliver Ditson (1914) found in Choice Sacred Songs

5:5-7, 9
CLARK, Palmer John
This Is My Commandment
Keyboard: LOW:c$^\#$1 - d2; HIGH:e1-f2
Remich (1915)

6:00
MENDELSSOHN, Felix (ed. M.B.Stearn)
Bread Of Life (from Lauda Sion Op. 73)
Organ: c1-f2
Coburn Press (1971) found in Lift Up Your Voice

6:00
OLDS, W.B.
The Bread Of Life
Keyboard: d#1 - g2
Carl Fischer (1946)

6:51 (adapted) (Isaiah 55:1)
KIESERLING, Richard
I Am The Bread Of Life
Piano: LOW:d1 - eb2; HIGH:f#1 - g2
Huntzinger (1930) found in Selected Songs For General Use

6:51
TOOLAN, S. Suzanne
I Am The Bread Of Life
Keyboard (with guitar chords): a1-e2
GIA (1976) G-2054

8:00
FISCHER, Irwin
Ye Shall Know The Truth
Piano/Organ: c1 - gb2
Coburn Press, found in Eleven Scripture Songs

8:12
SEE: Ephesians 5:14
HUMPHREYS, Don
Light Of The World

8:12
SEE: Revelation 3:20
MacDERMID, James
Arise, Shine For Thy Light Is Come

9:3-5
ELGAR, Edward
Neither Hath This Man Sinned (from The Light Of Life)
Keyboard: c-d1
Novello

9:4
SEE: Psalm 27:4
TALMA, Louise
Cantata: All The Days Of My Life

10:10, 14 (John 17:17, 24)
ELGAR, Edward
I Am The Good Shepherd (from The Light Of Life)
Keyboard: c - eb1
Novello

10:11-16 (Scottish Psalter, 1650)
    NEVIN, George
    I Am The Good Shepherd
    Organ: b^{b}1 - e2
    Oliver Ditson (1920)

10:14, 16a
    BURROUGHS, Bob
    I Am The Good Shepherd
    Keyboard: d1-d2
    Hope (1970) 501 found in New Testament Songs

11:1-44 (taken from)
    BARKER, Clement W.
    The Raising Of Lazarus
    Keyboard: LOW:b1-e2; HIGH:d1-g2
    R.D.Row (1946)

11:1, 3, 4, 17, 15, 41-44
    DAVIS, Katherine K.
    The Raising Of Lazarus
    Keyboard: b1-e2
    Carl Fischer (1947)

11:25, 26
    BUXTEHUDE, Dietrich
    I Am The Resurrection
    English/German Continuo, 2 Violins: E-d1
    Concordia 97-4821

11:25,26
    HAMMERSCHMIDT, Andreas (ed. Harold Mueller)
    I Am The Resurrection
    English/German String Quartet & Continuo: d1-f2
    Concordia 97-6317

12:33, 40, 44
    SEE: Luke 4:18, 21
    SULLIVAN, Arthur (ed. M.B.Stearns)
    The Spirit Of The Lord Is Upon Me

12:35
    SEE: Psalm 27:4
    TALMA, Louise
    Cantata: All The Days Of My Life

13:35
    SEE: John 15:12
    HUSTAD, Don
    This Is My Commandment

14:1
> SNYDER, Virginia
> Let Not Your Heart Be Troubled
> Piano/Organ: $c^{\#}1$ - g2
> Elkan-Vogel (1947)

14:1-2
> CHADWICK, G.W.
> Let Not Your Heart Be Troubled
> Keyboard: LOW:a1-e2; HIGH:c1-g2
> Arthur P. Schmidt (1915)

14:1, 2, 3
> JEWELL, Lucina
> In My Father's House Are Many Mansions
> Piano: c1-e2
> Oliver Ditson (1902) found in Sacred Songs; also found in
>   Choice Sacred Songs (Oliver Ditson, 1930)

14:1, 2, 3
> REIFF, Stanley
> Let Not Your Heart Be Troubled
> Piano/Organ: b1-e2
> Oliver Ditson (1924) found in Choice Sacred Songs

14:1, 2, 27
> HAEUSSLER, Paul
> Let Not Your Heart Be Troubled
> Piano: LOW:c1-e2; HIGH:d1 - $f^{\#}2$
> Boosey (1928)

14:1-3, 19, 20
> RUTENBER, C.B.
> Let Not Your Heart Be Troubled
> Organ: c1-d2
> G. Schirmer (1921)

14:1, 27
> SPEAKS, Oley
> Let Not Your Heart Be Troubled
> Piano/Organ: LOW:a1-e2; MED:c1-g2; HIGH:d1-a3
> G. Schirmer (1919)

14:1, 27 (John 16:33)
> THOMPSON, William H.
> Peace I Leave With You
> Piano: b1-d2
> Oliver Ditson (1948)

14:2, 3, 4, 27
> MacDERMID, James
> In My Father's House Are Many Mansions
> Keyboard: LOW:a1-d2; MED:b1-e2; HIGH:d1-g2
> Forster (1937)

14:2, 3, 4, 27
WARD-STEPHENS
In My Father's House Are Many Mansions
Piano: dl-g2
Chappell (1917) found in the <u>Ward-Stephens Musical Settings</u>
  <u>Of Sacred Words</u>

14:6
SEE: John 3:5, 6, 7, 16
MacDERMID, James
God So Loved The World

14:6, 8-9 (Luke 7:22)
WARREN, Clara
Hast Thou Not Known Me?
Keyboard: LOW:b^{b}1 - e^{b}2; MED:c1-f2
R.D.Row (1948) [Free Library]

14:16
FISCHER, I.
If Ye Love Me, Keep My Commandments
Piano/Organ: dl-f2
Composers Facsimile Edition

14:18-21
ROW, R.D.
I Will Not Leave You Comfortless
Piano: LOW:b^{b}1 - e^{b}2; HIGH:c1-f2
R.D.Row (1947)

14:18, 28
PINKHAM, Daniel
I Will Not Leave You Comfortless
Latin/English   Flute, Guitar: c1 - b^{b}3
E.C.Schirmer (1971) found in <u>Two Motets</u>

14:23
BENDER, Jan
If A Man Loves Me
Piano/Organ: el-e2
Concordia

14:27
GOUNOD, Charles
The Peace Of God
Keyboard: b1-d2
Oliver Ditson (1903) found in <u>Sacred Songs</u>

14:27 (John 16:6, 33)
ROBERTS, John Varley (ed. Carl Deis)
Peace I Leave With You
Organ: LOW:a1-d$^\#$2; HIGH:c1 - f$^\#$2
G. Schirmer (1936)

15:00
    HAMBLEN, Bernard
    This Is My Commandment
    Keyboard: LOW:c1-c2; HIGH:f1-f2
    R.D.Row (1946)

15:1-3, 5-7
    MacDERMID, James
    I Am The True Vine
    Keyboard: LOW:b1-e2; HIGH:d1-g2
    Forster (1946)

15:4
    HERBST, Johannes (arr. Karl Kroeger)
    Abide In Me (Bleibet in mir)
    English/German   Keyboard: e1-f2
    Boosey & Hawkes (1978) found in Three Sacred Songs

15:7, 9, 10, 12
    LaFORGE, Frank
    If Ye Abide In Me
    Piano/Organ: LOW:d1-d2; HIGH:g1-g2
    G. Schirmer (1942)

15:12 (John 13:35; James 5:16)
    HUSTAD, Don
    This Is My Commandment
    Keyboard: d1-e2
    Hope (1980) found in Everything For The Church Soloist

15:1-6
    DOIG, Don
    I Am The Vine
    Keyboard: c1 - e^{b}2
    Hope (1980) found in Everything For The Church Soloist

16:6, 22
    SEE: John 14:27
    ROBERTS, John (ed. Carl Deis)
    Peace I Leave With You

16:33
    SEE: Luke 23:28, 29a
    SULLIVAN, A.
    Daughters Of Jerusalem

16:33
    SEE: John 14:1, 27
    THOMPSON, William H.
    Peace I Leave With You

17:1, 5, 11, 21, 23
    HEAD, Michael
    Thus Spake Jesus
    Organ: LOW:b1-e2; HIGH:d#1 - g#2
    Boosey & Hawkes (1955)

17:17, 24
    SEE: John 10:10, 14
    ELGAR, Edward
    I Am The Good Shepherd

19:26-27
    JOHNSON, Hall (arr.)
    Take My Mother Home
    Piano
    Carl Fischer (1940) V-1473

19:30
    ANTES, John (ed. & arr. Donald McCorkle
    And Jesus Said: It Is Finished
    Organ/Piano: bb1 - g2
    Boosey & Hawkes (1963)

20:13, 15
    SEE: Matthew 28:5-7
    PHILLIPS, Madalyn
    He Is Risen, As He Said

20:13
    MENDELSSOHN, Felix
    Ye Have Taken Away My Lord
    English/German   Keyboard: DUET: 2 high voices
    John Church [Presser] (1907) found in Sacred Duets, Vol. I

20:29
    SEE: Job 23:3, 8-9
    ROWLEY, Alec
    O, That I Knew Where I Might Find Him

21:00
    KOCH, Frederick
    Feed My Lambs
    Keyboard: a1-e2
    Boosey & Hawkes

21:15
    FAULKNER, George
    Feed My Sheep
    Organ: LOW:c1-e2; HIGH:e1 - g#2
    Carl Fischer (1957) V-2113, high; V-2114, low

ACTS

2:14b, 16-17, 21-23, 32-33, 36
ELGAR, Edward
I Have Prayed To Thee (from The Kingdom)
Keyboard: c-f1
Novello

3:1-3
RICHNER, Thomas
Rise Up And Walk
Keyboard: c#1 - g2
Flammer (1975) found in Songs Of Praise By Contemporary
   Composers

3:1-8
WARREN, Clara
Rise And Walk
Keyboard: LOW:bb1 - c2; HIGH:d1-e2
R.D.Row (1963)

9:2 (Psalm 114:12-14; II Timothy 2:19; Philippians 4:5)
MENDELSSOHN, Felix
But The Lord Is Mindful Of His Own (from St. Paul)
Keyboard: a1-d2
G. Schirmer; also in Anthology Of Sacred Song - Alto

26:26
FLOYD, Carlisle
For I Am Persuaded
Piano/Organ: g-a1
Boosey & Hawkes

27:22, 24, 28 (Isaiah 45:22-23, 28; Philippians 2:11)
MacDERMID, James
God That Made The World
Keyboard: LOW:c1 - eb2; HIGH:e1-g2
Forster (1958)

ROMANS

5:8
SEE: Psalm 118:24
WARREN, Clara
Let Us Keep The Feast

6:3, 4
SOLER, Joseph
An ignoratis quia quicumque (Two Songs)
Latin   Piano: g-g1
Southern (1972)

6:14
  SEE: Romans 14:11
  BARKER, Clement
  Draw Nigh To God

8:00
  SEE: John 3:13
  MOZART, W.A. (ed. E.B.Stein)
  Behold The Son Of God, K.146

8:31-34
  HANDEL, G.F.
  If God Be For Us (Messiah)
  Keyboard: f#1 - a♭3
  Carl Fischer; G. Schirmer; Novello

8:31, 35, 37-39
  BURNS, William K.
  If God Be For Us (in Two Sacred Songs)
  Organ/Piano: LOW:d1-f2; HIGH:f1-a3
  Abingdon (1967)

8:35, 38-39
  DOIG, Don
  Who Shall Separate Us?
  Keyboard: d1 - e♭2
  Hope (1976) found in Everything For The Church Soloist

8:35, 37-39
  PINKHAM, Daniel
  Who Shall Separate Us From The Love Of Christ (II of Letters
    From Saint Paul)
  Organ/Piano (String Quartet): c#1 - a♭3
  E.C.Schirmer (1971) 142

8:38, 39 (Numbers 6:24-26)
  FLOYD, Carlisle
  For I Am Persuaded (from Pilgrimage)
  Keyboard: g-f1
  Boosey & Hawkes (1959)

10:15
  HANDEL, G.F.
  How Beautiful Are The Feet (Messiah)
  Keyboard: f#1 - f2
  Carl Fischer; G. Schirmer; Novello; also in Anthology Of
    Sacred Song - Soprano

10:15
  WOOLER, Alfred
  How Beautiful On The Mountains
  Piano (Organ) and Violin: e1-f2
  Oliver Ditson (1927)

10:18
   HANDEL, G.F.
   Their Sound Is Gone Out (Messiah)
   Keyboard: f1-g2
   Carl Fischer; G.Schirmer; Novello

11:33, 36
   SEE: Psalm 1:4; 1, 2, 24
   BAUMGARTEN, H. Leroy
   O Lord, My God, Thou Art Very Good

12:1, 2
   McAFEE, Don
   A Living Sacrifice
   Keyboard: c1-g2
   Hope (1970) 501, found in New Testament Songs

12:11, 12, 18
   DISTLER, Hugo
   My Dear Brethren, Meet The Demands Of This Time, Op. 17, #3
   German/English   Organ: c1-a3
   Concordia (1969) 97-4925, found in Three Sacred Concertos

13:8-10
   TELEMANN, G.P.
   Hemmet den Eifer, verbannet die Rache
   German   Continuo, Flute: e1-g2
   Barenreiter (1973)

13:11, 12
   PINKHAM, Daniel
   Now It Is High Time To Awake (VI of Letters From Saint Paul)
   Organ/Piano (String Quartet): b1-a3
   E.C.Schirmer (1971) 142

14:11 (James 4:8; Romans 6:14)
   BARKER, Clement
   Draw Nigh To God
   Keyboard: LOW:d1 - e^b2; HIGH:f1 - g^b2
   Carl Fischer (1935)

I CORINTHIANS

 2:9-10
   FAULKNER, William M.
   Eye Hath Not Seen
   Piano/Organ: e1-f2
   Carl Fischer (1956)

2:9 (Hebrews 11:10)
  GAUL, A.R.
  Eye Hath Not Seen
  Piano/Organ: b1-d2
  G. Schirmer, in Five Solos From The Holy City

2:9
  GAUL, Alfred R.
  Eye Hath Not Seen (from The Holy City)
  Keyboard: d1-f2
  G. Schirmer (1929) found in Anthology of Sacred Song - Alto;
    also in 52 Sacred Songs (G. Schirmer, 1939); Sacred Songs
    (Oliver Ditson, 1903); Everybody's Favorite Sacred Songs
    (Amsco, 1940)

2:9, 10
  STEARNS, Peter Pindar
  Eye Hath Not Seen (from Three Sacred Songs)
  Oboe, Horn, Cello: b1-g2
  American Composers Alliance

3:16, 17 (Psalm 115:3)
  MENDELSSOHN, Felix
  For Ye Know Not
  Keyboard: a-d1
  G. Schirmer

5:7-8 (I Corinthians 15:20-22)
  SCOTT, John Prindle
  Christ Is Risen
  Piano/Organ: LOW:c1-d2; MED:d1-e2; HIGH:f1-g2
  Flammer (1920)

6:11
  SEE: Isaiah 42:6-7
  BROWN, Allanson G. Y.
  Behold! The Former Things Are Come To Pass

9:24-27
  TELEMANN, G.P.
  Ein jeder lauft, der in den Schranken kauft
  German   Continuo & Oboe: f1-g2
  Barenreiter (1957) 3627

10:16
  SEE: Psalm 118:24
  WARREN, Clara
  Let Us Keep The Feast

11:23-26
  JOHNSON, Gary (arr. Joseph Linn)
  In Remembrance Of Me
  Keyboard: c1-d2
  Lillenas (1980) found in Scripture Solos For All Seasons

13:00
  BEHRENS, Jack
  I Corinthians 13
  Organ: e^b1 - a3
  Candian Music Centre

13:00
  BITGOOD, Roberta
  The Greatest Of These Is Love
  Keyboard: LOW:c1-d2; HIGH:e^b1 - f2
  H.W.Gray (1936)

13:00
  BRAHMS, Johannes
  Though I Speak With Tongues (View Erste Gesang), Op. 121
  German/English   Piano:a^b1 - g2
  Weaner-Levant; also found in Select Vocal Solos For The Church
    Musician (Abingdon, 1964) APM 308

13:00
  HASKINS, V.
  Love Never Faileth
  Keyboard: d1-g2
  G. Schirmer

13:00 (based on)
  HOPSON, Hal
  The Gift Of Love
  Keyboard: d1-d2
  Hope (1972) 911; also found in Everything For The Church
    Soloist; and in Everything For The Wedding Soloist

13:00 (based on)
  HOPSON, Hal
  The Gift Of Love
  Keyboard: DUET
  Hope, found in Folk Songs For Weddings

13:00
  MOE, Daniel
  The Greatest Of These Is Love
  Organ/Piano: LOW:b1-$d^{\#}2$; HIGH:d^b1 - $f^{\#}1$
  Augsburg (1958) 11:0702 high; 11:0703 low

13:00
  PENHORWOOD, Edwin
  The Greatest Of These Is Love
  Organ: b^b1 - e^b2
  Hinshaw (1976) HMV 104

13:00
  ROOT, Frederic
  Love Never Faileth
  Keyboard: f1-g2
  Summy (1907)

13:00
WARD-STEPHENS
Love Never Faileth
Piano: d1-f2
Chappell (1917) found in The Ward-Stephens Musical Settings
Of Sacred Words

13:00
WARE, Harriet
The Greatest Of These
Piano: LOW:d1 - f$^{\#}$2; HIGH:e^{b}1 - a^{b}3
Boston Music (1947)

13:00
WETZLER, Robert
The Greatest Of These Is Love (from Two Scriptural Songs)
Organ (Flute): c1-e2
AMSI (1979)

13:1-7
McAFEE, Don
If I Am Without Love
Keyboard: d1 - g$^{\#}$2
Hope (1970) 501, found in New Testament Songs

13:4-5, 13
SEE: Matthew 22:37-39
VanDYKE, M.
Love

13:4-7, 13 (paraphrase from The Living Bible)
LYNN, Lorna
The Greatest Of These Is Love
Piano or Guitar: a1-a2
Golden Music (1980)

15:00
SEE: Psalm 98
GORE, Richard
O Sing Unto The Lord A New Song

15:20, 26-28 (Colossians 3:1-3)
BACH, J.S. (ed. M.B.Stearns)
Awake All Ye People (from Cantata #15)
Keyboard: g-e2
Coburn Press (1971) found in Lift Up Your Voice

15:20, 22 (Isaiah 35:10; and other)
BACH, J.S.
Now Christ Is Risen
Keyboard: DUET
R.D.Row (1960) found in Sacred Duet Masterpieces

15:20
SEE: Job 19:25, 26
HANDEL, G.F.
I Know That My Redeemer Liveth

15:20-22
SEE: I Corinthians 5:7-8
SCOTT, John Prindle
Christ Is Risen

15, 20, 23 (adapted)
HANDEL, G.F. (arr. Carl Fredrickson)
Awake Thou That Sleepest
Keyboard: $d^b1 - e^b2$
R.D.Row (1959) found in Sacred Song Masterpieces

15:50-58
TELEMANN, G.P.
Jauchzt, ihr Christen, seid vergnugt
German   Violin & Continuo: d1-g2
Barenreiter (1971)

15:51-54
HANDEL, G.F.
Behold I Tell You A Mystery/The Trumpet Shall Sound
Keyboard: a-el
Carl Fischer; G. Schirmer; Novello

15:54-56
HANDEL, G.F.
Then Shall Be Brought To Pass/O Death Where Is Thy Sting
Keyboard: DUET:A-T
Carl Fischer; G. Schirmer; Novello

15:57 (and other)
GLUCK, Christoph (arr. Fredrickson)
Thanks Be To God
Piano/Organ: DUET
R.D.Row (1960) found in Sacred Duet Masterpieces

II CORINTHIANS

3:9-12
PISK, Paul
The Spirit Of God
Piano/Organ: c1-f2
American Composers Alliance

6:16
BARKER, Clement W.
Temple Of Glory
Keyboard: LOW:c1-e2; HIGH:$e^b1 - g2$
R.D.Row (1963)

12:7-10 (based on)
FETTKE, Tom
Three Times I Asked Him
Keyboard: $ab1 - f2$
Lillenas (1980) found in Scripture Solos For All Seasons

GALATIANS

5:1, 25 (II Timothy 1:7; and other)
BARKER, Clement
If We Live In The Spirit
Keyboard: LOW:c1 - e^b2; HIGH:e^b1 - g^b2
Carl Fischer (1935)

5:25 (based on, Croly)
HUSTAD, Donald
Spirit Of God
Piano: LOW:c1-d2; HIGH:b^b1 - c2
Fred Bock (1964) found in Everything For The Church Soloist
(Hope, 1980); also in The Sanctuary Soloist (Fred Bock, 1980)

6:14 (Watts)
HOPE, Lawrence
When I Survey The Wondrous Cross
Keyboard: d^b1 - f2
Turner & Phillips (1904)

6:14 (Watts)
LORENZ, E.J.
When I Survey The Wondrous Cross
Keyboard: c1-f2
Lorenz (1896)

6:14 (Watts)
MURRAY, Lyn
When I Survey The Wondrous Cross
Keyboard: LOW:c1-d2; HIGH:e1-f2
Fred Bock Music (1964) found in The Sanctuary Soloist

6:14 (Watts)
THOMSON, Sydney
When I Survey The Wondrous Cross
Organ: f1-f2
G. Schirmer (1922)

EPHESIANS

3:14-15
SCHUTZ, Heinrich
Ich benge meine knie
German   Continuo: DUET
Barenreiter (1963) 1705

4:7 (Psalm 121)
HARKER, F. Flaxington
I Will Lift Up Mine Eyes To The Hills, Op. 34, #2
Piano: LOW:c1-f2; HIGH:e^{b}1 - a^{b}3
Flammer (1923)

4:31, 32
DAVIS, Katherine K.
Be Ye Kind, One To Another
Keyboard: c1 - e^{b}2
Galaxy (1948) 1.1696.7

5:2, 8, 11, 15, 19
POWELL, Robert J.
Walk In Love
Keyboard: LOW:b1-d2; HIGH:d1-f2
Concordia (1980) 97-5578, high; 97-5579, low, found in Seven
    Wedding Songs

5:14 (John 8:12)
HUMPHREYS, Don
Light Of The World
Keyboard: LOW:b^{b}1 - e2; HIGH:e^{b}1 - g2
R.D.Row (1960) found in Songs For Christian Service, Book I

5:14 (I Thessalonians 5:5, 16-23)
WARD-STEPHENS
Awake Thou That Sleepest
Piano: LOW:b1 - g$^{\#}$2; HIGH:d^{b}1 - a^{b}3
Chappell (1917); also found in The Ward-Stephens Musical
    Settings Of Sacred Words

6:00
HUMPHREYS, Don
Put On The Whole Armour Of God
Keyboard: LOW:c1 - e^{b}2; HIGH:d1-f2
R.D.Row (1955) found in Songs For Christian Science Service
    Book I

6:11
SEE: Psalm 18:32, 37
VAUGHAN-WILLIAMS, Ralph
The Pilgrim's Psalm

6:16-17 (adapted)
    BACH, J.S. (arr. Carl Fredrickson)
    Be Strong In The Lord
    Keyboard: d1 - e^{b}2
    R.D.Row (1959) found in Sacred Song Masterpieces

PHILIPPIANS

1:3-11
    BECK, John Ness
    Song Of Devotion
    Piano: LOW:c1 - f$^\#$2; HIGH:e1-a3
    G. Schirmer (1968)

2:00
    HUMPHREYS, Don
    Let This Mind Be In You
    Piano: a^{b}1 - f2
    Willis (1965) found in Sing To The Lord

2:5-11
    SEE: Isaiah 9:6
    PENDLETON, Emmet
    Christ Is Lord

2:11
    SEE: Acts 27:22, 24, 28
    MacDERMID, James
    God That Made The World

4:00
    LANE, Richard
    Rejoice In The Lord
    Keyboard: e^{b}1 - g2
    Coburn Press (found in Eleven Scriptural Songs)

4:4 (Isaiah 9:2, 6-7)
    DISTLER, Hugo
    O Rejoice In The Lord At All Times, Op. 17, #2 (in Three
        Sacred Concertos)
    Organ: c1-g2
    Concordia (1969) 97-4925

4:4-7
    PINKHAM, Daniel
    Rejoice In The Lord Alway (V of Letters From Saint Paul)
    Organ or Piano: d1-g2
    E.C.Schirmer (1971) 142

4:5
  SEE: Acts 9:2
  MENDELSSOHN, Felix
  But The Lord Is Mindful Of His Own

4:7
  SEE: Matthew 25:1-6
  DENCKE, Jeremiah
  Go Ye Forth In His Name

4:8 (adapted)
  MacGIMSEY, Robert
  Think On These Things
  Organ or Piano: LOW:b^{b}1 - e^{b}2; HIGH:e1-g2
  Carl Fischer (1956)

4:8-9 (adapted)
  SKILLINGS, Otis
  Whatever Is True
  Keyboard: c1-f2
  Lillenas (1980) found in Scripture Solos For All Seasons

COLOSSIANS

3:1, 2
  FOSTER, Myles
  If Ye Then Be Risen With Christ
  Keyboard: DUET
  John Church (Presser, 1907) found in Sacred Duets, Vol. 2

3:1-3
  SEE: I Corinthians 15:20, 26-28
  BACH, J.S. (ed. M.B.Stearns)
  Awake, All Ye People (from Cantata #15)

3:1-4
  SOLER, Joseph
  Fraters: Si consurrexistis cum Christo (Two Songs)
  Latin   Piano: f-e2
  Southern Music (1972)

3:12-17 (adapted)
  SMITH, G. Alan
  Because You Are God's Chosen Ones
  Keyboard: d1-e2
  Hope (1980) 911, found in Everything For The Wedding Soloist;
    also found in Everything For The Church Soloist (Hope,
    1980) 804

3:16
   PINKHAM, Daniel
   Let The Word Of Christ Dwell In You (III of Letters From
      Saint Paul)
   Organ or Piano (or String Quartet):   c1-g2
   E.C.Schirmer (1971) 142

I THESSALONIANS

   5:1-6
   PINKHAM, Daniel
   But Of The Times And The Seasons (IV of Letters From Saint
      Paul)
   Organ or Piano (or String Quartet):   c#1 - a3
   E.C.Schirmer (1971) 142

   5:5, 16-23
   SEE: Ephesians 5:14
   WARD-STEPHENS
   Awake Thou That Sleepest

I TIMOTHY

   1:17
   SEE: Psalm 32:11
   HUHN, Bruno
   Be Glad, O Ye Righteous

II TIMOTHY

   1:7
   SEE: Galatians 5:1, 25
   BARKER, Clement
   If We Live In The Spirit

   1:7
   SEE: II Chronicles 20:15, 17
   KOCH, Frederick
   Be Not Afraid

   1:12 (Malachi 4:1-2)
   SCOTT, John Prindle
   I Know In Whom I Have Believed
   Keyboard: LOW:a1-d2; HIGH:d1-g2
   Presser (1914)

2:19
SEE: Acts 9:2
MENDELSSOHN, Felix
But The Lord Is Mindful Of His Own

HEBREWS

1:5
HANDEL, G.F.
Unto Which Of The Angels Said He
Keyboard: Tenor:f-g1
Carl Fischer; G. Schirmer; Novello

2:6
PURCELL, Henry
Lord, What Is Man (from Four Sacred Songs)
Piano (Organ): LOW:b^{b}1 - f2; HIGH:D1-3
International Music; Also found in 40 Sacred Songs

2:20
PETER, John Frederik (ed. & arr. Thor Johnson and Donald
    McCorkle)
The Lord Is In His Holy Temple
English/German   Piano: e^{b}1 - e^{b}2
Boosey & Hawkes (1963)

4:12
SEE: John 1:1
MacDERMID, James
He Sent His Word

8:10
SEE: Deuteronomy 32:11
MENDELSSOHN, Felix
God Hath Led His People On

10:22, 23
SEE: I John 3:1
BURNS, William K.
His Children (Four Meditative Songs)

11:1-2, 13, 16b (Hebrews 12:1-2a)
LOVELACE, Austin
Faith Is
Keyboard: d1-a3
Augsburg (1979) 11-9497, found in Three Solos For High Voice

11:3
SEE: John 1:1
MacDERMID, James
He Sent His Word

11:10
    SEE: I Corinthians 2:9
    GAUL, A.R.
    Eye Hath Not Seen

12:1-2a
    SEE: Hebrews 11:1-2, 13, 16b
    LOVELACE, Austin
    Faith Is

12:1, 2
    PINKHAM, Daniel
    Wherefore Seeing (I of <u>Letters From Saint Paul</u>)
    Organ or Piano (or String Quartet): $f^{\#}1 - a^{b}3$
    E.C.Schirmer (1971) 142

JAMES

1:17 (J. Smith)
    RIDER, Dale
    Every Good And Perfect Gift
    Organ or Piano: d1-g2
    Chantry

1:17-22
    TELEMANN, Georg Philipp
    Ew'ge Qwelle, milder Strom
    German   Continuo & Flute: $d^{\#}1 - e2$
    Barenreiter (1953) 3629

4:8
    SEE: Romans 14:11
    BARKER, Clement
    Draw Nigh To God

5:16 (Matthew 4:23; Matthew 5:1, 2; Matthew 6:6-13)
    CURRAN, Pearl G.
    Prayer
    Keyboard: d1-g2

5:16
    SEE: John 15:12
    HUSTAD, Don
    This Is My Commandment

I PETER

4:13, 14
    SEE: Psalm 63:6
    ELGAR, Edward
    The Sun Goeth Down

I JOHN

1:1, 5, 6, 7, 9
BAUMGARTNER, H. Leroy
This We Declare Unto You, Op. 49, #1 (from <u>Behold What Manner</u>
    <u>Of Love</u>)
Keyboard: d1-g2
Concordia (1955)

2:15
WARD-STEPHENS
Love Not The World
Piano: e^{b}1 - a^{b}3
Chappell (1917) found in <u>The Ward-Stephen Musical Settings Of</u>
    <u>Sacred Words</u>

2:25 (I John 3:1-2; and other)
CRUIKSHANK, Helen M.
Behold What Names Of Love
Keyboard: LOW:c1 - e^{b}2; HIGH:d1-f2
R.D.Row (1958)

3:1 (Hebrews 10:22, 23)
BURNS, William K.
His Children (from <u>Four Meditative Songs</u>)
Keyboard: e1-g2
Abingdon (1972) APM 515

3:1
SEE: Matthew 4:4
FICHTHOIN, Claude
Behold What Manner Of Love

3:1-2
SEE: I John 2:25
CRUIKSHANK, Helen M.
Behold What Manner Of Love

3:1-3
BAUMGARTNER, H. Leroy
Behold What Manner Of Love, Op. 49, #2 (in <u>Behold What Manner</u>
    <u>Of Love</u>)
Keyboard: e^{b}1 - g^{b}2
Concordia (1955)

3:1-3
HATCH, Wilbur
Behold! What Manner Of Love
Piano or Organ: c1 - a^{b}3
Shawnee (1955) A-5046

3:1-3
  PARIS, Harry Allen
  Behold, What Manner Of Love
  Piano/Organ: b$\flat$1 - e$\flat$2
  Huntzinger (1938)

3:1-3
  SEE: Genesis 1:26, 27
  MacDERMID, James
  Behold What Manner Of Love

3:2
  STEARNS, Peter Pindar
  Beloved, Now Are We The Sons Of God
  Oboe, Horn, Cello: f1 - e$\flat$2
  American Composers Alliance

4:7
  HEAD, Michael
  Beloved, Let Us Love One Another
  Piano/Organ: a1-d2
  Boosey & Hawks

4:7
  MYERS, Gordon
  Beloved, Let Us Love One Another
  Piano/Organ: e$\flat$1 - e$\flat$2
  Eastlane Music Corporation

4:7, 8 (based on)
  PROULX, Richard
  Beloved, Let Us Love
  Organ: d1-f2
  Augsburg (1970) 11-0715

4:7, 8, 11, 14, 16, 20, 21
  FISCHER, Irwin
  Love One Another
  Keyboard: e1-f2
  American Composers Alliance (1952)

4:7-12, 18-21
  BAUMGARTNER, H. Leroy
  Love Is Of God, Op. 49, #3 (in Behold What Manner Of Love)
  Keyboard: d1 - f$\sharp$2
  Concordia (1955) 97-9327

4:16
  HUMPHREYS, Don
  God Is Love
  Keyboard: LOW:c1-e2; HIGH:d1-f2
  R.D.Row (1951) found in Songs For Christian Science Service,
    Book I

5:4, 7, 10-12
BAUMGARTNER, H. Leroy
This Is The Victory, Even Our Faith, Op. 49, #4 (in <u>Behold What Manner Of Love</u>)
Keyboard: d1-g2
Concordia (1955)

<u>REVELATION</u>

1:00
SEE: Psalm 98
GORE, Richard
O Sing Unto The Lord A New Song

2:7 (Revelation 22:1, 2)
VAUGHAN-WILLIAMS, Ralph
The Song Of The Leaves Of Life And The Waters Of Life (from <u>Pilgrim's Progress</u>)
Piano: d1-e2
Oxford (1952)

2:10 (Jeremiah 1:8)
MENDELSSOHN, Felix
Be Thou Faithful Unto Death (<u>Saint Paul</u>)
Keyboard: d1-g2
G.Schirmer; also in <u>Anthology Of Sacred Song</u> - Tenor

3:10-12
MacDERMID, James
My New Name
Keyboard: b1-f2
Forster (1923)

3:20 (Matthew 11:27-28)
BRYANT, Verna Mae
Behold! I Stand At The Door
Organ or Piano: LOW:b^{b}1 - d2; HIGH:d1 - f$^{\#}$2
G. Schirmer (1955)

3:20 (John 8:12; Isaiah 59:19)
MacDERMID, James
Arise, Shine For Thy Light Is Come
Keyboard: LOW:a^{b}1 - d^{b}2; MED:b^{b}1 - e^{b}2; HIGH:d1-g2
Forster (1936)

5:8-10 (text by Parks)
ROGERS, Sharon Elery
Song Of The Redeemed
Keyboard: e1-g2
Hope (1970) 501, found in <u>New Testament Songs</u>

7:14, 15
GAUL, A.R.
These Are They Which Came Out Of Great Tribulation (The Holy
City)
Keyboard: e1 - g#2
G. Schirmer, in Anthology Of Sacred Song - Soprano

8:00
SEE: John 3:13
MOZART, W.A. (ed. M.B. Stearns)
Behold The Song Of God, K. 146

14:3 (Revelation 15:3; text by Parks)
ROGERS, Sharon Elery
A Song Of Victory
Keyboard: d1-g2
Hope (1970) 501, found in New Testament Songs

15:3
SEE: Revelation 14:3
ROGERS, Sharon Elery
A Song Of Victory

20:17
SEE: John 4:23, 24
ROBERTS, J.E.
God Is A Spirit

21:00
HARKER, F. Flaxington
God Shall Wipe Away All Tears, Op. 49, #2
Piano: LOW:a♭1 - f2; HIGH:c1-a3
G. Schirmer 81938)

21:00 (adapted)
HOFFMEISTER, Leon Abott
Behold The Tabernacle Of God
Piano/Organ: f1 - e♭2
G. Schirmer (1932) found in Seventeen Sacred Songs

21:1, 4, 5, 6
MITCHELL, Raymond E.
The Tabernacle Of God Is With Men
Piano: LOW:b♭1 - d2; HIGH:d1 - f#2
Huntzinger (1929) found in Selected Sacred Songs For General
Use

21:1-7
ROMER, Charles
New Heaven - New Earth
Keyboard (optional C Instrument): b1-d2
Lillenas (1980) found in Scripture Solos For All Seasons

21:1, 2, 3
  SHELLY, Harry Rowe
  And I, John, Saw The Holy City (from cantata, <u>The Inheritance</u>
    <u>Divine</u>)
  Organ: e^{b}1 - a^{b}3
  G. Schirmer (1895)

21:3, 4
  PERRY, Rob Roy
  God Shall Wipe Away All Tears
  Piano: b^{b}1 - e^{b}2
  G. Schirmer (1939) found in <u>52 Sacred Songs</u>

21:3, 4, 5
  SULLIVAN, A.
  The Lord Is Risen (The Light Of The World)
  Keyboard: b1-d2
  G. Schirmer, in <u>Anthology Of Sacred Song</u> - Alto

21:3, 4, 6
  RIMA, Caro
  God Shall Wipe Away All Tears
  Keyboard: LOW:g$^\#$ - c2; MED:b1 - c$^\#$2; LOW:d$^\#$1 - f$^\#$2
  Witmark (1913)

21:4
  FIELD, J.T.
  God Shall Wipe Away All Tears
  Organ: b1-d2
  G. Schirmer (1907) found in <u>Album Of 12 Sacred Solos</u> (Boston)

21:4
  SEE: Psalm 34:4
  STEVENSON, Frederick
  I Sought The Lord

21:7
  SEE: Psalm 18:32, 37
  VAUGHAN-WILLIAMS, Ralph
  The Pilgrom's Psalm

22:1, 2
  SEE: Revelation 2:7
  VAUGHAN-WILLIAMS, Ralph
  The Song Of The Leaves Of Life And The Water Of Life

22:1-4
  BUTT, James
  River Of Life
  Organ/Piano: c$^\#$1 - e2
  Sphemusations (1965)

22:1, 14, 17
　　FISCHER, Irwin
　　Come, Take The Water Of Life
　　Keyboard:　e1-g2
　　American Composers Alliance (1960)

22:1, 14, 17
　　JOY, Jeanne Alden
　　The River Of The Water Of Life
　　Keyboard:　LOW:b^{b}1 - e^{b}2; HIGH:e^{b}1 - f2
　　R.D.Row (1947)

22:5
　　SEE:　Psalm 27:4
　　TALMA, Louise
　　Cantata:　All The Days Of My Life

22:14, 16
　　SHELLY, Harry Rowe
　　I Jesus, Have Sent Mine Angel
　　Organ:　b^b - d^{b}1
　　G. Schirmer (1895)

COMPOSER INDEX

ABT, Franz - Matthew 10:29-31.
ADAMS, Joseph H. - Psalm 23.
ADDISON, Joseph - Psalm 19:1-6.
ADLER, Samuel - II Samuel 1:19-27; Proverbs 31:20, 28-30; Hosea
    2:21, 22.
ALBRECHT, M. - Matthew 6:9-13.
ALLETSEN, Frances - Psalm 27:1, 3, 5; Psalm 42.
ANCIENT GALIC FOLK HYMN - Matthew 6:9 - 13.
ANDERSON, Leroy and Alfred Heller - Matthew 6:9-13.
ANDREWS, Mark - Joel 2:12-13, 15-17; Psalm 23.
ANONYMOUS (ed. & arr. Marilyn Gambosi) Exodus 15:3.
ANTES, John - John 19:30.
ARCADELT, Jacob - Psalm 23.
ARCHER, Violet - Psalm 13:1-3; Psalm 23; Psalm 104:31-34; Wisdom
    Of Solomon 3:1-3.
AVERY, Lawrence - Ruth 1:16-17.
AVERY, Richard and Donald Marsh - Ruth 1:16, 17.

BACH, J. S. - Psalm 115:13-15; Psalm 137; Matthew 26:26-29; Luke
    12:24, 27, 29, 32; I Corinthians 15:20, 26-28; Ephesians
    6:16-17.
BAIN, James - Psalm 23.
BANKS, Harry C. - Micah 6:7-8.
BANTOK, Granville - Psalm 150; Matthew 6:9-13.
BARKAN, Emanuel - Song Of Songs 2:8-13.
BARKER, Clement - Psalm 67; Isaiah 2:22; Isaiah 1:18; Ezekiel
    13:3; Matthew 3:16; John 11:1-44; Romans 1:11; II Corinthians
    6:16; Galatians 5:1, 25.
BARNES, A. M. - Psalm 55:6.
BARNES, Milton - Matthew 6:9-13.
BARTLETT, Floy Little - Psalm 121.
BAUMGARTNER, H. Leroy - Psalm 26:8; Psalm 27:7-8, 9, 11, 13-14;
    Psalm 91:1-2, 5-6, 9-10, 14-16; Psalm 104:1, 3, 24; I John
    1:1, 5, 6, 7, 9; I John 3:1-3; I John 4:7-12, 18-21; I John
    4:7, 14-18; I John 5:4-5, 11, 14-15; I John 5:4, 7, 10-12.
BEALE, James - Proverbs 12:19; Proverbs 22:17-18; Proverbs
    24:30-31, 33-34; Proverbs 26:21-23.
BEAMONT, V. - Deuteronomy 31:6.
BEAUMONT, Vivian - Psalm 31:19, 24.
BECK, John Ness - Psalm 40; Philippians 1:3-11.
BEDELL, Robert L. - Psalm 130.

BEECH, Robert L. - Psalm 13.
BEETHOVEN, L. - Matthew 11:28-30.
BEHRENS, Jack - I Corinthians 13.
BELCHER, S. - Luke 2:8-15.
BENATI, (?) - Psalm 103.
BENDER, Jan - Psalm 128:1-4; Matthew 4:10; Matthew 22:4; Matthew
    25:1-13; Mark 10:14; Mark 10:14-15; Luke 21:25, 26, 33;
    John 14:23.
BEN-HAIM, Paul - Psalm 23.
BENNET, S. - Psalm 139:1-4.
BERLINSKI, Herman - Psalm 23.
BERMAN, Judith M. - Song of Songs 8:6-7.
BERNARD, Cristopher - Psalm 51:10, 11; Psalm 130.
BERTRAND - Brown - Mark 6:50.
BETTS, Lorne - Psalm 23; Song Of Songs 8:6-7.
BIBER, Heinrich - Psalm 127.
BILCHICK, Ruth Coleman - Song of Songs 2:11-13.
BINDER, A. W. - Psalm 23.
BITGOOD, Roberta - Psalm 46:10a; I Corinthians 13.
BIZET, Georges - John 1:29.
BLACK, Jennie Prince - Ruth 1:16-17.
BLAIR, Kathleen - Psalm 23; Psalm 42.
BLOCH, Ernst - Psalm 22; Psalm 114; Psalm 137.
BOEX, Andrew J. - Luke 2:8; Luke 2:13-14.
BOHM, Carl - Psalm 23.
BONE, Gene and Howard Fenton - Psalm 1; Psalm 119:105.
BOWLING, Blanche - Psalm 1; Isaiah 54:13.
BRAHMS, Johannes - Ecclesiastes 3:19-22; Ecclesiastes 4:1-3;
    Ecclesiasticus 41:1-2; I Corinthians 13:1-13.
BRITTON, D. Guyer - Psalm 100.
BOONES, Martin - Psalm 23.
BROD, Max - Psalm 126.
BROONING, Mortimer - Matthew 5:1-12.
BROWN, Allanson G. Y. - Psalm 119:165-166, 175-176; Isaiah
    42:6-7.
BROWN, Russell J. - Psalm 23.
BRYANT, Verna Mae - Revelation 3:20.
BUCH, Robert Fairfax - Psalm 18:1-6, 49; Psalm 18:2-3, 6.
BUCK, Dudley - Job 22; Psalm 27:1, 3, 5; Psalm 27:1, 5, 6;
    Jeremiah 31:6, 16.
BUGATCH, Samuel - Song Of Songs 2:1-5.
BURGON, Geoffrey - Luke 2:29-32.
BURKHARD, Willy - Luke 1:46-47.
BURNAM, Edna Mae - Psalm 121.
BURNS, William - Psalm 121; Psalm 130; Luke 1:46-49; Romans 8:31,
    35, 37-39; I John 3:1.
BURROUGHS, Bob - Matthew 1:21; Matthew 9:36b-37; John 3:16, 17;
    John 10:14, 16a.
BUSAROW, Donald - Psalm 91:4, 11-12.
BUSS, Duane - Psalm 23.
BUTLER, Eugene - Psalm 69:1-3, 5, 16-17, 29-30; Psalm 97:1, 2,
    4-6, 8, 11; Psalm 130:1-3, 5-6.

BUTT, James - Joshua 1:5-7; Psalm 1; Psalm 23; Psalm 90:1, 2, 4, 16, 17; Psalm 150; Malachai 4:2; Revelation 22:1-4.
BUXTEHUDE, Dietrich - Psalm 31:2, 3, 4; Psalm 33:3; Psalm 51:10-12; Psalm 57; Psalm 73:25, 26; Psalm 96; Psalm 98:1-6; Luke 2:29-32; John 3:14-15; John 3:16; John 11:25-26.

CADZOW, Dorthy - Matthew 6:9-13.
CALDER, Lee - Isaiah 12:3, 4.
CAMPBELL-TIPTON, Louis - Psalm 9:1, 2, 10.
CAMPION, Edward - Isaiah 53:5.
CAMPION, Thomas - Psalm 130.
CARMICHAEL, Ralph - Psalm 23.
CARR, Arthur - Matthew 21:9.
CARTWRIGHT, Marion - Psalm 147.
CASSLER, G. Winston - Ruth 1:16-17; Psalm 103; Psalm 135.
CESTI, Marc Antonio - Psalm 8.
CHADWICK, G. W. - Psalm 46:9, 10; John 14:1-2.
CHAJES, Julius - Psalm 134; Psalm 137.
CHAMBERS, Brent - Psalm 57:9-11.
CHARLES, Ernst - Psalm 27:1, 4, 6; Psalm 69; Isaiah 55:1, 3.
CHILDS, David - Psalm 81:1-4; Psalm 83:1-4, 13, 18; Psalm 91:1-4; Psalm 92:1-5; Psalm 121:1-8; Psalm 123:1-5; Psalm 148:1-6.
CLARK, Henry - Psalm 23.
CLARKE, Palmer John - John 5:5-7, 9.
CLERVOIS, Roger - Psalm 54.
CLOKEY, Joseph - Song Of Songs 8:6.
COENEN, William - Matthew 11:28; Matthew 11:28-30.
COOK, Gerald - Ruth 1:16-17.
COMBS, C. Whitney - Matthew 28:1-6.
CORNELIUS, Peter - Job 14:32-33; Psalm 18; Psalm 25:1; Psalm 30.
CORTESE, Luigi - Psalm 8.
CORY, George - Matthew 6:9-13.
CORYELL, Marian - Isaiah 61:10.
COSTA, M. - Psalm 30:1, 2, 11; Psalm 84:10.
COUPERIN, Francois - Psalm 12; Psalm 19:10; Psalm 68:1-6, 17, 18; Psalm 122.
COWEN, F. H. - Psalm 65:9, 11, 13; Psalm 103:13, 14.
CRAFF, Leta Bishop - Isaiah 33:24.
CRAWFORD, John - Psalm 23.
CRESTON, Paul - Psalm 23.
CROWE, B. - Psalm 121.
CRUIKSHANK, Helen M. - I John 2:25.
CUMMING, Richard - Exodus 15 (from).
CURRAN, Pearl G. - James 5:16.

DAME, William - Matthew 6:9-13.
DARKE, Harold - Psalm 65:9.
DAVIS, Katherine K. - Psalm 84:1-3; Psalm 103:1-4; Proverbs 3:5-6; Mark 10:17-24; John 11:1, 3, 4, 7, 41; Ephesians 4:3, 32.

DAVYE, John J. - Psalm 23; Psalm 91.
DAY, Stanley A. - Matthew 18:1-4, 6.
DEACON, Mary - Psalm 23.
DeBIZE, Theodore - Psalm 140.
deLANGE, S. - Psalm 84:1, 2, 10, 11.
DEMAREST, Alisen - Psalm 139.
DEMAREST, C. Agnew - Psalm 34:18-19, 21-22.
DENCKE, Jeremiah - Psalm 45:1-2; Matthew 25:1-6; Luke 1:46-47.
DEWEY, Richard A. - Ruth 1:16.
DIAMOND, David - II Samuel 18:33.
DIETTERICH, Philip - Psalm 34:1-6.
DINN, Freda - Psalm 127.
DISTLER, Hugo - Psalm 92:2-3; Romans 12:11, 12, 18; Philippians
    4:4.
DOIG, Don - Psalm 103:11-17; John 15:1-6; Romans 8:35, 38-39.
DUBOIS, Theodore - Lamentations 1:12, 13; Matthew 27:46.
DUKE, John - Psalm 116:1-5, 7-8; Luke 1:46-55.
DUNGAN, Olive - Psalm 46.
DVORAK, Anton - Psalm 23; Psalm 25:16-18, 20; Psalm 55:1-8;
    Psalm 61:1, 3-4; Psalm 97:2-6; Psalm 98:1, 7-8; Psalm
    119:114-115, 117, 120; Psalm 121:1-4; Psalm 137:1-5;
    Psalm 139:4, 23-24; Psalm 144:9; Isaiah 40:1.

EARLS, Paul - Matthew 6:9-13.
EBEN, Petr - Ruth 1:16, 17.
EDMUNDS, John - Psalm 113.
EDWARDS, Clara - Psalm 27.
EGGERT, Fred E. - Ecclesiastes 12:1-8.
ELGAR, Edward - Psalm 63:6; Isaiah 52:9; Luke 24:36c, 49; John
    9:3-5; John 10:10, 14; Acts 2:14b, 16-17, 21-23, 32-33, 36.
ELLIS, James G. - Psalm 23; Luke 9:28-29, 35.
ENGEL, James - Ruth 1:16-17.
ENGLERT, Andrew Lloyd - Psalm 119:105.
ESPINA, Noni - Psalm 23.
EVANS, Vincent - Psalm 51.
EVILLE, Vernon - Psalm 23, Psalm 121; Psalm 137.

FAULKNER, George - John 21:15.
FAULKNER, William M. - I Corinthians 2:9-10.
FAURE, Gabriel - Psalm 103:1-4.
FELCIANO, Richard - Psalm 92:12.
FERRIS, William - Psalm 108; Psalm 127:4-6; Psalm 128:4-6;
    Ecclesiastes 47:2.
FETTKE, Tom - II Corinthians 12:7-10.
FICHTHOIN, Claude - Matthew 4:4.
FIELD, J. T. - Revelation 21:4.
FISCHER, Irwin - Psalm 34:8; Psalm 90; Psalm 104:1, 2, 5, 24,
    30; Psalm 119:12, 18, 28, 35, 59, 68; Psalm 139:9-11, 14,
    17; Psalm 145; Psalm 148:1, 3, 7, 9, 11-13; Proverbs 3:13,
    16, 17, 19, 21; Isaiah 52:7, 9; Isaiah 63:7; Matthew 19:14;
    John 3:16; John 8; John 14:16; I John 4:7, 8, 11, 14, 16,
    20, 21; Revelation 22:1, 14, 17.

FISHER, William Arms - Matthew 6:25-33.
FLOWERS, Geoffrey - Psalm 23; Matthew 6:9-13.
FLOYD, Carlisle - Job 14:1, 2, 7-12; Psalm 54:1; Psalm 69:1-3,
    14-17, 20; Psalm 139:1-4, 6-10, 23-24; Psalm 146:1-2; Acts
    26:36; Romans 8:38, 39.
FOLKEMER, Stephen P. - Psalm 145:1-3, 8, 9, 13b, 14, 17, 18, 21.
FORSYTH, Josephine - Matthew 6:9-13.
FOSS, Lukas - Song Of Songs 3:1, 3; Song Of Songs 4:16; Song Of
    Songs 7:11; Song Of Songs 8:6.
FOSTER, Myles B. - Lamentations 1:12; Matthew 6:31, 32b, 33.
FRANCO, Johan - Matthew 6:9-13.
FREDERICKSON, Carl - Isaiah 61:1-3.
FREED, Isadore - Psalm 8.
FREUDENTHAL, Josef - II Samuel 23:1-5; Psalm 23; Psalm 24:1-5;
    Psalm 67; Psalm 95; Psalm 119:50; Micah 6:6-8.
FROMM, Herbert - II Samuel 19:27; Psalm 1; Psalm 42:1-4a; Psalm
    92; Psalm 121; Psalm 149:1-4.
FRYXELL, Regina - Psalm 67.

GARDNER, Adelaide - Psalm 23.
GARLICK, Anthony - Psalm 4; Psalm 17; Psalm 23; Psalm 28.
GASKILL, Clarence - Matthew 6:9-13.
GASLINI, Giorgio - Luke 1:46-47.
GATES, Cecil - Matthew 6:9-13.
GAUL, Alfred R. - Psalm 42:2, 3; Psalm 96:7, 8; Daniel 9:9;
    Matthew 25:34; I Corinthians 2:9; Revelation 7:14, 15.
GIDEON, Miriam - Psalm 127; Psalm 128; Proverbs 31:10, 25, 28,
    31.
GIESEKE, Richard W. - Ruth 1:16, 17.
GILBERT, N. - Psalm 23.
GLUCK, C. - I Corinthians 15:57.
GOEMANNE, Noel - Ecclesiastes 3:1-8.
GOETZ, Marty - Psalm 23.
GOLDMAN, Edward - Psalm 23; Psalm 98; Psalm 150.
GOLDMAN, Maurice - Ruth 1:16-17.
GOODE, Jack - Psalm 23; Psalm 147.
GORE, Richard - Ruth 1:16-17; Psalm 33:3; Psalm 98.
GOUNOD, Charles - Ruth 1:16-17; Psalm 23; Luke 1:46-55; John
    14:27.
GRAFF, Leta Bishop - Isaiah 33:24.
GREENE, Maurice - Psalm 1:1, 4; Psalm 3:8; Psalm 4:8; Psalm 68:19;
    Psalm 84:4, 5; Psalm 103:1, 2-4; Psalm 103:20; Psalm 113:3,
    4; Psalm 119:1, 5, 18; Psalm 119:4-5, 19; Psalm 121:6;
    Isaiah 60:19; Malachi 1:11.
GREENBAUM, Matthew - Psalm 84.
GREENFIELD, Alfred - I Chronicles 29:10-11, 13-14.
GRIMM, Heinrich - Matthew 21:9.
GROTON, Frederic - Ruth 1:16-17.

HAEUSSLER, Paul - John 14:1, 2, 27.
HALLQUIST, Gary - Ruth 1:16.

HAMBLEN, Bernard - Psalm 86; Psalm 119; Isaiah 40:28-31; John 15;
    Matthew 6:9-13.
HAMMERSCHMIDT, Andreas - Psalm 67:5-8; John 11:25-26.
HANDEL, G. F. - Exodus 15:2; Job 19:25-26; Psalm 2:1-2; Psalm
    2:4, 9; Psalm 5:8; Psalm 9:9-10; Psalm 22:7; Psalm 23;
    Psalm 41:1-2; Psalm 51:10-12; Psalm 57:10; Psalm 68:18;
    Psalm 69:20; Psalm 84:12; Psalm 95:1-2; Psalm 95 (adapted);
    Psalm 95:6, 7, 8; Psalm 97:10; Psalm 99:9; Psalm 103:21;
    Psalm 135:1-2; Psalm 135:5; Psalm 145:2, 9; Isaiah 7:14;
    Isaiah 9:2-6; Isaiah 25:5, 6; Isaiah 35:5, 6; Isaiah 40:1-3;
    Isaiah 40:4; Isaiah 53:3; Isaiah 55:1, 3; Isaiah 60:2, 3;
    Haggai 7; Zechariah 9:9-10; Luke 2:8-13; Romans 8:31-34;
    Romans 10:15; Romans 10:18; I Corinthians 15:20, 23;
    I Corinthians 15:51-53; I Corinthians 15:51-54; Hebrews 1:5.
HANDY, William Christopher - Psalm 126:1-2, 5-6.
HANKS, Billie Jr. - Psalm 19.
HANSON, Howard - Psalm 6; Psalm 8; Psalm 46; Psalm 47.
HARKER, F. Flaxington - Psalm 13; Isaiah 40:11; Isaiah 52:7;
    Isaiah 60:1-3, 13, 21; Luke 2:10-14; Matthew 28:1-7;
    Ephesians 4:7; Revelation 21.
HART, Theron Wolcott - Mark 5:24-29, 34.
HARTLEY, Walter - Psalm 12:1-4, 9; Psalm 40:1-4; Psalm 43:1-3;
    Psalm 63:1-5; Psalm 145:1-3, 8-10, 21.
HARRIS, Cuthbert - Psalm 69:1.
HASIDIC FOLK SONG - Isaiah 40:3-5.
HASKINS, V. - I Corinthians 13.
HATCH, Wilbur - I John 3:1-3.
HAUSMAN, Ruth L. - Mark 10:13-16.
HAYDN, Joseph - Genesis 1:1; Psalm 84:1, 2, 4; Proverbs 3:1, 56.
HEAD, Michael - Exodus 23:20, 22, 25; Job 22; Psalm 57; Psalm
    100; Psalm 121: Matthew 6:9-13; John 17:1, 5, 11, 21, 23;
    I John 4:7.
HEALY, William - Matthew 6:9-13; Matthew 11:28-30.
HEILLER, Anton - Matthew 6:9-13.
HELDER, Bartholomaeus - Psalm 23.
HELFMAN, Max - Song Of Songs 2:10-13; Song Of Songs 8:6-7.
HENSCHEL, George - Matthew 6:9-13.
HERBERT, Mariel - Psalm 96.
HERBST, Johannes - Psalm 71:16; Isaiah 60:16; John 1:29; John
    15:4.
HILDACH, Eugen - Ruth 1:16-17.
HINES, Jerome - Matthew 6:9-13.
HOFFMEISTER, Leon Abbott - Psalm 9; Psalm 13; Matthew 6:9-13.
HOLLER, John - Psalm 23.
HONEGGER, Arthur - Psalm 34; Psalm 138; Psalm 140.
HOPE, Lawrence - Galatians 6:14.
HOPEKIRK, Helen - John 4:23, 24.
HOPSON, Hal H. - Psalm 121; I Corinthians 13.
HORVIT, Michael - Psalm 68:4.
HOVHANESS, Alan - Psalm 130.
HOVLAND, Egil - Luke 1:46-55.
HOWELL, Charles T. - Psalm 137:1-5.

HUHN, Bruno - Psalm 32:11; Psalm 47:1-2, 6-7.
HUMMELL, Ferdinand - Psalm 23.
HUMPHREYS, Don - Genesis 1:27; Psalm 19:14; Psalm 23; Psalm 27:1,
    4-6; Psalm 34; Psalm 36; Psalm 37; Psalm 90; Psalm 91;
    Psalm 106:1-4; Psalm 107: Psalm 121; Isaiah 35; Isaiah
    55:6; Isaiah 60:1; Philippians 2; Ephesians 5:14; Ephesians
    6; Matthew 5; I John 4:16.
HUSTAD, Don - John 15:12; Galatians 5:25.

ISAACSON, Michael - Psalm 23.
ISENSEL, Paul B. - Matthew 6:9-13.

JACKSON, Stanley - Psalm 121.
JEFFERIES, George - Psalm 104:1, 2, 24, 33, 34.
JENNINGS, Kenneth - Psalm 121.
JENSEN, Adolf - Psalm 121.
JEWELL, Lucina - John 14:1, 2, 3.
JOHNSON, David N. - Matthew 6:9-13.
JOHNSON, Gary - I Corinthians 11:23-26.
JOHNSON, Hall - Jeremiah 8:22 (arranger); John 19:26-27 (arr).
JONES, Kelsey - Psalm 49.
JORDAN, Alice - Psalm 103.
JORGENSEN, Philip - Matthew 6:9-13.
JOY, Jeanne Alden - Revelation 22:1, 14, 17.
JUDASSOHN, S. - Psalm 100.

KAHN, E. I. - Psalm 13; Psalm 126.
KALMANOFF, Martin - Psalm 23; Isaiah 11:17.
KAUFMAN, Julius - Psalm 145:1, 5-18.
KAVANAUGH, Patrick - Matthew 5:1-12.
KAYDEN, Mildred - Psalm 121.
KENDRICK, Virginia - Psalm 121; Isaiah 45.
KINGSLEY, Gershon - Psalm 9:2-3; Psalm 23; Song Of Songs 2:10-12;
    Amos 5:24.
KINSCELLA, Hazel Gertrude - Psalm 23:4.
KLASS, Lillian V. - Isaiah 9:1, 5, 6.
KOCH, Frederick - II Chronicles 2:15, 17; John 21.
KOCH, John - Psalm 23; Psalm 67; Psalm 100; Psalm 121; Psalm 150.
KRAPF, Gerhard - Isaiah 12; Luke 5:1-11; Luke 6:36-42; Luke 7:
    11-17; Luke 14:16-24; Luke 16:19-31.
KREBS, Karl August - Matthew 6:9-13.
KRESERLING, Richard - John 6:51.

LADERMAN, Ezra - Psalm 7:14-15; Psalm 39:13a; Psalm 61:1; Psalm
    69:4b; Psalm 104:5.
LAFFERTY, Karen - Matthew 6:30.
LaFORGE, Frank - Psalm 36:5-7, 11; Psalm 100; Psalm 103; Psalm
    116:12-14, 17-19; Psalm 119:33; Isaiah 34:1; Isaiah 40:28-
    31; Matthew 5:14-16, 43-45, 48; Matthew 11:28; Matthew
    19:1-2, 13-15; Luke 2:8-14; John 15:7, 9, 10, 12.

LAGOURGUES, Charles - Psalm 92.
LaMONTAINE, John - Psalm 23; Song Of Songs 2:1-3a; Song Of Songs
    2:3b-5; Song Of Songs 2:6; Song Of Songs 2:8-10a; Song Of
    Songs 2:10b-13; Song Of Songs 2:14; Song Of Songs 2:16-17;
    Matthew 1:23.
LANE, Richard - Philippians 4.
LANSING, A. W. - Psalm 42.
LEDERER, Charles - Psalm 104.
LEICHTLING, Alan - Proverbs 1:7-9; Proverbs 2:19-22.
LEKBERG, Sven - Psalm 13; Psalm 95:1-7; Psalm 121; Psalm 139:1,
    4, 8; Matthew 21:8-9.
LEPKE, Charma Davis - Revelation 15.
LIDDLE, Samuel - Psalm 23; Psalm 42; Psalm 84.
LILJESTRAND, Paul - Ruth 1:16.
LISZT, Franz - Isaiah 25:8, 9.
LORENZ, E. J. - Galatians 6:14.
LOVELACE, Austin - Hebrews 11:1-2, 13, 16b.
LOWE, A. F. - Psalm 91:1, 2, 4, 9, 11.
LOWE, Augustus - Psalm 23.
LUCKE, Katherine - Psalm 1.
LULLY, Jean Baptiste - Psalm 119:135, 136.
LUTKIN, Peter (arr. William Stickler) - Numbers 6:24.
LYNES, Frank - Isaiah 55:6.
LYNN, Lorna - I Corinthians 13:4-7, 13.
LYON, James - Psalm 8.

MacDERMID, James - Genesis 1:26, 27; Deuteronomy 32:1-3;
    I Chronicles 29:11-13; Job 22:21; Psalm 36; Psalm 46; Psalm
    91:1, 5, 6, 9, 10, 11, 12; Psalm 100; Psalm 119; Psalm 127:1;
    Psalm 139:7-12; Psalm 148:1-6, 9, 11, 13; Proverbs 3:5-6,
    19-20, 25-26; Proverbs 8; Isaiah 26:3, 4, 8-9; Isaiah 26:3-4,
    13-14; Isaiah 35; Isaiah 40:6-8, 28-31; Isaiah 55:1, 3,
    10-11; Isaiah 55:6; Isaiah 61:1, 2; Jeremiah 31:31, 33, 34;
    Zephaniah 3; John 1:1; John 3:5, 6, 7, 16; John 14:2, 3,
    4, 27; John 15:1-3, 5-7; Acts 27:22, 24, 28; Revelation
    3:10-12; Revelation 3:20.
MacGIMSEY, Robert - Daniel 3; Matthew 6:9-13; Philippians 4:8.
MADER, Clarence - Psalm 23; Psalm 40:1-4, 8, 9b, 10b, 11-12, 16;
    Proverbs 3:13-23.
MALOTTE, Albert Hay - Psalm 23; Matthew 5:3-6; Matthew 6:9-13.
MANNER, Charles F. - Psalm 119:33, 34, 37.
MARCELLO, Benedetto - Psalm 42.
MARKS, Christopher - Psalm 130.
MAROT, Clement - Psalm 138.
MARZO, Edwardo - Psalm 25.
MATESKY, Thelma - Psalm 133; Psalm 138.
MATTHEWS, Thomas - Psalm 23.
MAYFIELD, Larry - Matthew 6:9-13.
McAFEE, Don - Psalm 8:1, 3-8; Psalm 24:1-5; Psalm 47:1, 5-8;
    Psalm 139; Matthew 22:37-39; John 1:1-5; Romans 12:1, 2;
    I Corinthians 13:1-7.

McARTHUR, Edwin - Psalm 103:1-3; John 4:23, 24.
McFETTERS, Raymond - Psalm 100.
McGUIRE, Bobby - Luke 22:17-20.
MEEK, Kenneth - Psalm 23.
MENDELSSOHN, Felix - Deuteronomy 4:29; Deuteronomy 32:11;
    I Kings 18:36-37; Psalm 37:1, 4-5, 7; Psalm 43:3-5; Psalm
    51; Psalm 55; Psalm 84:1; Psalm 91; Psalm 95; Psalm 121;
    Isaiah 49:7, 10; Isaiah 52:7; Isaiah 54:10; Jeremiah 23:29;
    Jeremiah 29:13; Matthew 13:43; Matthew 23:37; John 6;
    John 20:13; Acts 9:2; I Corinthians 3:16-17; Revelation
    2:10.
MERBECKE, John - Matthew 6:9-13.
MILHAUD, Darius - Psalm 129.
MILLER, Merle - I Kings 3:5, 7, 9, 10-13.
MITCHELL, Raymond E. - Revelation 21:1, 4, 5, 6.
MOE, Daniel - I Corinthians 13.
MOLIQUE, B. - Psalm 5:8; Psalm 145:1, 3, 16, 18-20.
MOURANT, Walter - John 4:23, 24.
MOZART, W. A. - John 3:13.
MUELLER, Carl F. - Psalm 23; Psalm 51; Psalm 51:10-13; Psalm
    100; Psalm 139.
MULLIGAN, Harold - Psalm 61.
MURRAY, Lyn - Galatians 6:14.
MYERS, Gordon - Psalm 127:1; Matthew 6:9-13; I John 4:7.
MYLES, Foster - Colossians 3:1, 2.

NEIDLINGER, W. H. - Psalm 91:1, 9-10, 11, 14, 16.
NELHYBEL, Vaclav - Psalm 1; Psalm 18:2; Psalm 22:11; Psalm 25:5;
    Psalm 61:1-2.
NEVIN, George - John 10:11-16.
NYSTEDT, Knut - Matthew 27:45-46.

O'CONNOR, Morris G. - Psalm 23; Psalm 91.
OLDS, W. B. - John 6.
ORE, Charles W. - Psalm 1; Psalm 4; Psalm 23; Psalm 25.
ORLANDO, Henry - Psalm 49.
OVERBY, Rolf Peter - Song Of Songs 7:11-13.
OWENS, Jim - II Chronicles 7:14.

PAER, Ferdinando - Psalm 112.
PARIS, Harry Allen - I John 3:1-3.
PARKER, Clifton - Job 11:13-19; Psalm 89:15, 16; Psalm 89:16;
    Psalm 121.
PARKER, Horatio - Isaiah 40:1.
PEETERS, Flor - Ruth 1:16-17; Matthew 6:9-13.
PELOQUIN, C. Alexander - Job 19:25-26.
PELZ, Walter - Psalm 33:20-22; Psalm 84:4, 10-12.
PENDLETON, Emmet - Ruth 1:16-17; Psalm 50:14; Isaiah 9:6;
    Matthew 6:33.

PENN, Marilyn - Psalm 93.
PENORWOOD, Edwin - I Corinthians 13.
PERGOLESI, Giovanni - Psalm 10.
PERRY, Julia - Isaiah 52:7.
PERRY, Rob Roy - Revelation 21:3, 4.
PETER, Johann F. - Psalm 25:5; Isaiah 55:3; Isaiah 60:20;
    Habakkuk 2:20; Hebrews 2:20.
PHILLIPS, Louis Baker - Psalm 90.
PHILLIPS, Madalyn - Matthew 28:5-7.
PICKET, Fredrick - Isaiah 40:6-8.
PINKHAM, Daniel - Job 14:1-2; Psalm 80; Ecclesiastes 1:2;
    Ecclesiastes 9:7-9; Song Of Songs 8:6; John 14:18, 28;
    Romans 8:35, 37-39; Romans 13:11, 12; I Thessalonians 5:1-6;
    Philippians 4:4-7; Colossians 3:16; Hebrews 12:1-2.
PISK, Paul - II Chronicles 6:14, 19-21; Jeremiah 5:15-22;
    II Corinthians 3:9-12; James 3:13-18.
POHLE, David - Psalm 42:1-2, 12.
POWERS, George - Psalm 51:10-12, 15.
POWERS, Margaret Westlake - Psalm 46:1-6, 10.
POWELL, Robert J. - Psalm 13:1-6; Psalm 33:21; Psalm 89:1, 5,
    8-9, 11, 14-15; Psalm 107:1-2, 43; Psalm 128:1; Ephesians
    5:2, 8, 11, 15, 19.
PROULX, Richard - Matthew 6:9-13; I John 4:7-8.
PURCELL, Henry - Psalm 6:1-4; Psalm 8:4; Psalm 23:1; Joel 2:15;
    Luke 2:42; Hebrews 2:6.

RAIGORDSKY, Natalie - Psalm 121.
RAKSIN, David - Psalm 3:1-4.
RANZZINI - Psalm 13.
REGER, Max - Psalm 119:1-5, 8.
REINTHALER, C. - Psalm 42:5.
REMA, Caro - Revelation 21:3, 4, 6.
REPP, Ray - Psalm 121.
REZNICK, Hyman - Song Of Songs 8:6-7.
RHEINTHALER, C. - Deuteronomy 4:29.
RICHARDS, Stephen - Psalm 137.
RIDDLE, Peter - Psalm 23.
RIDER, Dale - James 1:17.
RIKER, Franklin - Psalm 51:10-13; Isaiah 1:2, 4, 18-19.
ROBERTS, J. E. - Deuteronomy 4:29; John 4:23, 24.
ROBERTS, J. Varley - Isaiah 55:6, 7; John 14:27.
ROBINSON, McNeils - John 1:1-14.
ROBYN, Alfred - Psalm 85:6-11.
ROCHBERG, George - Song Of Songs 2:10, 11, 12, 13b; Song Of
    Songs 4:1; Song Of Songs 7:11; Song Of Songs 8:6, 7.
ROGERS, Bernard - Psalm 68.
ROGERS, Faith Helen - Psalm 91:1, 5-7, 11, 12.
ROGERS, James - Psalm 13:1; Psalm 119:165, 174-176; Psalm 126:5,
    6; Psalm 130.
ROGERS, Sharon Elery - Matthew 21:9; Revelation 5:8-10;
    Revelation 14:3.

ROMER, Charles - Revelation 21:1-7.
ROOT, Frederic - I Corinthians 13.
ROREM, Ned - II Samuel 1:19-27; Psalm 100; Psalm 120; Psalm 134;
     Psalm 140; Psalm 142; Psalm 148; Psalm 150; Matthew 6:9-13;
     Matthew 27:62-66; Luke 2:9-15.
ROSENMUELLER, Johann - Psalm 134:1-4; Jeremiah 1:1-5.
ROW, Richard D. - Psalm 138; John 14:18-21.
ROWLEY, Alec - Job 23:3, 8-9; John 20:29.
RUBBRA, Edmund - Psalm 6; Psalm 23; Psalm 150.
RUBENSTEIN, Anton - Isaiah 40:1-3.
RUTENBER, C. B. - Psalm 121; Matthew 9:28-30; John 14:1-3, 19,
     20.

SACCO, John - Psalm 27:13, 14.
SACCO, Peter - Psalm 13; Psalm 18; Psalm 23; Psalm 8; Matthew
     5:9-10.
SAINT-SAENS, Camille - Psalm 19:14; Psalm 40:1.
SAMMA, Leo - Ruth 1:16-17; Song Of Songs 2:10-13; Song Of Songs
     3:9-11; Song Of Songs 4:9-11.
SANDRESKY, Margaret - Luke 1:46-47.
SAVIONI, Mario - Luke 1:46-47.
SCARLATTI, Alessandro - Matthew 11:28-30.
SCHALET, H. - Psalm 6.
SCHALITT - Psalm 22:2.
SCHIAVONE, John - Psalm 128.
SCHILLING, Hans Ludwig - Psalm 150.
SCHINHAM, Jan Philip - Psalm 139.
SCHMUTZ, Albert D. - Psalm 145; Isaiah 12; Isaiah 40:28-31;
     Isaiah 60:1-3, 18-19.
SCHNECKER, P. A. - Psalm 33.
SCHUTZ, Heinrich - Ruth 1:16-17; I Samuel 2:1, 2; II Samuel
     18:33; Psalm 3:6-9; Psalm 4:1; Psalm 4:2; Psalm 6; Psalm
     9:12, 13; Psalm 13:5-6; Psalm 18:2-7; Psalm 27:4; Psalm
     29:12; Psalm 30:5-6; Psalm 31:2, 3; Psalm 34:1-7; Psalm
     34:2-5, 7; Psalm 34:2-7; Psalm 37:1-5; Psalm 37:25; Psalm
     40:14-18; Psalm 47:1-6; Psalm 51; Psalm 51:10; Psalm 70;
     Psalm 78:1-3; Psalm 96:1-4; Psalm 100:1-4; Psalm 111;
     Psalm 107:2-4; Psalm 145:3-4; Isaiah 41:10; Matthew 11:28-
     30; Luke 1:46-47; Luke 2:8-14; Luke 2:10-12; Luke 2:29-30;
     Luke 2:48, 49; Luke 5:5; Luke 21:34-36; Ephesians 3:14-15.
SCHULTZ, A. L. - Matthew 19:14.
SCOTT, Charles P. - Psalm 118:14, 15; Luke 18:15, 16.
SCOTT, John Prindle - Psalm 8; Psalm 23; Psalm 91; Psalm 103:
     13-17; Psalm 130; Ecclesiastes 12:1-7; Isaiah 2:4; Isaiah
     15:3, 6-8; Isaiah 26:3-4, 11-12; Isaiah 40:3, 6-8; Isaiah
     52; Isaiah 60; Matthew 3:1, 2, 7, 8, 11, 12; Matthew
     6:28-34; Matthew 25:34-36; Matthew 25:41-45; Matthew
     28:5-6; Luke 2:8-15; Luke 24; I Corinthians 5:7-8;
     II Timothy 1:12.
SEATON, Annette - Psalm 62:1, 5-7.
SECCHI, ? - Isaiah 55.

SEEGER, Charles - Psalm 137.
SELBY, Peter H. - Deuteronomy 32:1-4, 9-12.
SESSIONS, Roger - Psalm 140.
SHAWN, Allen - Isaiah 26.
SHELLEY, Harry Rowe - Psalm 23; Psalm 91:1-2; Revelation 21:2, 3;
    Revelation 22:14, 16.
SHENK, Louis - Matthew 6:9-13.
SIBELIUS, Jean (SEE: R.D.Row - Matthew 6:9-15)
SIEGEL, Arsene - Psalm 83:1-5, 13-15, 18.
SIFLER, Paul - Psalm 130.
SINGER, Guy - Ruth 1:16-17.
SINZHEIMER, Max - Psalm 128.
SKILLINGS, Otis - Philippians 4:8-9.
SMART, Henry - Psalm 23.
SMITH, G. Alan - Colossians 3:12-17.
SNYDER, Virginia - John 14:1.
SOLER, Joseph - Romans 6:3, 4; Colossians 3:1-4.
SOWERBY, Leo - Psalm 13:1-6; Psalm 23; Psalm 39; Psalm 61:1-5;
    Psalm 91; Psalm 100; Psalm 121; Psalm 142.
SPEAKS, Oley - Psalm 13:1, 3, 5; Psalm 27; Psalm 137:1-5; Isaiah
    26:3; Matthew 28:1-6; John 14:1, 27.
SPICKER, Max - Psalm 42:5; Psalm 71:1, 9, 12, 18.
SPENCER, William R. - Psalm 23.
SPIRITUAL - Exodus 8:1; Jeremiah 8:22; Matthew 24:29.
STAINER, John - John 3:16, 17.
STANFORD, Charles Villiers - Psalm 46:8-10; Psalm 121; Psalm 124;
    Psalm 130; Ecclesiasticus 24:3-7, 12-14.
STARER, Robert - Psalm 31:1, 9, 15-16; Psalm 51:1; Psalm 136:1-9.
STEBBINS, G. Waring - Isaiah 1:18, 20, 28.
STEARNS, Peter P. - Psalm 23; Psalm 104:1, 24; Psalm 121;
    I Corinthians 2:9, 10; I John 3:2.
STEPHENSON, Richard T. - Psalm 103:1-5, 8, 13.
STEVENSON, Frederick - Psalm 34:4; Psalm 81:9-11; Wisdom Of
    Solomon 18:14, 15.
STICKLER, William - Psalm 42:2.
STRANDBERG, Newton - Psalm 100.
STRICKLAND, Lily - Psalm 42; Isaiah 55:1, 3, 12.
SUBEN, Joel - Psalm 100.
SULLIVAN, Arthur - Isaiah 5:8; Proverbs 3:5-6; Luke 4:18, 21;
    Luke 15:17-19; Luke 23:28, 29a; Revelation 21:3, 4, 5.
SWIFT, Robert - Isaiah 40:28-31.

TALMA, Louise - Psalm 27:4.
TATE, Phyllis - Psalm 23.
TAYLOR, Raynor - Psalm 23.
TCHAIKOVSKY, Peter - Psalm 23.
TELEMANN, G. P. - Psalm 34:2-4; Psalm 100; Psalm 121; Isaiah
    60:1-6; I Corinthians 9:24-27; Romans 13:8-10; I Corinthians
    15:50-58; James 1:17-22.
THIMAN, Eric - Psalm 1; Psalm 23; Psalm 134; Proverbs 3:13, 15,
    18; Isaiah 26:3, 4; Isaiah 35:1, 2, 6-8, 10; Isaiah 36:3, 4.

THOMPSON, Randall - Luke 1:46-47.
THOMPSON, William H. - John 14:1, 27.
THOMSON, Sydney - Galatians 6:14.
THOMSON, Virgil - Psalm 23; Song Of Songs 2:14; Song Of Songs
    3:1, 2; Song Of Songs 6:3; Song Of Songs 6:13; Song Of Songs
    8:13.
THORNE, Francis - Isaiah 40:3-5; Luke 1:46-47; Luke 2:29.
TIMMINGS, William - Psalm 51:9-11.
TOCH, Ernst - Ecclesiastes 3:1-8.
TOOLAN, Suzanne - John 6:51.
TOPLIFF, Robert - Matthew 6:25, 26, 28, 29.
TRIPLETT, Robert - Psalm 23; Psalm 89.
TWINN, Sydney - Psalm 121.

UNDERHILL, Charles - Mark 10:13, 14.

VAN DE WATER, Beardsley - Psalm 23; Luke 8:10; Luke 15:11-25;
    Luke 18:10-14.
VAN DYKE, May - Psalm 113:3; Isaiah 55:6, 7; Matthew 22:37-39.
VAN NAYS, Rena - Psalm 139:7-10, 12, 14, 23-24.
VAN VOLLENHOVEN, Hanna - Psalm 27:1.
VAN WOERT, Rutger - Isaiah 45:1, 2, 22.
VAUGHAN-WILLIAMS, Ralph - Psalm 18:32, 37; Psalm 23; Psalm 31:5;
    Ecclesiasticus 44; Ephesians 6:13; Revelation 2:7;
    Revelation 22:1-2.
VIADANA, Lodovico - Exodus 15:1-2.
VIVALDI, Antonio - Psalm 86:4-6, 12.
VOGEL, Howard - Song Of Songs 7:6.

WARD-STEPHEN - Psalm 139; Matthew 5:3; Matthew 5:5; Matthew 5:6;
    Matthew 5:7; Matthew 5:9; Matthew 5:10; John 14:2, 3, 4, 27;
    Ephesians 5:14.
WARE, Harriet - I Corinthians 13.
WARREN, Clara - Psalm 118:24; John 14:6, 8-9; Acts 31:8.
WARREN, Raymond - Luke 7:36-40, 47-48.
WATTS, Winter - Ruth 1:16-17.
WAY, Arthur - Job 22:21.
WEAVER, Powell - Psalm 98; Psalm 150.
WEINBERGHER, Jaromis - Psalm 150; Luke 24:13-31.
WEINER, Lazar - Ruth 1:16-17; Psalm 130.
WEINHORST, Richard - Isaiah 26:3-4.
WENZEL, Eberhard - Psalm 90.
WERNICK - Psalm 122:2, 3, 6-8.
WESLEY, Samuel S. - Psalm 5:8; Psalm 103:1.
WEST, A. John - Psalm 42.
WETZLER, Robert - Psalm 128; Isaiah 61; Isaiah 61:1-3;
    I Corinthians 13.
WIKEHART, Lewis - Psalm 96.
WHITE, Louie L. - Ruth 1:16-17.

WIANT, Bliss - Isaiah 61:1-3.
WIEMAR, Wolfgang - Psalm 70; Psalm 103.
WILDER, Alec - Psalm 137.
WILLAN, Healey - Matthew 6:9-13.
WILLIAMSON, Inez McCane - Matthew 6:9-13.
WILSON, John F. - Proverbs 31:25-31.
WINTON, Mary - Psalm 23.
WOLFE, Jacques - Ezekiel 37; Matthew 5:3-11.
WOOD, Don - Matthew 5:1-10, 12.
WOOLER, Alfred - Job 36:5, 6, 7; Psalm 6:33-37; Psalm 12; Psalm
     13; Psalm 27:1, 2, 3, 5; Psalm 43:1, 2, 3, 4; Psalm 54;
     Psalm 57; Psalm 61:1; Psalm 130; Romans 10:15.
WRIGHT, Norman S. - Psalm 8.
WYNER, Yehudi - Psalm 39:4-5; Psalm 66; Psalm 66:1-4; Psalm
     119:25-32.

YARDUMIAN, Richard - Psalm 130.
YOUNG, Gordon - Ruth 1:16-17.
YOUNG, Walter E. - Isaiah 1:6, 10.

ZAIMONT, Judith Lang - Psalm 23; Proverbs 31:10, 11, 17, 20, 26,
     28, 30.

SONG TITLE INDEX

Abide In Me – Johannes Herbst
Acquaint Now Thyself With Him – Michael Head
Acquaint Now Thyself With Him – James MacDermid
Acquaint Now Thyself With Him – Arthur Way
Acquaint Thyself With Him – Dudley Buck
Adagio Ma Non Troppo – Walter S. Hartley
Ad Te Levavi Occulos Meus – Francois Couperin
Agnus Dei – Georges Bizet
All Flesh Is Grass – Frederick Pickete
Allegro – Walter S. Hartley
Allegro Con Brio – Walter S. Hartley
Alleluia – Ferdinant Hummel
Also hat Gott die Welt geliebt – Dietrich Buxtehude
An Angel Speaks To The Shepherd – Ned Rorem
And A Very Great Multitude – Sven Lekberg
And I, John, Saw The Holy City – Harry Rowe Shelley
And In That Day Thou Shalt Say – Albert D. Schmutz
And Jesus Said: It Is Finished – John Antes
And Lo! The Angel Of The Lord Came Upon Them – G.F. Handel
And The Angel Said Unto Them – G.F. Handel
And Suddenly There Was With The Angel – G.F. Handel
And There Were Shepherds – Andrew J. Boex
And There Were Shepherds Abiding In The Fields – Frank LaForge
And There Will Be Sound – Jan Bender
And Thou Shalt Know It – Johannes Antes
Andante Con Moto – Walter S. Hartley
Andante Molto – Walter S. Hartley
Angels Roll The Rock Away – John Prindle Scott
Ani Chavatselet Hasharon – Amvel Bugatch
Answer Me When I Call – Charles Ore
Arise, O Lord – Lenn Abbott Hoffmeister
Arioso – S. Judassohn
Arise, Shine – John Prindle Scott
Arise, Shine, For Thy Light Is Come – F. Flaxington Harker
Arise, Shine, For Thy Light Is Come – Don Humphreys
Arise, Shine, For Thy Light Is Come – James MacDermid
Arise, Shine, For Thy Light Is Come – Albert Schmutz
As It Began To Dawn – C. Whitney Combs
As It Began To Dawn – F. Flaxington Harker
As The Hart Panteth – Kathleen Blair
As The Rain Cometh Down – James MacDermid
As Pants The Hart – A.W. Lansing

As Pants The Hart - Henry Smart
As Pants The Hart - Lily Strickland
As Pants The Wearied Hart - Benedetto Marcello
Ascribe Unto The Lord Worship and Power - A.R. Gaul
At The Time Of The Banquet - Gerhard Krapf
Attendite, Popule Meus, Legum Meam - Heinrich Schutz
Aus der Tiefer - Berhard Christopher
Ave Maria (English text Magnificat) - Charles Gounod
Awake All Ye People - J.S. Bach
Awake, O North Wind - Lukas Foss
Awake Thou That Sleepest - G.F. Handel
Awake Thou That Sleepest - Ward-Stephens

Balm In Gilead - Spiritual, arr. Burleigh
Balm In Gilead - Spiritual, arr. Johnson
Be Exalted, O God - Brent Chambers
Be Glad, O Ye Righteous - Bruno Huhn
Be Merciful Unto Me - Michael Head
Be Merciful, Even As Your Father Is Merciful - Gerhard Krapf
Be Not Afraid - Bertrand-Brown
Be Not Afraid - Frederick Koch
Be Not Afraid - Heinrich Schutz
Be Not Far From Me - Vaclav Nelhybel
Be Not Far From Me, O God - Rutger Van Woert
Be Of Good Courage - Vivian Beaumont
Be Still, And Know - Margaret Westlake Powers
Be Still And Know That I Am God - Roberta Bitgood
Be Still And Know That I Am God - Olive Duncan
Be Strong In The Lord - J.S. Bach
Be Thou Faithful Unto Death - Felix Mendelssohn
Be Ye Kind, One To Another - Katherine K. Davis
Beatitudes, The - Mortimer Browning
Beatitudes, The - Don Humphreys
Beatitudes, The - Albert Hay Malotte
Beatitudes, The - Patrick Kavanaugh
Beatitudes, The - Don Wood
Beatus Vir - Ferdinando Paer
Because You Are God's Chosen Ones - G. Alen Smith
Begone Satan - Jan Bender
Behold, A Virgin Shall Be With Child - John LaMontaine
Behold A Virgin Shall Conceive/O Thou That Tellest - G.F. Handel
Behold And See - G.F. Handel
Behold, God Is Mighty - Alfred Wooler
Behold, How Fair And Pleasant - Howard Vogel
Behold, How Good And How Pleasant - Thelma Matesky
Behold, I Send An Angel - Michael Head
Behold, I Stand At The Door - Verna Mae Bryant
Behold I Tell You A Mystery/The Trumpet Shall Sound - G.F. Handel
Behold! The Former Things Are Come To Pass - Allanson G.Y. Brown
Behold The Lamb Of God - Clement W. Barker
Behold The Son Of God - W.A. Mozart

Behold The Tabernacle Of God - Leon Abbott Hoffmeister
Behold The Wicked Man - Ezra Laderman
Behold! Thou Art Fair - George Rochberg
Behold, Thus Is The Man Blessed - William Ferris
Behold What Manner Of Love - H. Leroy Baumgartner
Behold What Manner Of Love - Claude Fichthoin
Behold! What Manner Of Love - Wilbur Hatch
Behold, What Manner Of Love - James MacDermid
Behold, What Manner Of Love - Harry Allen Paris
Behold What Names Of Love - Helen M. Cruikshank
Beloved, Let Us Love One Another - Michael Head
Beloved, Let Us Love One Another - Gordon Myers
Beloved, Let Us Love - Richard Proulx
Beloved, Now Are We The Sons Of God - Peter Pindar Stearns
Benedican Dominum in Omni (Trois Psaumes) - Arthur Honegger
Benedictio Nuptialis - Richard Felciano
Beside Still Waters - Mary Deacon
Bird's Song, The - Ralph Vaughan-Williams
Bless The Lord - Frank LaForge
Bless The Lord Oh My Soul - Clement Barker
Bless The Lord, O My Soul - Katherine K. Davis
Bless The Lord, O My Soul - Gabriel Faure
Bless The Lord, O My Soul - Alice Jordan
Bless The Lord, O My Soul - Edwin McArthur
Bless The Lord, O My Soul - Peter Pindar Stearns
Bless Thou The Lord - Benati
Blessed, The - Jacques Wolfe
Blessed Are The Meek - Ward-Stephens
Blessed Are The Merciful - Ward-Stephens
Blessed Are The Peacemakers - Peter Sacco
Blessed Are The Peacemakers - Ward-Stephens
Blessed Are The Poor In Spirit - Ward-Stephens
Blessed Are They - G.F. Handel
Blessed Are They That Dwell In Thy House - Maurice Greene
Blessed Are They Which Are Persecuted - Ward-Stephens
Blessed Are They Which Do Hunger - Ward-Stephens
Blessed Are Those Who Fear The Lord - Robert Powell
Blessed Are Those Who Fear The Lord - Max Sinzheimer
Blessed Be Thou, Lord God Of Israel - Alfred Greenfield
Blessed Is The Man - Maurice Greene
Blessed Is The Man - Katharine Lucke
Blessed Is The Man - Vaclav Nelhybel
Blessed Is The Man - Charles W. Ore
Blessed Is The People - Clifton Parker
Blessed Virgin's Expostulation, The - Henry Purcell
Blow Ye The Trumpet - Henry Purcell
Bone Come A-Knittin' - Jacques Wolfe
Bow Down Your Ear - Secchi
Bread Of Life - Felix Mendelssohn
Bread Of Life, The - W.B. Olds
Bring To Jehovah - Heinrich Schutz
Bring Ye All The Tithes Into The Storehouse - James MacDermid

Bringt her dem Herren - Heinrich Schutz
Brother James's Air - James Bain (arr. Phyllis Tate)
Brother James's Air - James Bain (arr. Arthur Trew)
But The Lord Is Mindful Of His Own - Felix Mendelssohn
But Thou Didst Not Leave His Soul In Hell - G.F. Handel
But Who May Abide The Day Of His Coming - G.F. Handel
But Of The Times And The Seasons - Daniel Pinkham
By Night On My Bed - Lukas Foss
By The Rivers Of Babylon - Alec Wilder
By The Waters Of Babylon - Oley Speaks
By Waters Of Babylon - J.S. Bach
By Waters Of Babylon - Julius Chajes
By Waters Of Babylon - Anton Dvorak
By Waters Of Babylon - Vernon Eville
By Waters Of Babylon - Charles T. Howell

Cantata: All The Days Of My Life - Louise Talma
Cantata de Psaumes - Darius Milhaud
Contemus Domino - Lodovico Viadana
Christ Is Lord - Emmet Pendleton
Christ Is Risen - John Prindle Scott
Christ Whose Glory - James Butt
Christmas Prophecy - Bob Burroughs
Clouds And Darkness - Anton Dvorak
Come, Let Us Make A Joyful Noise - G.F. Handel
Come, My Beloved - Lukas Foss
Come, My Beloved - Rolf Peter Overby
Come, My Beloved - George Rochberg
Come Near Ye Nations - Frank LaForge
Come Now And Let Us Reason Together - G. Waring Stebbins
Come, Take The Water Of Life - Irwin Fischer
Come To Me - Ludwig Beethoven
Come To The Waters - G.F. Handel (solo)
Come To The Waters - G.F. Handel (duet)
Come Unto Me - William Coenen
Come Unto Me - G.F. Handel
Come Unto Me - Frank LaForge
Come Unto Me - C.B. Rutenber
Come Unto Me - Alessandro Scarlatti
Come Unto Me, All Ye That Labor - Healey Willan
Come Ye Blessed - A.R. Gaul
Come Ye Blessed - John Prindle Scott
Comfort Ye, My People - Anton Dvorak
Comfort Ye My People - Anton Rubenstein (solo)
Comfort Ye My People - Anton Rubenstein (duet)
Comfort Ye/Every Valley - G.F. Handel
Commission, The - Bob Burroughs
Communion Song - Bobby McGuire
Confitebor tibi, Domini (Trois Psaumes) - Arthur Honegger
Consider, And Hear Me - F. Flaxington Harker
Consider, And Hear Me - Alfred Wooler

Consider The Lilies - John Prindle Scott
Consider The Lilies - Robert Topliff
Courage - James Butt
Create In Me - George Powers
Create In Me A Clean Heart - Christoph Bernhard
Create In Me A Clean Heart - Dietrich Buxtehude
Create In Me A Clean Heart - Vincent Evans
Create In Me A Clean Heart - Carl F. Mueller
Create In Me A Clean Heart - Franklin Riker

Daily Will I Love Thee (Herzlich lieb hab ich dich) - Heinrich
     Schutz
Daughters of Jerusalem - A. Sullivan
David Mourns For Absalom - David Diamond
David's Psalm - Martin Broones
Days Of All Thy Sorrow, The - Johann F. Peter
De David - Newton Strandberg
De Profundis - Paul Sifler
Delight Thyself In The Lord - Irwin Fischer
Depart From Me - John Prindle Scott
Der 134th Psalm - Johann Rosenmuller
Domines Salvum Fac Regem - Francois Couperin
Doth Not Wisdom Cry - James MacDermid
Draw Nigh To God - Clement Barker
Drop, Drop Slow Tears - Raymond Warren

Earth Is The Lord's, The - Josef Freudenthal
Earth Is The Lord's, The - Don McAfee
Eighth Psalm, The - Norman S. Wright
Ein jeder lauft, der in den Schranken kauft - G.P. Telemann
Eili, Eili! Sanctuary - Shalitt
Enter In The Wilderness - Hasidic Folk Song
Entreat Me Not - Frederic Groton
Entreat Me Not To Leave Thee - Lawrence Avery
Entreat Me Not To Leave Thee - Richard T. Gore
Entreat Me Not To Leave Thee - Charles Gounod
Entreat Me Not To Leave Thee - Louie White
Entreat Me Not To Leave Thee - Gordon Young
Erhoere mich, wenn ich rufe - Heinrich Schutz
Eripe me Domine, ab homine malo (Trois Psaumes) - Arthur Honegger
Es danken dir, Gott, die Voeller - Andreas Hammerschmidt
Every Day Will I Give Thanks - G.F. Handel
Every Good And Perfect Gift - Dale Rider
Every Valley - G.F. Handel
Ew'ge Qwelle, milder Strum - G.P. Telemann
Except The Lord Build The House - Gordon Myers
Exultavit cor meum - Heinrich Schutz
Eye Hath Not Seen - William M. Faulkner
Eye Hath Not Seen - A.R. Gaul
Eye Hath Not Seen - Peter Pindar Stearns

Faith Is - Austin Lovelace
Father Abraham, Have Mercy On Me - Gerhard Krapf
Fear Not, Little Flock - J.S. Bach
Fear Not Ye, O Israel - Dudley Buck
Fear Of The Lord, The - Alan Leichtling
Feed My Lambs - Frederick Koch
Feed My Sheep - George Faulkner
Feurchte dich nicht - Heinrich Schutz
Fili Mi Absalom - Heinrich Schutz
I Corinthians 13 - Jack Behrens
First Easter Morn, The - John Prindle Scott
First Psalm - Gene Bone and Howard Fenton
Five Phrases from the Song of Solomon - Virgil Thomson
For Behold Darkness Shall Cover The Earth - G.F. Handel
For I Am Persuaded - Carlisle Floyd
For Look, As High As The Heaven - G.F. Handel
For The Mountains Shall Depart - Blanche Bowling
For The Mountains Shall Depart - James MacDermid
For The Mountains Shall Depart - Felix Mendelssohn
For This Our Truest Interest - G.F. Handel
For Ye Know Not - Felix Mendelssohn
Fraters: Si Consurrexistis cum Christo - Josep Soler
Frohlochet - Heinrich Schutz
From The End Of The Earth - Ezra Laderman
From Psalm 49 - Henry Orland

Garment Of Praise - Carl Frederickson
Gift Of Love, The - Hal Hopson (solo)
Gift Of Love, The - Hal Hopson (duet)
Give Ear Of Ye Heaven - Peter H. Selby
Give God The Father - Heinrich Schutz
Give Thanks Unto The Lord - Robert Starer
Glorious Jerusalem - Horatio Parker
Glory To God In The Highest - F. Flaxington Harker
Go Down Moses - Spiritual
Go Forth In His Name - Jeremiah Dencke
Go Thy Way, Eat Thy Bread With Joy - Daniel Pinkham
God Be Merciful To Me - Alfred Wooler
God Be Merciful Unto Me - John Koch
God Hath Led His People On - Felix Mendelssohn
God Is A Constant Sure Defense - G.F. Handel
God Is A Spirit - Helen Hopekirk
God Is A Spirit - Edwin McArthur
God Is A Spirit - J.E. Roberts
God Is A Spirit - Charles P. Scott
God Is My Salvation - Lee Calder
God Is My Shepherd - Anton Dvorak
God Is Of Love - Don Humphreys
God Is Our Refuge - James MacDermid
God Is Our Refuge and Strength - Howard Hanson
God, My Father - Theodore DuBois

God Of Love My Shepherd Is, The - Eric H. Thiman
God Shall Wipe Away All Tears - J.T. Field
God Shall Wipe Away All Tears - F. Flaxington Harker
God Shall Wipe Away All Tears - Franz Liszt
God Shall Wipe Away All Tears - Rob Roy Perry
God Shall Wipe Away All Tears - Caro Rima
God So Loved The World - I. Fischer
God So Loved The World - James MacDermid
God So Loved The World - John Stainer
God That Made The World - James MacDermid
God's Love - Bob Burroughs
God's Tender Mercy Knows No Bounds - G.F. Handel
God's Time - John Sacco
Good Shepherd, The - Beardsley Van De Water
Good Tidings - Robert Wetzler
Great Commission, The - Bliss Wiant
Great Is Our Lord - Marion L. Cartwright
Great Is The Lord - Bruno Huhn
Great Is The Lord - Heinrich Schutz
Great Peace Have They - Allanson G.Y. Brown
Great Peace Have They - Jean Baptiste Lully
Great Peace Have They Which Love The Law - James Rogers
Greatest Of These, The - Harriet Ware
Greatest Of These Is Love, The - Roberta Bitgood
Greatest Of These Is Love, The - Lorna Lynn
Greatest Of These Is Love, The - Daniel Moe
Greatest Of These Is Love, The - Edwin Penhorwood
Greatest Of These Is Love, The - Robert Wetzler

Habe dein Lust an dem Herren - Heinrich Schutz
Halleluya - Yehudi Wyner
Happy Are They Who Dwell In Your House - Walter L. Pelz
Happy Are You Who Fear The Lord - John Schiavone
Happy Is The Man - Clarence Mader
Happy Is The Man (Psalms) - Eric Thiman
Happy Is The Man (Proverbs) - Eric Thiman
Hark, My Beloved - Emanuel Barisan
Hast Thou Not Known - Frank LaForge
Hast Thou Not Known - Albert Schmutz
Hast Thou Not Known - Robert Swift
Hast Thou Not Known Me? - Clara Warren
Haste Thee, Lord God, Haste To Save Me - Heinrich Schutz
Haste Thee, O God, To Save Me - Heinrich Schutz
Have Mercy Upon Me, O Lord - Robert Starer
He Hath Shewed Thee O Man - Harry C. Banks
He Is Risen, As He Said - Madalyn Phillips
He Maketh Wars To Cease - George Chadwick
He Maketh Wars To Cease - John Prindle Scott
He Restoreth My Soul - Kathleen Blair
He Sent His Word - James MacDermid
He Sent His Word And Healed Them - Don Humphreys

He Shall Be Like A Tree - Blanche Bowling
He Shall Feed His Flock - G.F. Handel
He Shall Feed His Flock - F. Flaxington Harker
He Shall Give His Angel Charge - John Prindle Scott
He Shall Give His Angels Charge Over Thee - Donald Busarow
He That Dwelleth In Heaven/Thou Shalt Break Them - G.F. Handel
He That Dwelleth In The Secret Place - H. Leroy Baumgartner
He That Dwelleth In The Secret Place - Don Humphreys
He That Dwelleth In The Secret Place - W.H. Neidlinger
He That Dwelleth In The Secret Place - Harry Rowe Shelly
He Was Cut Off - G.F. Handel
He Was Despised - G.F. Handel
Healing Of The Woman In The Throng, The - Theron Wolcott Hart
Hear Me, O Lord - Heinrich Schutz
Hear Me Speedily, O Lord! - Hanna Van Vollenhoven
Hear Me When I Call - Vaclav Nelhybel
Hear My Cry - Harold Vincent Mulligan
Hear My Cry, O God - Leo Sowerby
Hear My Cry, O Lord - Leo Sowerby
Hear My Cry, O Lord! - Alfred Wooler
Hear My Prayer - Anton Dvorak
Hear My Prayer - Felix Mendelssohn
Hear My Prayer, O Lord - Anton Dvorak
Hear My Voice - Vaclav Nelhybel
Hear, O Heavens, And Give Ear O Earth - Franklin Liker
Hear, O Lord, When I Cry With My Voice - H. Leroy Baumgartner
Hear, O My People - Frederick Stevenson
Hear Thou My Prayer - Bernard Hamblen
Hear Ye Israel - Felix Mendelssohn
Heavens Declare His Glory, The - Billie Hanks, Jr.
Hemmt den Eifer, verbannet die Rache - G.P. Telemann
Herb, wenn ich nur dich habe - Dietrich Buxtehude
Herr, auf dich traue ich - Dietrich Buxtehude
Der Herr ist mein Hirt - Wolfgang Wiemar
Herr, Nun Lasset du deinen deiner - Dietrich Buxtehude
Heutet euch - Heinrich Schutz
His Children - William K. Burns
His Left Hand Is Under My Head, And His Right Hand Doth Embrace
    Me - John LaMontaine
Hosanna To The Son Of David - Arthur Carr
Hosianna, dem Sohne David - Heinrich Grimm
Hour Cometh, The - Walter Mourant
How Beautiful Are The Feet - G.F. Handel
How Beautiful Are The Feet - Julian Perry
How Beautiful Are Thy Dwellings - S. deLange
How Beautiful On The Mountain - Alfred Wooler
How Beautiful Upon The Mountains - Irwin Fischer
How Beautiful Upon The Mountains - F. Flaxington Harker
How Beautiful Upon The Mountains - Felix Mendelssohn
How Excellent Is Thy Loving Kindness - F.H. Cowen
How Excellent Is Thy Loving Kindness - Don Humphreys
How Excellent Is Thy Name - Don McAfee

How Long, O Lord Wilt Thou Forget Me? - James Rogers
How Long Will Thou Forget Me, O Lord - Robert L. Beech
How Long Wilt Thou Forget Me - Robert J. Powell
How Long Wilt Thou Forget Me - Leo Sowerby
How Long Wilt Thou Forget Me - Oley Speaks
How Long Wilt Thou Forget Me, O Lord? - Leon Abbott Hoffmeister
How Long Wilt Thou Forget Me, O Lord - Sven Lekberg
How Lovely Are Thy Dwellings - Katherine K. Davis
How Lovely Are Thy Dwellings - Samuel Liddle
How Lovely Are Thy Dwellings Fair - Eric Thiman
How Lovely Is Thy Dwelling Place - Franz Josef Haydn
How Many Hired Servants - Arthur Sullivan
Hymn Of The Last Supper - Victoria Demarest

I Am The Bread Of Life - Richard Kieserling
I Am The Bread Of Life - S. Suzanne Toolan
I Am The Good Shepherd - Bob Burroughs
I Am The Good Shepherd - Edward Elgar
I Am The Good Shepherd - George Nevin
I Am The Resurrection - Dietrich Buxtehude
I Am The Resurrection - Andreas Hammerschmidt
I Am The Rose Of Sharon And The Lily Of The Valley - John
    LaMontaine
I Am The True Vine - James MacDermid
I Am The Vine - Don Doig
I Believe - C. Alexander Peloquin
I Have Prayed To Thee - Edward Elgar
I Have Seen Water - William Ferris
I Jesus, Have Sent Mine Angel - Harry Rowe Shelly
I Know In Whom I Have Believed - John Prindle Scott
I Know That My Redeemer Liveth - G.F. Handel
I Lift Up My Eyes - Ray Repp
I Lift Up My Eyes To The Hills - Hal H. Hopson
I Lift Up My Eyes To The Hills - Kenneth Jennings
I Love The Lord - John Duke
I Love Thee, Lord, My Strength - Peter Cornelius
I Sat Down Under The Shadow - John LaMontaine
I Shall Not Want - James G. Ellis
I Shall Not Want - Samuel Liddle
I Sought The Lord - Don Humphreys
I Sought The Lord - Frederich Stevenson
I Speak Of Things - Jeremiah Dencke
I Waited For The Lord - Camille Saint-Saens
I Waited Patiently For The Lord - Clarence Mader
I Will Betroth Her Unto Me - Samuel Adler
I Will Bless The Lord At All Times - Heinrich Schutz
I Will Dwell In The House Of The Lord - Vernon Eville
I Will Extol Thee - Albert D. Schmutz
I Will Extol Thee My God - B. Molique
I Will Extol Thee O Lord - M. Costa
I Will Follow - Richard Avery and Donald Marsh

I Will Give Thanks Unto The Lord - Campbell-Tipton
I Will Give Thanks Unto The Lord - Gershon Kingsley
I Will Go In The Strength Of The Lord - Johannes Herbst
I Will Lay Me Down In Peace - Maurice Greene
I Will Lift Up Mine Eyes - Anton Dvorak
I Will Lift Up Mine Eyes - Vernon Eville
I Will Lift Up Mine Eyes - Michael Head
I Will Lift Up Mine Eyes - Stanley Jackson
I Will Lift Up Mine Eyes - Virginia Kendrick
I Will Lift Up Mine Eyes - John Koch
I Will Lift Up Mine Eyes - Sven Lekberg
I Will Lift Up Mine Eyes - Natalie Raigorodsky
I Will Lift Up Mine Eyes - C.B. Rutenber
I Will Lift Up Mine Eyes - Sydney Twinn
I Will Lift Up Mine Eyes - Leo Sowerby
I Will Lift Up Mine Eyes - Peter Pindar Stearns
I Will Lift Up Mine Eyes - Margery Watkins
I Will Lift Up Mine Eyes To The Hills - F. Flaxington Harker
I Will Lift Up Mine Eyes Unto The Hills - Edna Mae Burnham
I Will Lift Up Mine Eyes Unto The Hills - Don Humphreys
I Will Lift Up Mine Eyes Unto The Hills - Clifton Parker
I Will Lift Up My Eyes - Floy Little Bartlett
I Will Magnify Thee - Julius Kaufmann
I Will Make An Everlasting Covenant - Johann Peter
I Will Not Leave You Comfortless - Daniel Pinkham
I Will Not Leave You Comfortless - R.D. Row
I Will Praise Thee With My Whole Heart - Thelma Matesky
I Will Sing Of The Mercies Of The Lord - Robert J. Powell
I Will Sing Of Thy Great Mercies - Felix Mendelssohn
I Will Sing Of Thy Steadfast Love - Robert F. Triplett
I Will Sing New Songs of Gladness - Anton Dvorak
I Will Worship The Lord - Robert Fairfax Birch
Ich Benge meine knie - Heinrich Schutz
Ich bin jung gewesen - Heinrich Schutz
Ich danke dem Herrn von ganzem Herzen - Heinrich Schutz
Ich habe meine Augen auf zu dem Bergen - G.P. Telemann
Ich, Liege und Schlafe - Heinrich Schutz
Ich will den Herren loben allezeit - Heinrich Schutz
Ich will den Herren loben allezeit - G.P. Telemann
If A Man Loves Me - Jan Bender
If God Be For Us - William K. Burns
If God Be For Us - G.F. Handel
If I Am Without Love - Don McAfee
If I Take The Wings Of The Morning - Irwin Fischer
If My People Will Pray - Jimmy Owens
If Thou Prepare Thine Heart - Clifton Parker
If We Live In The Spirit - Clement Barker
If With All Your Hearts - Felix Mendelssohn
If With All Your Hearts - J.E. Roberts
If Ye Abide In Me - Frank LaForge
If Ye Love Me, Keep My Commandments - Irwin Fischer
If Ye Then Be Risen With Christ - Myles Foster

Ihr Volkers, Hoert - G.P. Telemann
Il faut que de tour mes espirits - Clement Marot
In His Hands Are All The Corners Of The Earth - Felix Mendelssohn
In My Father's House Are Many Mansions - Lucina Jewell
In My Father's House Are Many Mansions - James MacDermid
In My Father's House Are Many Mansions - Ward-Stephens
In Remembrance Of Me - Gary Johnson
In Te, Domine, Speravi - Heinrich Schutz
In The Beauty Of Holiness - M. VanDyke
In The Beginning - Joseph Haydn
In The Beginning Was The Word - McNeil Robinson
In The End Of The Sabbath - Oley Speaks
In Thee, O God, Do I Put My Trust - Max Spicker
Incline Thine Ear - Ernest Charles
Incline Your Ear - Lily Strickland
Inhabitants Shall Not Say I Am Sick, The - Leta Bishop Graff
Intreat Me Not To Leave Thee - Wintter Watts
Is It Nothing To You? - Myles B. Foster
Is Not His Word Like A Fire - Felix Mendelssohn
Isaiah - Stefan Wolpe
It Is A Precious Thing To Thank Our God - Hugo Distler

Jauchzet dem Herrn, alle Welt - G.P. Telemann
Jauchzet, ihr Christen, seid vergnugt - G.P. Telemann
Jerusalem - Felix Mendelssohn
Jesus Said To The Widow, "Do Not Weep" - Gerhard Krapf
Joy To The World - Powell Weaver
Jubilate deo omnis terra - Heinrich Schutz
Jubilate Dominio - Dietrich Buxtehude

Keep Not Thou Silence, O God - Peter Sacco
Keep Thou Not Silence, O God - Arsene Siegel
King Of Love, The - James Butt
King Of Love, The - John Crawford
King Of Love My Shepherd Is, The - Charles Gounod
King Of Love My Shepherd Is, The - John Holler
King Of Love My Shepherd Is, The - Harry Rowe Shelly
King Of Love My Shepherd Is, The - William Spence
Know Ye That The Lord He Is God - D. Guyver Britton

Labor Of Thy Hands, The (#1) - Miriam Gideon
Labor Of Thy Hands, The (#3) - Miriam Gideon
Lamentation - Paul Pisk
Lamentation Of David - Herbert Fromm
Laments - Samuel Adler
Lamp Unto My Feet, A - Josef Freudenthal
Last Words Of David, The - Josef Freudenthal
Laudate Nomen - G. Winston Cassler
Lead Me In Thy Truth - Johann F. Peter

Lead Me, Lord - G.F. Handel
Lead Me, Lord - B. Molique
Let Not The Wise Men Glory In His Wisdom - James MacDermid
Let Not Your Heart Be Troubled - G.W. Chadwick
Let Not Your Heart Be Troubled - Paul Haeussler
Let Not Your Heart Be Troubled - Stanley Reiff
Let Not Your Heart Be Troubled - C.B. Rutenber
Let Not Your Heart Be Troubled - Virginia Snyder
Let Not Your Heart Be Troubled - Oley Speaks
Let The Beauty Of The Lord - Irwin Fischer
Let The Children Come Unto Me - Jan Bender
Let The Word Of Christ Dwell In You - Daniel Pinkham
Let This Mind Be In You - Don Humphreys
Let Us Keep The Feast - Clara Warren
Let Us Now Praise Famous Men - Ralph Vaughan-Williams
Let Us Sing Unto The Lord - Joseph Freudenthal
Lied der Ruth - Petr Eben
Lift Thine Eyes - Felix Mendelssohn
Lift Up Thine Eyes - Adolf Jensen
Light - Frederick Stevenson
Light Of The World - Don Humphreys
Like As A Father - F.H. Cowen
Like As A Father - John Prindle Scott
Like As The Hart - John A. West
Like As The Hart - S. Liddle
Like As The Hart Desireth - Frances Allitsen
Lion And The Lamb, The - Martin Kalmanoff
Living Sacrifice, A - Don McAfee
Lobe den Herrn, meine Seele - Wolfgang Wiemer
Look Away From Me - Ezra Laderman
Look Unto Me, Saith Our God - Virginia Kendrick
Lord Bless You, The - J.S. Bach
Lord Bless You And Keep You, The - Peter Lutkin
Lord By Wisdom Founded The Earth - Alan Leichtling
Lord By Wisdom Hath Founded The Earth, The - Irwin Fischer
Lord, Create In Me A Clean Heart - Heinrich Schutz
Lord God Of Abraham - Felix Mendelssohn
Lord, How Long Wilt Thou Forget Me? - Ranzzini
Lord, I Have Loved The Habitations Of Thy House - H. Leroy
    Baumgartner
Lord, In Thee Do I Trust - Dietrich Buxtehude
Lord Is A Mighty Warrior, The- Anonymous
Lord Is In His Holy Temple, The - John Frederik Peter
Lord Is My Light - Frances Allitsen
Lord Is My Light, The - Dudley Buck
Lord Is My Light, The - Clara Edwards
Lord Is My Light, The - Don Humphreys
Lord Is My Light, The - Oley Speaks
Lord Is My Light, The - Alfred Woller
Lord Is My Rock, The - Vaclav Nelhybel
Lord Is My Shepherd, The - Adams
Lord Is My Shepherd, The - Jacob Arcadelt

Lord Is My Shepherd, The - Abraham Wolf Binder
Lord Is My Shepherd, The - Carl Bohm
Lord Is My Shepherd, The - Henry Leland Clarke
Lord Is My Shepherd, The - John J. Davye
Lord Is My Shepherd, The - Josef Freudenthal
Lord Is My Shepherd, The - Adelaide Gardner
Lord Is My Shepherd, The - N. Gilbert
Lord Is My Shepherd, The - Don Humphreys
Lord Is My Shepherd, The - Martin Kalmanoff
Lord Is My Shepherd, The - Gershon Kingsley
Lord Is My Shepherd, The - John Koch
Lord Is My Shepherd, The - Clarence Mader
Lord Is My Shepherd, The - Thomas Matthews
Lord Is My Shepherd, The - Kenneth Meek
Lord Is My Shepherd, The - Charles W. Ore
Lord Is My Shepherd, The - Peter Sacco
Lord Is My Shepherd, The - John Prindle Scott
Lord Is My Shepherd, The - Henry Smart
Lord Is My Shepherd, The - Leo Sowerby
Lord Is My Shepherd, The - Peter Pindar Stearns
Lord Is My Shepherd, The - Raynor Taylor
Lord Is My Shepherd, The - Peter Tchaikovsky
Lord Is My Shepherd, The - Robert Triplett
Lord Is My Strength, The - G.F. Handel
Lord Is My Strength, The - Bruno Huhn
Lord Is Nigh Unto Them, The - C. Agnew DeMarest
Lord Is Risen, The - C. Reinthaler
Lord Is Risen, The - A. Sullivan
Lord, Let Me Know My End - Yehudi Wyner
Lord, Lord Open To Us - Jan Bender
Lord, My Hope Is In Thee - Heinrich Schutz
Lord My Shepherd Is, The - Helder Bartholomaeus
Lord Reigns, The - Eugene Butler
Lord, Teach Me Thy Statues - Irwin Fischer
Lord Thou Art My Refuge - Anton Dvorak
Lord, To Thee Do I Lift My Soul - Antonio Vivaldi
Lord, What Is Man - Henry Purcell
Lord's Blessing, The - Josef Freudenthal
Lord's My Shepherd, The - Carl F. Mueller
Lord's Name Is Praised, The - Maurice Greene
Lord's Prayer, The - M. Albrecht
Lord's Prayer, The - Ancient Gaelic Hymn arr. Richard Proulx
Lord's Prayer, The - Leroy Anderson and Alfred Heller
Lord's Prayer, The - Granville Bantock
Lord's Prayer, The - Milton Barnes
Lord's Prayer, The - Dorothy Cadzow
Lord's Prayer, The - George Cory
Lord's Prayer, The - Paul Earls
Lord's Prayer, The - Geoffrey Flowers
Lord's Prayer, The - Josephine Forsyth
Lord's Prayer, The - Johan Franco
Lord's Prayer, The - B. Cecil Gates

Lord's Prayer, The - Bernard Hamblen
Lord's Prayer, The - Michael Head
Lord's Prayer, The - Georg Henschel
Lord's Prayer, The - Jerome Hines
Lord's Prayer, The - Leon Abbott Hoffmeister
Lord's Prayer, The - Paul R. Isensee
Lord's Prayer - David N. Johnson
Lord's Prayer, The - Philip Jorgensen
Lord's Prayer, The - Albert Hay Malotte
Lord's Prayer, The - John Merbecke
Lord's Prayer, The - Gordon Myers
Lord's Prayer, The - Richard Proulx (arr.)
Lord's Prayer, The - Ned Rorem
Lord's Prayer, The - Louis Shenk
Lord's Prayer, The - Jan Sibelius
Lord's Prayer, The - Healey Willan
Lord's Prayer, The - Inez McC. Williamson
Lord Preserveth the Souls, The/For Look As High As The Heaven
    Is - G.F. Handel
Lord Thou Hast Been Our Dwelling Place - Don Humphreys
Lord, Thou Hast Been Our Dwelling Place - Louis Baker Phillips
Lord To Thee Do I Lift My Soul - Antonio Vivaldi
Lord Will Not Be Ever Wroth, The - C. Rheinthaler
Lord, What Is Man - Henry Purcell
Love - Mary Van Dyke
Love Is Of God - H. Leroy Baumgartner
Love Never Faileth - V. Haskins
Love Never Faileth - Frederic Root
Love Never Faileth - Ward-Stephens
Love Not The World - Ward-Stephens
Love One Another - Irwin Fischer

Magnificat - Willy Burkhard
Magnificat - John Duke
Magnificat - Giorgio Gaslini
Magnificat - Egil Hovland
Magnificat - Mario Savioni
Magnificat - Francis Thorne
Make A Joyful Noise - Michael Head
Make A Joyful Noise - Frank LaForge
Make A Joyful Noise - James MacDermid
Make A Joyful Noise - Joel Suben
Make A Joyful Noise Unto The Lord - Frederick Koch
Make Me A Clean Heart - G.F. Handel
Man - Don Humphreys
Man That Is Born Of A Women - Carlisle Floyd
Man That Is Born Of A Woman - Daniel Pinkham
Mark The Perfect Man - Clement W. Barker
Mein Herz ist bereit - Dietrich Buxtehude
Meine Seele erhebt den Herren - Heinrich Schutz
Meister, wir haben die ganze Macht gearbeitet - Heinrich Schutz

Messenger Of Peace, The - John Prindle Scott
Mimaamakin - Lazar Weiner
Miserere et Jubilate - Violet Archer
Mourning Song - Ned Rorem
My Beloved Is Mine And I Am His - John LaMontaine
My Beloved Spake - Leo Samama
My Dear Brethren, Meet The Demands Of This Time - Hugo Distler
My Heart Is Ready, O God - William Ferris
My Lord What A Morning - Spiritual
My New Name - James MacDermid
My Prayer - Don Humphreys
My Shepherd Will Supply My Need - Virgil Thomson
My Son, Wherefore Hast Thou Done This To Us? - Heinrich Schutz
My Soul Doth Magnify - Margaret Sandresky
My Soul Doth Magnify The Lord - William K. Burns
My Soul Doth Magnify The Lord - Jeremiah Dencke
My Soul Doth Magnify The Lord! - Verna Hatch
My Soul Doth Magnify The Lord - Randall Thompson
My Soul Is Athirst For God - A.R. Gaul
My Soul Is Athirst For God - William Stickles
My Speech Shall Distill As The Dew - James MacDermid

Neither Hath This Man Sinned - Edward Elgar
New Heaven - New Earth - Charles Romer
New 23rd Psalm, The - Ralph Carmichael
Ninety-first Psalm, The - James MacDermid
Ninety And Nine, The - Edward Campion
Nisi Dominus aedificaverit domum - Heinrich I.F. Biber
Not A Sparrow Falleth - Franz Abt
Now Christ Is Risen - J.S. Bach
Now It Is High Time To Awake - Daniel Pinkham
Now Let All Christen Men Rejoice - Andrew J. Boex
Now Will I Praise The Lord - Philip Dietterich
Now Will I Praise The Lord - Heinrich Schutz
Nunc Dimittis - Geoffrey Burgon
Nunc Dimittis - Francis Thorne

O Be Joyful In The Lord - Leo Sowerby
O Clap Your Hands - Don McAfee
O Clap Your Hands, All Ye People - Howard Hanson
O Come Harken - Charles Villiers Stanford
O Come, Let Us Sing Unto The Lord - Sven Lekberg
O Come Let Us Worship - G.F. Handel
O Death How Bitter - Johannes Brahms
O Death Where Is Thy Sting - G.F. Handel
O Dieu donne moi deliverance - Theodore DeBeze
O Father In Heaven - Larry Mayfield
O Give Thanks - Robert J. Powell
O God Have Mercy - Felix Mendelssohn
O God, I Will Praise Thee - Heinrich Schutz

O Lamb Of God (Agnus Dei) - Georges Bizet
O Lord, Have Mercy Upon Me - Giovanni Pergolesi
O Lord, How Long Wilt Thou Forget Me - Peter Sacco
O Lord, How Manifold Are Thy Works - Irwin Fischer
O Lord, I Will Praise Thee - Gerhard Krapf
O Lord, Our Lord, How Excellent Thy Name - Howard Hanson
O Lord, My God, Thou Art Very Great - H. Leroy Baumgartner
O Lord, Rebuke Me Not - Henry Purcell
O Lord, Rebuke Me Not - Alfred Wooler
O Lord, Rebuke Me Not In Thine Anger - Howard Hanson
O Lord, Return - H. Schalit
O Lord Thou Hast Searched Me - Sven Lekberg
O Lord, Thou Hast Searched Me And Known Me - Carlisle Floyd
O Lord, Thou Hast Searched Me Out - S. Bennett
O Magnify The Lord (5th Chandos Anthem) - G.F. Handel
O Magnify The Lord (8th Chandos Anthem) - G.F. Handel
O My Dove, That Art In The Clefts Of The Rock - John LaMontaine
O Praise The Lord - Maurice Greene
O Praise The Lord (12th Chandos Anthem) - G.F. Handel
O Rejoice In The Lord At All Times - Hugo Distler
O Rest In The Lord - Felix Mendelssohn
O Sing Unto The Lord - Lewis Whikehart
O Sing Unto The Lord A New Song - Richard T. Gore
O That I Knew Where I Might Find Him - Alec Rowley
O Thou That Tellest - G.F. Handel
O Vos Omnes - Theodore DuBois
Oh, Lord, Our Heavenly King - James Lyon
Oh That I Had Wings - A.M. Barnes
Old Jerusalem - Julius Chajes
On Eagles Wings - Bernard Hamblen
On Laziness - James Beale
On Slander - James Beale
On The Way To Emmaus - Jaromir Weinberger
On Truth - James Beale
On Wisdom - James Beale
One Hundred Twenty-First Psalm - B. Crowe
One Hundredth Psalm, The - Carl F. Mueller
One Thing Befalleth The Beasts - Johannes Brahms
One Thing I Ask Of The Lord - Heinrich Schutz
Our Father - William Dame
Our Father - Clarence Gaskill
Our Father - Karl August Krebs
Our Father - Robert MacGimsey
Our Heart Shall Rejoice In The Lord - Robert Powell
Our Soul Waits For The Lord - Walter Pelz
Out Of My Soul's Depth - Thomas Campion
Out Of The Deep - J. Christopher Marks
Out Of The Deep Have I Called Unto Thee - Robert L. Bedell
Out Of The Depths - William K. Burns
Out Of The Depths - Eugene Butler
Out Of The Depths - Alan Hovhaness
Out Of The Depths - James H. Rogers

Out Of The Depths - John Prindle Scott
Out Of The Depths - Alfred Wooler

Pater Noster - Anton Heiller
Pater Noster - Flor Peeters
Path Of The Just, The - Clement W. Barker
Peace Be Unto You - Edward Elgar
Peace I Leave With You - William H. Thompson
Peace I Leave With You - John Varley Roberts
Peace Of God, The - Charles Gounod
Penitent, The - Beardsley Van De Water
People That Walk In Darkness, The - G.F. Handel
People Who Walked In Darkness - Lillian Klass
Pilgrim's Song - Ralph Vaughan-Williams
Pledge, The - Jennie Prince Black
Powerful Guardian - G.F. Handel
Praise - LeMar Barrus
Praise Him, All That In His House Attend - G.F. Handel
Praise, My Soul The King Of Heaven - C. Winston Cassler
Praise Of Exaltation - Ernest Charles
Praise The Lord - John Koch
Praise The Lord His Glories Show - Powell Weaver
Praise The Lord, O My Soul - Carlisle Floyd
Praise The Lord, O My Soul - Maurice Greene
Praise The Lord, O My Soul - George Jefferies
Praise The Lord, O My Soul - Samuel S. Wesley
Praise To The Lord - Heinrich Schutz
Praise Ye The Lord - Granville Bantok
Praise Ye The Lord - John Edmunds
Praise Ye The Lord - Irwin Fischer
Praise Ye The Lord - Herbert Fromm
Praise Ye The Lord - Don Humphreys
Praise Ye The Lord - Heinrich Schutz
Praised Be The Lord - Maurice Greene
Prayer - Pearl G. Curran
Prayer For Jerusalem, A - Richard F. Wernick
Precepts Of Micah, The - Josef Freudenthal
Prepare To Meet Thy God - Gershon Kingsley
Prepare Ye The Way Of The Lord - Francis Thorne
Psalm 1 - James Butt
Psalm 1 - Herbert Fromm
Psalm 4 - Anthony Garlick
Psalm VI (O Lord Rebuke Me Not) - Edmund Rubbra
Psalm 8 (O Lord, How Excellent Is Thy Name) - Isadore Freed
Psalm 13 - E.I. Kahn
Psalm 17 - Anthony Garlick
Psalm 22 (Elohim! Why Hast Thou Forsaken Me?) - Ernest Bloch
Psalm 22 - E. Goldman
Psalm 23 - Paul Ben-Heim
Psalm XXIII - Hermann Berlinski
Psalm 23 - Lorne Betts

Psalm 23 - Duane Buss
Psalm XXIII - Paul Creston
Psalm 23 - Geoffrey Flowers
Psalm 23 - Anthony Garlick
Psalm 23 - Marty Goetz
Psalm 23 - Jack Goode
Psalm 23 - Michael Isaacson
Psalm 23 - Augustus Lowe
Psalm 23 - G. O'Connor-Morris
Psalm XXIII - Peter Riddle
Psalm XXIII - Edmund Rubbra
Psalm 23 - Mary Winton
Psalm 23 - Judith Lang Zaimont
Psalm 28 - Anthony Garlick
Psalm 42 - Herbert Fromm
Psalm 49 - Kelsey Jones
Psalm 66 - Yehudi Wyner
Psalm 67 - Regina H. Fryxell
Psalm 67 - Jacques Wolfe
Psalm 68 - Bernard Rogers
Psalm 79 - Daniel Pinkham
Psalm 81 - David Childs
Psalm 83 - David Childs
Psalm 84 - Matthew Greenbaum
Psalm 90 - James Butt
Psalm 90 - Wenzel Eberhard
Psalm 91 - David Childs
Psalm 91 - G. O'Connor-Morris
Psalm 92 - David Childs
Psalm 92 - Charles Lagourgue
Psalm 93 - Marilyn Penn
Psalm 97 (O Sing Unto The Lord A New Song) - Edward M. Goldman
Psalm 103 - Richard T. Stephenson
Psalm 104 - Charles Lederer
Psalm 114 (Snatched Away By Jehovah) - Ernest Bloch
Psalm 119 - Yehudi Wyner
Psalm 121 - William K. Burns
Psalm 121 - David Childs
Psalm 121 - Herbert Fromm
Psalm 121 - Mildred Kayden
Psalm 123 - David Childs
Psalm CXXVI - Max Brod
Psalm 126 - E.I. Kahn
Psalm 127 - Freda Dinn
Psalm 128 - Robert Wetzler
Psalm 134 (Behold, Bless Ye The Lord) - Ned Rorem
Psalm 137 - Ernst Bloch
Psalm 137 - Stephen Richards
Psalm 137 - Charles Seeger
Psalm 139 - Don McAfee
Psalm 140 - Roger Sessions
Psalm 142 (I Cried To The Lord) - Ned Rorem
Psalm 142 - Leo Sowerby

Psalm 145 - Stephen P. Folkemer
Psalm 147 - Jack Goode
Psalm 148 - David Childs
Psalm 148 - Ned Rorem
Psalm 149 - Herbert Fromm
Psalm 150 - James Butt
Psalm 150 - Ned Rorem
Psalm CL - Edmund Rubbra
Psalm 150 - J. Weinberger
Psalm 150 in the form of a Ciacona - Hans Ludwig Schilling
Psalm Of David, A - Heinrich Schutz
Psalm Of Praise - Irwin Fischer
Psalm Of Praise, A - Raymond McFeeters
Psalm Of Praise, A - Ned Rorem
Psalm On The Eve Of Battle - David Raksin
Publican, The - Beardsley Van De Water
Put On The Whole Armour Of God - Don Humphreys

Raising Of Lazarus, The - Clement W. Barker
Raising Of Lazarus, The - Katherine K. Davis
Ransomed Of The Lord, The - Don Humphreys
Ransomed Of The Lord, The - James MacDermid
Recitative and Angel's Message To The Shepherds - Heinrich Schutz
Rejoice Greatly - G.F. Handel
Rejoice In The Lord - P.A. Schnecker
Rejoice In The Lord Alway - Daniel Pinkham
Remember Now Thy Creator - Fred E. Eggert
Remember Now Thy Creator - John Prindle Scott
Repent Ye - John Prindle Scott
Requiem - Violet Archer
Rest In The Lord - Don Humphreys
Resurrection - Ned Rorem
Rise And Walk - Clara Warren
Rise Up And Walk - Thomas Richner
Rise Up My Love - Gershon Kingsley
Rise Up My Love - George Rochberg
Rise Up My Love, My Fair One, And Come Away - John LaMontaine
River Of Life - James Butt
River Of The Water Of Life, The - Jeanne Alden Joy
Robe Of Righteousness, The - Marian Coryell
Ruth (to Naomi) - Gerald Cook
Ruth - Lazar Weiner

Sacrament - J.S. Bach
Salomons Prayer - Paul Pisk
Salmo VIII - Luigi Cortese
Salvation Belongeth Unto The Lord - Maurice Greene
Salvum me fac Deus - Francois Couperin
Sanctuary - A.F. Lowe
Save Me, O God - Eugene Butler

Save Me, O God - Ernst Charles
Save Me, O God - Cuthbert Harris
Save Me, O God, For The Waters Are Come - Carlisle Floyd
Save Me, O Lord - Roger Clerbois
Save Me, O Lord - Carlisle Floyd
Save Me, O Lord - Alfred Woller
Schaffe in mir, Gott, ein rein Herz - Dietrich Buxtehude
Seal Upon Thy Heart, A - Hyman Reznick
Search Me, O God - Anton Dvorak
Search Me, O God, And Know My Heart - Ward-Stephen
See Him, He Is The Lamb Of God - Johannes Herbst
Seek Ye First - Karen Lafferty
Seek Ye First The Kingdom Of God - William Arms Fisher
Seek Ye First The Kingdom Of God - M.B. Foster
Seek Ye The Lord - Frank Lynes
Seek Ye The Lord - J. Varley Roberts
Seek Ye The Lord While He May Be Found - Don Humphreys
Send Out Thy Light - Alfred Wooler
Set Me As A Seal - Judith Berman
Set Me As A Seal - Lorne Betts
Set Me As A Seal - Joseph Clokey
Set Me As A Seal - Lukas Foss
Set Me As A Seal - George Rochberg
Set Me As A Seal Upon Thy Heart - Max Helfman
Shadow Of Thy Wings, The - James MacDermid
Shadrach - Robert McGimsey
Shepherd, The - Julie L. Wolford
Shepherd's Psalm - Noni Espina
Sicut Moses - Dietrich Buxtehude
Sing, O Daughters Of Zion - James MacDermid
Sing To God - Michael Horvit
Sing To The Lord A New Song- Dietrich Buxtehude
Sing Unto The Lord - Peter Cornelius
Sing Unto The Lord - Emmet Pendleton
Sing Unto The Lord A New Song - James MacDermid
Sing Unto The Lord All The Earth - Muriel Herbert
Sing Ye A Joyful Song - Anton Dvorak
Singet dem Herrn - Dietrich Buxtehude
Singet dem Herrn - Heinrich Schutz
So Great Is His Mercy - Don Doig
So I Returned - Johannes Brahms
Solomon's Prayer - Merle Miller
Song Of Battle, A - Charles V. Stanford
Song Of David, A: Psalm 120 - Ned Rorem
Song Of Devotion - John Ness Beck
Song Of Hope, A - Charles V. Stanford
Song Of Hosanna - Sharon Elery Rogers
Song Of Joy - John Ness Beck
Song Of Moses, The - Richard Cumming
Song Of The Redeemed - Sharon Elery Rogers
Song Of Ruth - Maurice Goldman
Song Of Ruth - Gary Hallquist

Song Of Ruth - Emmet Pendleton
Song Of Songs, The - Ruth Coleman Bilchick
Song Of The Leaves Of Life And The Waters Of Life, The - Ralph
    Vaughan-Williams
Song Of Trust, A - Charles V. Stanford
Song Of Victory, A - Sharon Elery Rogers
Song Of Wisdom, A - Charles V. Stanford
Sorrow Of Death Compassed Me, The - Peter Sacco
Spacious Firmament, The - Joseph Addison
Spirit Of God - Donald Hustad
Spirit Of God, The - Paul Pisk
Spirit Of The Lord God Is Upon Me, The - James G. MacDermid
Spirit Of The Lord Is Upon Me, The - Arthur Sullivan
Suffer Little Children - Ruth L. Hausman
Suffer Little Children - Frank LaForge
Suffer Little Children - Charles P. Scott
Suffer Little Children - Charles D. Underhill
Suffer The Children To Come Unto Me - I. Fischer
Suffer The Little Children - Stanley A. Day
Suffer The Little Children - A. Schultz
Sun Goeth Down, The - Edward Elgar
Sun Shall Be No More Thy Light, The - Maurice Greene
Symphony #2 - Richard Yardumian

Tabernacle Of God Is With Men, The - Raymond E. Mitchell
Take My Mother Home - (arr.) Hall Johnson
Taste And See That The Lord Is Good - I. Fischer
Te Deum - Violet Archer
Teach Me, O Lord - Bernard Hamblen
Teach Me, O Lord - Frank LaForge
Teach Me, O Lord - Charles F. Manney
Temple Of Glory - Clement Barker
Tenebrae factae sunt - Knut Nystedt
Thanks Be To God - Christoph Gluck
Their Sound Is Gone Out - G.F. Handel
Then Shall Be Brought To Pass/O Death Where Is Thy Sting -
    G.F. Handel
Then Shall The Eyes Of The Blind/He Shall Feed His Flock -
    G.F. Handel
Then Shall The Righteous Shine - Felix Mendelssohn
There Is A Season To Everything - Ernst Toch
There Is A Spirit In Me - Peter Cornelius
There Were Shepherds - G.F. Handel
There Were Shepherds - John Prindle Scott
These Are They Which Came Out Of Great Tribulation - A.R. Gaul
They Shall Run And Not Be Weary - James MacDermid
They That Sow In Tears - William Christopher Handy
They That Sow In Tears - James H. Rogers
Thine, O Lord Is The Greatness - James MacDermid
Think On These Things - Robert MacGimsey
This Is My Commandment - John Palmer Clark

This Is My Commandment - Bernard Hamblen
This Is My Commandment - Don Hustad
This Is The Victory, Even Our Faith - H. Leroy Baumgartner
This Night I Lift My Heart To Thee - M. Costa
This We Declare Unto You - H. Leroy Baumgartner
Those Who Wait On The Lord - Annette Seaton
Thou Art Gone Up On High - G.F. Handel
Thou Didst Set The Earth - Ezra Laderman
Thou Hast Charged/O That My Ways - Maurice Greene
Thou Hast Ravished My Heart - Leo Samama
Thou Shalt Dash Them - G.F. Handel
Thou Visitest The Earth - Harold Parker
Thou Wilt Keep Him In Perfect Peace - James MacDermid
Thou Wilt Keep Him In Perfect Peace - Allen Shawn
Thou Wilt Keep Him In Perfect Peace - Oley Speaks
Thou Wilt Keep Him In Perfect Peace - Eric Thiman
Thou Wilt Keep Him In Perfect Peace - Richard Wienhorst
Though I Speak With Tongues - Johannes Brahms
Three Times I Asked Him - Tom Fettke
Thus Saith The Lord/But Who May Abide - G.F. Handel
Thus Spake Jesus - Michael Head
Thy Rebuke Hath Broken His Heart/Behold And See/He Was Cut Off/
    But Thou Didst Not Leave - G.F. Handel
Thy Mercy, Lord - G.F. Handel
Thy Mercy, O Lord, Is In The Heavens - Frank LaForge
Thy Right Hand Shall Hold Me - Richard D. Row
Thy Secret Place - Felix Mendelssohn
Thy Word Is A Lamp - Jean Bone and Howard Fenton
Thy Word Is A Lamp - Andrew Lloyd Englert
Thy Word Is A Lamp - James MacDermid
Time For Everything, A - Noel Goemanne
To Everything There Is A Season - Daniel Pinkham
To The Lord Our God Belong Mercies - A.R. Gaul
Transfiguration - James G. Ellis
Treasure In Heaven - Katherine K. Davis
Trois Psaumes - Arthur Honegger
Trust In The Lord - Katherine K. Davis
Trust In The Lord - Franz Josef Haydn
Trust In The Lord - Arthur Sullivan
Trust In The Lord With All Thine Heart - James MacDermid
Trust Ye The Lord - John Prindle Scott
Turn Thee To Me - Charles Ore
Turn Thee To Me And Have Mercy - Anton Dvorak
Turn Thy Face From My Sins - William Timmings
Twenty-Third Psalm, The - Mark Andrews
Twenty-Third Psalm, The - Violet Archer
Twenty-Third Psalm, The - Robert L. Bedell
Twenty-Third Psalm, The - Russell J. Brown
Twenty-Third Psalm, The - Albert Hay Malotte
Two Commandments, The - Don McAfee

Unto The Hills - Herbert Fromm
Unto Thee I Lift Up My Soul - Peter Cornelius
Unto Thee O Lord - Eduardo Marzo
Unto Thee Will I Cry - Henry Purcell
Usuequo Domine - Francois Couperin

Vanity Of Vanities - Daniel Pinkham
Voice In The Wilderness, The - John Prindle Scott
Voice Of Joy, The - Charles P. Scott
Voice Of My Beloved - Max Helfman
Voice Of My Beloved, The! Behold, He Cometh - John LaMontaine
Voice Of The Wilderness, The - Edward Elgar

Walk In Love - Robert J. Powell
Watchful's Song - Ralph Vaughan-Williams
Wedding Cantata - Leo Samama
Wedding Song - Jan Bender
Wedding Song - Richard W. Gieseke
Wedding Song - Flor Peeters
Wedding Song - Daniel Pinkham
Wedding Song - Heinrich Schutz
What Did I Not Steal - Ezra Laderman
What Shall I Render Unto The Lord - Frank LaForge
Whatever Is True - Otis Skillings
When All Things Began - Don McAfee
When I Consider The Heavens - John Prindle Scott
When I Survey The Wondrous Cross - Lawrence Hope
When I Survey The Wondrous Cross - E.J. Lorenz
When I Survey The Wondrous Cross - Lyn Murray
When I Survey The Wondrous Cross - Sydney Thomson
Where'er Thou Goest - Eugen Hildach
Wherefore Seeing - Daniel Pinkham
Whither Shall I Go - Rena Van Nuys
Whither Shall I Go From Thy Spirit - Alison Demarest
Whither Shall I Go From Thy Spirit - Carl F. Mueller
Whither Shall I Go From Thy Spirit - James G. MacDermid
Whither Shall I Go From Thy Spirit - Jan Philip Schinham
Whither Thou Goest - G. Winston Cassler
Whither Thou Goest - Richard A. Dewey
Whither Thou Goest - James Engel
Who Shall Separate Us? -- Don Doig
Who Shall Separate Us From The Love Of Christ - Daniel Pinkham
Whosoever Does Not Receive The Kingdom - Jan Bender
Why Art Thou Cast Down, O My Soul? - C. Reinthaler
Why Art Thou Cast Down, O My Soul - Max Spicker
Why Art Thou Cast Down, My Soul - Felix Mendelssohn
Wilderness, The - Eric Thiman
Wilderness, The - Walter E. Young
Wonders Of The Universe, The - Marc Antonio Cesti
Whoso Dwelleth - Leo Sowerby

Whoso Dwelleth In The Secret Place - Faith Helen Rogers
Why Art Thou Cast Down, O My Soul? - C. Reinthaler
Why Do The Nations - G.F. Handel
Wie der Hirsch schreyet - David Pohle
Wilt Thou Not Receive Us Again - Alfred Robyn
Wither Thou Goest - Paul Liljestrand
Wither Thou Goest - Leo Samama
Wither Thou Goest - Guy Singer
Woe Unto The Foolish Prophet - Clement Barker
Wohl denen, die ohne Tadel leben - Max Reger
Woman Of Valor, A - Samuel Adler
Woman Of Valor, A - Miriam Gideon
Woman Of Valor, A - Judith Lang Zaimont
Worthy Woman, A - John Wilson

Ye Are The Light Of The World - Frank LaForge
Ye Have Taken Away My Lord - Felix Mendelssohn
Ye People Rend Your Hearts/If With All Your Hearts - Felix
    Mendelssohn
Ye Shall Know The Truth - Irwin Fischer
Yea, Though I Walk Through The Valley - Hazel G. Kinscella